Two Guns From Harlem

Two Guns From Harlem: The Detective Fiction Of Chester Himes

Robert E. Skinner

Bowling Green State University Popular Press
Bowling Green, Ohio 43403

Cover design by Gary Dumm

For Patty--

This one's for you

Contents

Chester Himes at about age 35
Photo courtesy of Dr. Joseph S. Himes, Jr.

Introduction

In his critical study of Chester Himes, scholar Stephen F. Milliken has written:

One goal that every critic who discusses black American literature should set for himself, I feel, is to write in such a manner that no reader will be able to determine with any certainty whether the critic himself is black or white. If he does not, his comments will trigger automatic reactions of prejudice—some negative, some positive—that will almost certainly bar his opinions from whatever serious consideration they might merit.[1]

While I see the nobility of Milliken's sentiment, I do not find it a useful one in the case of Chester Himes. I can say with some assurance that my white middle-class origins are the reason that Himes has held such a fascination for me. Because of that, I approached his work with the awe and wonder of an outsider discovering a totally new world. It is doubtful that I could effectively communicate that sense of new discovery without an admission of how far removed culturally I am from Himes' particular viewpoint.

While very few white readers may have ever wished to trade places with their Black neighbors, there is no doubt that some of us still harbor a tremendous curiosity about what Black life is like. In spite of the fact that Blacks have been a part of American life since 1619, no one could be naive enough to deny that there are profound differences in the lifestyle, customs, and thinking of American Blacks and whites. Without a doubt these differences—and the lack of understanding that exists on both sides—have contributed to the difficulties that Blacks have met as they have tried to assert themselves as equal citizens.

With the exceptions of Frank Yerby and a very few others, most American Black writers have taken it upon themselves to write about the Black experience. They have written eloquently and powerfully of the plight of the American Negro, and a few—Wright, Baldwin, Ellison most notably—have attained lasting international fame. In my opinion, Chester Himes belongs in this latter group and is the one best equipped to make a white reader understand the frustrations of the urban American Black.

Himes wrote in the 1940s and early '50s with tremendous passion and resentment of the pain attached to the life of the Negro intellectual as he attempted to make himself felt and become accepted in an often bigoted and hostile society. In the later '50s and into the '60s, Himes described forcefully

1

and sometimes frighteningly the lot of the poverty-stricken city-bred Negro who is preyed upon by an uncaring white establishment and the scheming wolves of his own race.

Unlike many of his contemporaries, Himes was willing to express bold opinions and insisted on expressing them in a way that tended to excite the unfavorable comment of both white critics and the more moderate members of his own race. A man ahead of his time, Himes consistently wrote more truth than his readers were ready to hear.

By the time he began to write crime fiction in the late 1950s, Himes was nearly washed up as a writer. He was in his late 40s and needed money desperately when the publishing house of Gallimard asked him to try his hand at what was for him a totally new field of endeavor. The French, who often have been more appreciative of our artists than we have, ourselves, were wildly enthusiastic about Himes and awarded him one of their most prestigious literary awards. From the French he gained a sense of worth and a financial security that were denied him by his countrymen.

On our side of the Atlantic, Himes still managed to attract unfavorable comment from members of the white literary establishment. In an early issue of *The Armchair Detective,* critic Marvin Lachman commented that "frequently the mystery elements are subordinate to sheer sex and mayhem. Also, because of the author's undisguised hatred of whites he would lead the Negro as a detective into areas as segregated as those before World War II."[2]

But more often, critics looked at Himes' work and recognized it as something beyond the common run of crime story. Unlike Lachman, who viewed Himes' detective fiction within the narrow boundaries usually reserved for the genre (and possibly from the vantage point of unrealized prejudice), white critics like Raymond Nelson and Edward Margolies and Black scholars like John A. Williams began to recognize that Himes' thrillers were really exercises in socio-political thought and were in keeping with his earlier protest style.

It is interesting to me that virtually all of the substantive examinations of Himes' work that have appeared during the past 20-odd years have been performed by white scholars. Perhaps they felt as I do, that Himes has something to say to the white reader and, despite his anger, it is nevertheless worth hearing.

In his crime novels, Himes is writing in a tradition that was established by white writers more than 20 years before he began working in the field. Because that genre is cluttered with the hack work of Carroll John Dalys and Richard Prathers, it is important to recognize that Himes himself did not stoop to hack work.

Like Dashiell Hammett before him, Himes was writing to a certain extent from hard-won experience. He took his experience as a Black man in an unforgiving urban world and fused it together with his unique experience as a criminal and habitue of the ghetto *demi-monde.* The result is a sometimes surreal depiction of a frightening and sordid world where the term "good" is a very relative one. Criminal Harlem was a place Himes had been: a place where he was one of the characters.

In a way, Himes' writing can be seen as a harbinger of life as it exists today. In our time, criminal life has taken on a nihilism that is starkly reminiscent of Himes' fictional world. Parts of our largest cities virtually have been taken over by amoral and vicious criminals, whose response to any outside threat is instantaneous and horrible violence. As I write these paragraphs, the newspapers are full of the Los Angeles drug and gang wars that are true "wars" in every sense of the word.

From both popular culture and literary perspectives, Himes' crime series deserves a thorough examination. Indeed, Himes continues to enjoy a high literary reputation in France, where his known work has never gone out of print and where two volumes of his previously unpublished work have been recently translated and published.

During the past two years, interest in Chester Himes has had a resurgence here in America. His first two novels, long out of print, were reissued recently by Thunder's Mouth Press, and most of the Harlem series has been made available again through Allison & Busby, a British publisher. A few magazine articles have recently appeared which offer strikingly new appraisals of Himes' work.

My own interest in Himes initially came from a long-time interest in the development of the hard-boiled crime novel. While attempting to view his series from what is essentially a pop culture background, I have tried to bring a new perspective to the examination of Chester Himes. In so doing, I am attempting to create a new interest in one of the most fascinating series of novels ever written in this country.

Chapter I
Criminal, Convict, Writer:
The Early Life Of Chester Himes

It is one of the great ironies of Chester Himes' life that it did not begin in the gutter. For the time in which he was born, Himes had an unusually auspicious and hopeful start in life. He was born in Jefferson City, Missouri, on July 29, 1909, "across the street from the entrance to Lincoln Institute, where my father, Professor Joseph Sandy Himes, taught blacksmithing and wheelwrighting as head of the Mechanical Department."[1]

Himes' mother, Estelle Bomar Himes, "was an octoroon, or perhaps whiter. I remember her as looking like a white woman who had suffered a long siege of illness; she had hazel eyes, a sallow complexion, and auburn hair."[2] Being descended from a wealthy southern family with an aristocratic English heritage, Mrs. Himes was extraordinarily status-conscious. Himes remembered that "much of her nagging and scolding and punishing and pushing us stemmed from her desire for us to live up to our 'heritage.' "[3]

During the seven years that they lived at Alcorn College in Mississippi, Estelle Himes refused to let her children play with other faculty children because she considered them to "be 'country' and not very 'cultured.' " To make up for the lack of elementary educational facilities for Blacks in Alcorn, Mrs. Himes set up a school for her two youngest sons in their home. She was a strict taskmaster and demanded a great deal as she drilled her sons unceasingly.[4]

Himes' father was the complete antithesis of his mother. Physically he was rather short and bowlegged with an ellipsoidal skull, Arabic face, and hooked nose.[5] He was as black as his wife was white. This difference in their backgrounds was to create untold misery in the family and, in large measure, helped to mold Himes into the man he later became.

Himes had two brothers, Eddie and Joseph. Eddie was at least eight years older than Chester, and Joseph was Chester's elder by one year. All were light-skinned and rather handsome, like their mother. It is interesting that each went on to distinguish himself in his chosen field of endeavor. Eddie left home at an early age and, years later, became an executive of the waiters' union in New York. Joseph became an internationally famous sociologist who is still active today.

4

Call it pride or insecurity or sheer arrogance: Estelle Himes almost made it a practice to create dissension wherever the family went. Himes noted that when they lived in Mississippi, they were the only car owners of any color in their county, a fact that did not endear them to the cracker farmers who populated the district. When the Himeses went for rides in the country, they were forever getting into rows with these farmers who were angered when engine noise frightened their mule teams. When these rural types reached for their shotguns, Himes' mother would beat them to the draw with her revolver and disarm them. These incidents eventually resulted in Joseph Himes' dismissal from the college where he worked.

Just prior to the job loss, an event occurred that severely traumatized the family and provided Himes with his first real understanding of the double standard under which Black Americans lived. In school Himes and his brother Joseph were to have worked together on a chemistry experiment one day. Chester, however, had gotten into trouble before class and as punishment was forbidden to participate. Somehow the experiment went wrong, and Joseph was badly hurt in the explosion.

The boy was rushed by his parents to the nearest hospital but the doctors there refused to treat Negroes. The sight of his muscular father begging, in tears, for the adamant white doctors to help his son was one that haunted Chester for the rest of his life. Himes was further troubled by the guilty feeling that, if he had been there, the accident never would have happened.

The family soon moved to St. Louis where Joseph could get special treatment at the Barnes Hospital. Chester started high school where his naturally aggressive nature began to come into play. He later remembered playing "football, baseball, soccer, basketball, any game that you can name, with suicidal intensity. The other boys on the playground either ganged up on me or refused to play with me; the gym teacher stopped me from playing all games in school."[6] He was also unpopular with his teachers and began to cut class on a regular basis. He admitted that he was "lonely, shy, and insufferably belligerent."[7]

After two years in St. Louis, the Himes family moved again, this time to Cleveland, Ohio, where Joseph, Sr., hoped to find work while they stayed with some of his relatives. As one might predict, Himes' mother did not get along at all with her in-laws. Her contempt for their "blackness" and her own exclusivity began to drive a deeper wedge between her and her husband.

Himes graduated from high school. Because any graduate of a public high school was eligible to attend Ohio State University, he planned to go there and study medicine. In order to earn money to allow him to go, he took a job as a busboy at an exclusive hotel restaurant in the city. It was during this period, when things most seemed to be going well for him, that he first began his explorations of the seamy side of life.

He noted in his autobiography that, while on this job, inconclusive flirtations with white female co-workers drove him to see a Black prostitute on Cleveland's notorious Scovil Avenue. Shortly after this unsatisfying experience, Himes actively began trying to get dates with young white women. He was unsuccessful, and his frustrations mounted.

His life took an unfortunate turn one day when he inadvertently stepped into an empty elevator shaft. He broke his left arm at the wrist, fractured three vertebrae, broke his jaw and shattered most of his teeth, and suffered many internal injuries. The accident cost him four months in the hospital in a body cast and extra time in a back brace after his release.

Himes found himself treated with extreme generosity on all sides. The Ohio State Industrial Commission held the hotel completely responsible for the accident. The Commission paid for all of his medical bills and put him on total disability with a pension. At the same time, the hotel management offered to continue his salary of 50 dollars a month through his convalescence.

Himes later recounted that "I discovered that had I rejected the pension given me by the Industrial Commission I could have sued the hotel for a considerable sum of money. But when the Industrial Commission offered the pension and the hotel promised to continue paying my salary, my father persuaded me to sign the waivers to all rights for additional claims."[8]

Joseph, Sr.'s, advice created an additional rift in his marriage. As a conservative man by nature, he was inclined to accept the offers of the Commission and the hotel. On the other hand, Himes' mother felt that her son had not been treated with fairness. She hated all manner of condescension from white people and faced it with extreme antagonism. Himes was frank in admitting in his autobiography that he inherited this quality from her.

Soon Estelle Himes went to the hotel and got into an altercation with the management. She accused them of taking advantage of her son's youth and inexperience; as a result the hotel retaliated by ceasing payment of Chester's salary. Himes' father attacked Estelle bitterly for her action when she returned home, increasing the alienation that they felt from one another.

Himes recovered sufficiently from his accident to begin classes at Ohio State in the fall of 1926. Using the money he had saved, he bought himself a raccoon coat, a fancy suit, a pipe, and a Ford roadster. In spite of the sophisticated figure he cut, he was too insecure to make friends among the other students, many of whom were from upwardly-mobile middle-class homes. He began to visit prostitutes, who he discovered were younger and better looking than the ones he had seen in Cleveland. Perhaps as a consequence of his youthful womanizing, his grades began a downward slide. By Christmas of that year he was in serious danger of being dropped from the university.

Somehow he managed to pull himself together to complete the first semester successfully, but school was beginning to bore him. The segregation and discrimination he found at the university bothered him so much that he was badly depressed. This first experience in the wider world marked the beginning of his inability to accept the unequal status accorded Blacks.

At home for the holidays, he found his mother and father more at odds than ever. He stayed away from home, spending much of his time in sexual liaisons with black domestic servants. In his autobiography he made an interesting comment about this period, particularly where women and skin color are concerned. He noted that "black women were easy to pick up and made exciting bedmates; maids were the easiest and good-looking whores were the hardest. I liked black women; black, black women. I always have."[9]

It is hard to justify this statement when it is contrasted with attitudes reflected in his later life and work. In his early writing, his protagonists are fascinated to the point of self-destruction with the idea of sexual relations with white women. In his Harlem crime series, as we will later discuss, he equated light skin color with irresistible sexuality in Black women. Even more interestingly, the people with the lightest skins in the Harlem crime stories, women and men alike, are typically the most evil. The characters with the blackest skin are the "squares" and therefore the victims.

In his personal life, he made it a practice of engaging in romantic liaisons with white women even before he left the United States. He met his first long-term white lover on the ship going to Paris, and later, after innumerable other experiences with white women in Europe, he actually married an Englishwoman with whom he remained until his death in 1984.

Himes resented the importance of skin color among his fellow Black students, later commenting "I despised the in-group class distinction based on color and the degree of white blood in one's veins...I liked dark black people, I was accepted by them as just another person. I was at ease with them. Among them, I felt as black as the next person and as good as anyone. The 'light-bright-and-damn-near-white' social clique got on my ass."[10]

While he was a student at Ohio State, Himes took a group of these proper, light-skinned young Black people down to the ghetto one night to meet some of his pimp and prostitute friends as a joke. The gag backfired on him, and some of the girls in the group reported Himes to the dean of men. He was called in and forced to withdraw for reasons of "ill health and failing grades."

The chagrined young man returned to Cleveland, where he had a relapse from his injuries. He was laid up for the entire winter, trapped in the house with his violently quarrelling parents.

When the summer came, he recovered sufficiently to leave home. An acquaintance introduced him to Bunch Boy, a professional gambler. Bunch Boy made quite an impression on young Himes, so much so that Himes used him as a character in some of his early short stories and in several novels. Bunch Boy had converted the upper story of a house on Cleveland's Cedar Avenue near Ninety-fifth Street into a gambling club. All forms of gambling were available there, including bookmaking.

Bunch Boy employed, among others, a Johnny Perry to run his blackjack game. Perry, whom Himes described as a handsome, soft-spoken married man with a superficial air of culture, was certainly the model for Johnny Perry, the heroic gambler of *The Crazy Kill*.

Himes began hanging around the place and eventually he became an employee. While working there, he met a big snaggle-toothed red-brown man named Val, whom he also used as a character in *The Crazy Kill*. From Val, Himes learned to become a competent blackjack player.

As he began to make the rounds with these gangsters and toughs, Himes met many successful pimps and madams and learned how to get along in the underworld. Soon he was making money from pimping and bootlegging as well as from gambling. He met other gamblers and gangsters named Abie the Jew, Red Johnny, Four-Four, Chink Charlie, and Dummy, all of whom eventually became characters in the Harlem series.

Sometime in 1928, Himes was walking down the street in Cleveland and saw a vivacious young woman named Jean Johnson leaning against the front gate of her house. Their gazes locked, and it was love at first sight.[11] He went to work for a landprop, or madam, who gave him a job selling whiskey in a joint in back of Bunch Boy's place. The major reason for his taking the job was that it provided him with an apartment where he could live with Jean. However, he often became infuriated when the low-life clientele began to try to buy her from him. He bought his first gun, an Owl's Head .32 revolver, and carried it with him everywhere.[12] Himes remarked that "I was fortunate that it didn't shoot straight, because I shot at quite a number of people."[13] His wild behavior eventually angered his boss to the point that she fired him and put them out of their apartment.

Himes found himself broke and desperate for money. With some friends he broke into a National Guard armory and stole a case of Colt .45 automatic pistols and ammunition. Their plan was to sell them to Blacks employed in the steel mills in Warren and Youngstown, Ohio. Shortly after the theft, however, they were arrested and taken back to Cleveland.

He was saved from immediate imprisonment after a sympathetic female judge heard the overwrought pleas of his mother. Mrs. Himes apparently told in some detail all the family's misfortunes over the past several years. Himes got a suspended sentence and returned home in time to see his parents separate. Shortly thereafter, the family completely disintegrated when Joseph, Jr., left for Oberlin College and Chester moved out to begin living with Jean Johnson again.

In September of 1928, Himes and a friend stole a car and drove to Columbus, where he spent some time hanging around the Ohio State campus flirting with coeds. During this period he stole a freshman identity card and used it to pass bad checks. Again, he was quickly apprehended, brought to trial, and sent to jail. At a later hearing, another judge allowed himself to be swayed by a story of mitigating circumstances. Himes was placed in the custody of his divorced father with a two-year suspended sentence and a five-year bench parole.

The young man began living with his father in a rented room on Eighty-ninth Street off Cedar Avenue in Cleveland. His father had fallen far from the days when he was a respectable college professor. By now he was working at janitorial jobs and living in a very rundown room. Himes stayed out of the room as much as he could to escape the miasma of his father's defeat.

The golden promise of Chester's childhood was gone now, and the young man was very near going over an emotional precipice. He became violent and walked the streets with a chip on his shoulder. He vandalized a bar when he was refused service and pistol-whipped the manager with a large revolver he had begun carrying.

Not too long after that, he heard a Negro chauffeur at Bunch Boy's bragging about the wealth of his boss, who lived in the exclusive white neighborhood of Cleveland Heights. Himes conceived of a desperate plan by which he would rob the family and leave the country. Subsequently, he went to the home at 10:30 one night and forced his way into the house at gunpoint. Once inside, he stuck up all of the family members and servants he found there. He took away a sizeable amount of cash and jewelry and escaped in the Cadillac automobile he found in the garage. After several near-misses with disaster, he managed to get a train to Chicago where he soon was arrested after an unsuccessful attempt to fence the jewelry.

The detectives took Himes back to the police station where they handcuffed his feet together and hung him upside down from an open door. There they systematically beat him about the ribs and testicles with revolvers wrapped inside their hats. The irony of the story is that the Chicago police were attempting to get Himes to confess to a local robbery. When he confessed to the Cleveland crime to keep them from killing him, they were caught off guard.

Chester Himes was returned to Cleveland where he stood trial for armed robbery and was sentenced on December 27, 1928. The unfortunate youngster found himself in front of a merciless judge this time, who sentenced him to 20 to 25 years at hard labor in the Ohio State Penitentiary. Himes later complained that this judge "had hurt me as much as I could ever be hurt if I lived a hundred thousand years."[14]

With that stroke of a pen, Chester Himes' life as a criminal was over. Looking in retrospect, it is surprising to realize that the part of his life that provided him with so much grist for his writing career lasted only about one year.

Once in prison, he discovered much the same life as he had known on the outside. Gambling and prostitution were the major occupations of the inmates. Having had a fair amount of experience with both, Himes found that he fit right in. While he was much smaller physically than many of the other inmates, Himes had developed into an extremely violence prone man while he was out on the street. He wrote that he had such violent seizures of rage that men twice his size would back off from him. He became indispensable to the other cons because he "helped the gambling to be accepted, I could talk, I kept it clean, headed off fights, stopped the cheating, protected the 'chumps,' and personally paid off arguments before they erupted into violence."[15]

One or two years after Himes entered prison, probably about 1931, he began to write. Ironically, we have little information about how and why he started. In his autobiography he noted that "I began writing in prison...[it] protected me, against both the convicts and the screws. The black convicts had both an instinctive respect for and fear of a person who could sit down at a typewriter and write...the screws could never really kill a convict who was a public figure..."[16]

Himes's brother Joseph suggests that the reasons for his embarking on a writing career were less dramatic and probably the result of a number of differing factors. He believes that his brother's drive to become a writer had its roots in their childhood. When Joseph Himes, Sr., was on the faculty of the Branch Normal School in Pine Bluff, Arkansas, both boys got a "significant course" in English fundamentals from Miss Ernestine Copeland, a member of the college English department. "We analyzed the language," he remembers, "parsing and diagramming the sentences, studying composition, and the other elements of writing and reading the language. This experience quickened Chester's interest in reading and writing, and gave him a strong language foundation for writing."[17]   Reading was a nightly pastime in the Himes family, with everyone gathered around the stove reading newspapers, magazines, the *Encyclopedia Britannica,* and anything else that was handy. Chester developed a decided preference during these years for the works of Edgar Allen Poe and similar exciting and romantic fiction.

Joseph believes that when his brother was imprisoned and found himself confronted with an empty future, "he took himself in hand and decided that he had to do something with his life. The alternative was too ghastly to consider. Even at this time he may have thought of writing as what he would like to do."[18]

Estelle Himes was devastated by what had happened to her youngest son and began to push him in the same direction. She often visited him in prison and persuaded prison officials to excuse him from hard labor and provide him with a place to develop his skills. She also furnished him with a typewriter, paper, pencils, and anything else he might need. More importantly, she visited him often and provided him with the encouragement he needed to push toward his new goal. Within a relatively short time, he began to experience success.

Research suggests that his first published story may have appeared in a Black owned magazine entitled *The Bronzeman.* Unfortunately, we know nothing about the story, including the title, because a complete set of this periodical is no longer available anywhere in the country, and copies have not been found in Himes' collected papers.

We do know from stories that have been identified as his that he became quite prolific during these prison years. A number of stories by Himes appeared in the 1932 and 1933 issues of such now-defunct Negro periodicals as *Abbott's* and *The Atlanta Daily World*. It is interesting to note in reading this early work that, like Dashiell Hammett in his early days, Himes chose to write about the things he knew best: crime and criminals.

But Himes wasn't writing the blood and thunder thriller that was typical of *Black Mask*. He was using his experience to write about men who usually were career criminals already in prison or on their way. Most of the stories are heavy on plot and character development and exhibit little of the blazing violence that characterizes his Harlem crime novellas.

At times the criminals resemble Himes himself: men with violence deeply imbedded in them. One of the most representative is Spats, the protagonist of "His Last Day," who remembers that "ten years in the big house had taught him not to take any chances, to shoot when the occasion called for shooting, and to shoot straight, and pay for his blanks with his freedom."[19]

At times, though, Himes seems to have been influenced by the "slick" magazine fiction of his day. In the story "Her Whole Existence: A Story of True Love," Himes writes about the love affair between socialite Mable Miles and racketeer Richard Riley. Though we are told that "Riley's power swings plenty votes" that would have "too much blood on them,"[20] Riley is totally unlike the proletarian characters who inhabit the rest of Himes' fiction. Riley seems drawn more in the mold of a Louis Joseph Vance hero, whose masculinity is leavened by a propensity for breaking into passionate Edwardian lovemaking:

"Lord you're beautiful Mable. You're more than just beautiful, you're bewitching. You're like a beautiful painting with the golden bronze of your complexion and the moonbeams playing hide-and-seek in your midnight hair. And brown-eyes like love itself..."

"Forgive me, Miss Miles, I'm sorry," he apologized. "I didn't intend to be rude, but you don't know how disturbingly beautiful you are with the moonlight falling across your face like that. I had to say something."[22]

As one might expect in a story with this type of dialogue, the pair are secretly married. Later, after Riley gets into a shooting scrape with police officers and kills one, they escape to Mexico, where they lead an idyllic life raising their small son and breeding horses. Finally, in the mold of the true Edwardian hero, Riley's personal honor can no longer allow him to live in hiding, and he decides to return to the States to give himself up. Mable remains outside, waiting faithfully for him to serve out his term because "she loves him, she will always love him—it is her life— *her whole existence*."[22]

In 1934 Himes made a major breakthrough with his sale of a story entitled "Crazy in the Stir" to *Esquire*. This put a temporary end to his writing for Negro periodicals, and in the beginning he even carefully hid his identity as a Black man. Continuing in the vein of his first publications, most of his early *Esquire* stories were about convicted criminals and prison life. Himes critic Stephen Milliken has noted that "the central characters were types *Esquire* readers might be expected to admire: white, mildly bigoted, tough and uncomplicated, rapidly drawn in crisp, authoritative strokes on the two levels, surface and immediately below...''[23] Himes became a regular contributor to *Esquire,* and it was not until 1936 that he was finally identified as a Black man.

On April 1, 1936, Himes was paroled to his mother after serving seven and a half years of his term. This hopeful change in his life was somewhat diminished by the news that the State of Ohio was stopping disability payments he had been awarded at the time of his accident. This was unfortunate because, instead of saving it, he had used the money to pay for his brother Joseph's undergraduate and graduate education.

On August 13, 1937, he married Jean Johnson and, in his words, "we began slowly starving together."[24] He was trying to sell stories to magazines, but was finding it slow going. Although *Esquire* continued to buy occasional stories from him, increasingly he found himself having to return to the less remunerative Black-owned periodicals. He published several stories a year all through the latter 1930s, but it was clear that he was going to have to find regular work in order to support his new wife.

During this period he met a number of people whose luck and industry would eventually make them successful and famous. He came to know his cousin, Henry Lee Moon, who would later become publicity director of the NAACP. He also made the acquaintance of Langston Hughes. Himes later complained, however, that these people were "of no help and offered very little encouragement."[25]

During the winter of 1937-38 he managed to get work as a laborer with the WPA. It was hard, cold, dirty work digging sewers and dredging drainage canals for the sum of $65.00 a month. He wrote letters of protest to the local and state headquarters of WPA and for his efforts was promoted to research assistant, a job that netted him an additional $30.00 a month.

His first assignment was to write vocational bulletins for the Cleveland Public Library. He also became interested in the CIO at this time, and research suggests that he did some kind of voluntary work for the organization's newspaper, the *Union Leader.* He is also believed to have written a brief history of the CIO. Although a unsigned pamphlet history of the organization that was published in 1937 has been discovered, it is impossible to positively identify it as Himes' work.

His work was sufficiently skillful that WPA promoted him to the status of professional writer, and he was assigned to write articles about Cleveland's history. An article he wrote about the Shaker and Mennonite religious sects, which included some rather unfortunate humorous remarks, got him into trouble with his superiors. As a result, he was demoted back to research assistant status.

Never one to accept anything willingly he saw as a personal injustice, Himes wrote a number of angry letters to the state and national directors of WPA and to President Franklin Roosevelt. Apparently the letters had some effect because an investigator was sent from Washington, and Himes was eventually reinstated as a writer. He was transferred back to the Public Library where, as part of the WPA Writers' Project, he wrote a long history of Cleveland. Apparently the manuscript was never published and was subsequently lost because later efforts to uncover it have met with no success.

Another shadowy episode in this part of his life was an under-the-table job he had with the *Cleveland News*. Himes later claimed in his autobiography that the editor, N.R. Howard, assigned him to travel about the streets of the city and write vignettes based on conversations he heard. Himes claimed that the vignettes, totalling about fifty in number, appeared on the editorial page in a box entitled "This Cleveland." The articles, which he called prose poems, were supposedly published unsigned except for his initials. Himes claimed that he was anonymous to everyone but the editor because there would have been some sort of protest if it had been generally known that he was a Negro.

Recent research suggests that Himes was mistaken about much of this information. No series entitled "This Cleveland" ever appeared in the paper, and no series of any kind ever appeared in a box on the editorial page. So far it is impossible to attribute anything in this paper to Himes conclusively.

In 1940, the war in Europe was heating up, and war industry was booming in America. In the hopes of cashing in on the war boom, Himes convinced Ohio Governor Harold Burton to terminate his parole and restore his citizenship. One of his first acts was to register with the Democratic Party.

Thanks to the intercession of the Jelliffes, a white family who ran the Karamu settlement house and theater in Cleveland's ghetto, Himes got a job working as a cook and butler on the country estate of writer Louis Bromfield. Bromfield liked Himes, and after reading Himes' unpublished novel *Black Sheep*, he promised to help him get it published or made into a film. Bromfield was unsuccessful in this endeavor, but he did take Himes and Jean with him to Los Angeles in the fall of 1941 when he went there to write the screen adaptation of Hemingway's *For Whom The Bell Tolls*.

In spite of Bromfield's efforts to help him find writing work, Himes found that Hollywood was as color blind as anywhere else in the country. Thanks to introductions provided by Langston Hughes, however, Himes met a number of politically active Blacks in the Los Angeles area, among them Loren Miller and Welford Wilson. Through these people, Himes got a first-hand view of the intellectual   communist life in Southern California. As he later told John Williams, "I was given the works—taken to cell meeting (sic) all over town; to parties, to lectures and all that crap. I met all the local heroes of the Spanish Civil War and all the communist script writers—Dalton Trumbo and John Howard Lawson, etc."[26]

These people were probably trying to recruit Himes, because they housed, fed, and interviewed him. He was sent out to apply for work in Los Angeles companies that did not hire Blacks and was effectively used by them to prove points. Although he knew he was being used, Himes went along with it for awhile, gathering much of the material that he would later put to good use in the writing of *Lonely Crusade* (1947).

Tiring of this life, Himes and Jean moved to San Francisco where he got work at the Richmond Shipyards owned by the Henry J. Kaiser Company. Dissatisfied with this job, he moved around the Bay Area working as a warehouseman for an aircraft company and in a number of other menial capacities.

After a time, they moved back to Los Angeles at the specific request of Hall Johnson so Himes could work as a press agent for the filming of *Cabin in the Sky*. To Himes' chagrin, MGM refused to hire him on and instead hired a local Negro reporter for the job. Himes probably would have resented his working conditions bitterly had he gotten the job. The MGM lot was extremely Jim Crowed and all Blacks, from the janitors up to the actors, were completely segregated from the whites.

In the meantime, Jean Himes had gotten a good job as co-director of women's activities for the 18 USOs in the Los Angeles area. They had a pleasant house on a hill in the City Terrace area near the reservoir. Himes found work as a shipfitter at the San Pedro Harbor shipyard, and, on the surface, all appeared to be well with the couple.

However, Himes became increasingly frustrated. His work was unsatisfying, and he was forced to work with bigoted whites, many of whom had moved from poverty-stricken southern rural backgrounds in order to take advantage of the war production boom. To add to his problems, Himes was depressed because Jean not only had to work to help support them, but she also had a better-paying and more prestigious job. Their marriage began to suffer in consequence.

He began to write *If He Hollers Let Him Go*, which was based on his experiences in the shipyards, and in May of 1944 he was granted a Rosenwald Fellowship to complete it. He went to New York that June. There he became depressed and for a time got involved in drunkenness and affairs with many women. One affair, which would have far-reaching implications for him, was with an attractive white woman named Vandi Haygood, acting director of fellowships for the Rosenwald Foundation. When Jean joined him, her discovery of his infidelity almost caused her to take her own life.

As emotionally disastrous as this period was, it was not a total loss. Himes fell into the thick of New York literary society and met everyone from W.E.B. Dubois to Arthur Miller. Nineteen-forty-five was something of a landmark year for the young writer because it marked his first meeting with Richard Wright. Although Wright's towering ego grated on Himes, they became friends, and Himes became part of Wright's circle. Later, when *If He Hollers Let Him Go* appeared in print, Wright wrote the first and the most supportive review of the book.

Nineteen-forty-five was important for another reason. It marked the death of Estelle Bomar Himes at the age of 71. It is impossible to believe that this loss did not have a profound effect on Himes, though he later said little about it. His mother was undoubtedly the most profound influence of his life. Her pride, her arrogance, and her insistence on equal treatment all emerged in the personality of her son, who was about to embark on a career as a protest novelist. Although he found living with her impossible and her influence grating at times, Himes must have felt the loss keenly.

The appearance of Himes' first book should have marked a time of great joy in his life, but, like so much of Chester Himes' experience, it held more than its share of bitterness for him. He had had a rewarding experience working with his editor at Doubleday, Bucklin Moon, but Moon left to work on his own book before seeing the publication through. A female editor whom Himes never met took over and apparently was deeply offended by things in the book. The book was harshly edited without Himes' permission, and when it was finally released distribution was sabotaged. To add insult to injury, dissention within the ranks at Doubleday prevented him from being awarded the George Washington Carver Memorial Award.

During the summer of 1946, Himes and Jean went to live in the desert near Miford, California. In his memoirs, Himes describes the experience as an idyllic one, filled with lovemaking and work on his second book. It was probably the last golden moment in an already deteriorating marriage.

They returned east in the fall of 1946 and lived at Wading River, Long Island. There Himes finished *Lonely Crusade* while working as a caretaker for a New York doctor named Stafford.

In 1947, they took a room in Harlem at 421 West 147th Street, and Jean got a job as director of athletics at a Welfare Department Girls Camp. *Lonely Crusade* appeared on the stands to almost total scorn and rejection. Blacks, communists, conservative whites, and everyone else wrote scathing denunciations of Himes' ambitious novel. He was further humiliated when a scheduled radio interview on the prestigious Mary Margaret McBride program was cancelled without warning, and both Macy's and Bloomingdale's cancelled autograph signings. In many places, books were taken out of stock. Only about 1,400 copies were published, and it was many years before the novel was reprinted in the United States. Himes was crushed by the vitriolic response and vowed that he would leave the United States.

In May and June of 1948, he was invited to Yaddo, a writers' colony in Saratoga Springs. The distraught writer stayed drunk most of the time and was unable to get any writing done. While there, however, he was invited to the University of Chicago where he delivered a paper entitled "The Dilemma of the Negro Writer in the United States." At this lecture, the disappointed and emotionally wounded Himes said some things that shocked and astonished his racially mixed audience.

He postulated that given the nature of white racism, all American Blacks "must, of necessity, hate white people." He rounded out his argument by asserting:

If this plumbing for the truth reveals within the Negro personality homicidal mania, lust for white women, a pathetic sense of inferiority, paradoxical anti-Semitism, arrogance, Uncle Tomism, hate and fear and self-hate, this then is the effect of oppression on the human personality. These are the daily horrors, the daily realities, the daily experiences of an oppressed minority.[27]

The stunned audience sat transfixed in their seats, not daring to move. There was neither applause nor derision. Himes left the auditorium, went back to Yaddo, and stayed drunk for six more weeks. He was 39 years old.

Jean lost her job with the Welfare Department, and in consequence Himes worked at everything in order for the two of them to survive. Having to take responsibility for the support of his family brought him out of his slough of despond and, temporarily at least, saved his marriage. He worked as a caretaker in Sussex Village in New Jersey and as a bellhop at a hotel in New York. He took another caretaking job at a camp in Ware, Massachusetts, and at a country club on Lake Copake before moving on a whim to Bridgeport, Connecticut.

Bridgeport became the scene of one more event that was destined to drive Himes more deeply into despair and strengthen his resolve to leave the United States. On the eve of leaving Bridgeport in order to move back to New York City, Himes was involved in a trivial motor accident with the wife of a prosperous white doctor. Much to his surprise, he was jailed and his bail was set at $25.00.

With Jean in New York looking for an apartment and his only other friend in Bridgeport, his landlady, out of town for two more days, the penniless writer was faced with a humiliating and demoralizing imprisonment. Himes eventually was remanded to the county prison, where he was held incommunicado for some time before his frantic wife could effect his release.

He later wrote of this incident that it "shook me. It wasn't that it hurt so much. Nor was I surprised. I believed that the American white man—in fact all Americans, black or white—was capable of anything. It was just that it stirred up my anxiety, which had gradually settled down somewhat."[28]

During this time he got Margot Johnson as an agent and began working on what is probably his most autobiographical novel, *The Third Generation*. It was his least favorite book, and he told John Williams that "it is a subtly dishonest book, made dishonest deliberately for the purpose of making money. Strangely enough, it didn't live up to expectations."[29]

The next few years were something of a blur for Himes, and he wrote confusingly about them in his memoirs. He and Jean moved briefly to New York City, where he experienced a lot of frustration in attempting to sell his prison novel. In the spring of 1950 they moved to Stamford, Connecticut, where they worked on the farm of a Madison Avenue attorney named Halperin. Later that same year they moved briefly to Durham, North Carolina, where Joseph Himes had arranged for Chester to conduct a two-week seminar in creative writing at North Carolina College, a state teachers' college for Blacks.

Following a brief visit to New York City, where Himes discovered his novel *Cast the First Stone* had been rejected by Henry Holt, he and Jean went to Vermont. There they stayed briefly with Black writer William Smith. From Vermont, they went to White Plains, New York, where Himes got a job in the mailroom of *The Readers' Digest*. Finding himself less than adept at the work he was given, he soon left to take a job as a porter at the White Plains Y.M.C.A.

Thanks to her experience at Girls Camp, Jean was able to get work as recreational director of the New York State Women's Reformatory at nearby Mount Kisco. She had to live on the grounds of the Reformatory and was able to see Himes only for the two days each week that she got off. He roomed with the spinster daughter of a former A.M.E. bishop on the edge of White Plains.

This involuntary separation seems to mark the beginning of the end of their marriage. With publishers seemingly unanimous in their rejection of his novels *Cast the First Stone* and *The Third Generation*, Himes was at his lowest ebb. Lonely and despondent over the separation and the knowledge that his wife was essentially supporting him financially, he quit his job in White Plains and went to live with his older brother, Eddie, in New York City. Sheer economic necessity eventually drove him back to working as a janitor at the New Prospect Hotel in upstate New York.

Just when all seemed lost, Himes received a message from William Targ, vice president and editor-in-chief of the World Publishing Company, telling him that they were accepting his novel, *The Third Generation*, for publication. The sale put a $2,000.00 advance into the destitute writer's hands, and he quickly moved back to New York City.

With the money in his hands, what Himes most wanted was female companionship. In his memoirs, he put it more bluntly: he wanted to sleep with a white woman. It happened that Vandi Haygood, the white woman with whom he had enjoyed a brief affair in Chicago several years earlier, was now living in New York working as an executive for the International Institute of Education.

Vandi was beautiful, erratic, and sexually adventurous, and Himes used her to lose himself in an alcohol-soaked and drug-ridden debauch. He lived with her for 18 months, during which he spent all of his advance from *The Third Generation* and nearly ruined himself. By Christmas of 1952, their affair had degenerated into near hatred, with Himes physically abusing Vandi when it was apparent that she was seeing other men on the side. The affair was certainly one of the lowest points of his life and was the basis for his most depressing autobiographical novel, *The Primitive*.

He left Vandi and moved in briefly with Bill Smith in Vermont. While he was living here, his father died in Cleveland, and Himes, destitute as usual, had to borrow the money in order to attend the funeral.

With both of his parents dead, his wife gone, his affair with Vandi on the rocks, and very few friends in a position to help him, Himes had nothing to hold him in America any longer. Only the lack of money to leave held him back. This problem was solved when his agent, Margo Johnson, sold *Cast The First Stone* to Coward-McCann for a $1,200.00 advance. Hard on the heels of this good news came word from Bill Targ that New American Library had purchased the reprint rights to *The Third Generation* for $10,000.00, half of which was immediately available to Himes. With a confidence that only money could bring, Himes booked passage on the *Isle de France* and left America forever on April 3, 1953.

On the voyage he met an aristocratic white woman named Willa Thompson (he protected her identity with the pseudonym "Alva" in his memoirs) and, perhaps because of his terrible loneliness, began an affair with her that they continued when they reached Europe. She was a Boston socialite, member of the D.A.R., wife of a European dentist, and mother to four little girls whom she missed terribly. She was recovering from a nervous breakdown when they met.

They parted company after they reached Europe, though they corresponded with each other. In Paris Himes was briefly reunited with Vandi Haygood, and they resumed their affair. After Vandi left Paris, Willa came to Himes, and the two decided to live together.

The couple lived for seven months in London before moving to Mallorca for nine months. Together they wrote a long novel entitled *The Silver Altar* which was based on Willa's life and which Himes considered a beautiful love story. Himes made many attempts to sell it, but he found that he could not overcome his publisher's disgust at their living arrangements. Later he tried to submit the manuscript in her name, but found that no one would give the book a fair hearing. Years later, Beacon Press of Boston published a drastically revised version of the book which had been retitled *Garden Without Flowers*. Sole authorship was given to Willa, although Himes received some money for his efforts.

While living in Mallorca, Himes developed what he described as a "don't-give-a-goddamn attitude" and wrote *The Primitive*. Based on his self-destructive love affair with Vandi Haygood, the novel ends with the Himes character murdering the Vandi character. This book seems to have grown out of Himes' assertion that "the final answer of any black to a white woman with whom he lives in a white society is violence."[30] The real Vandi later killed herself with an overdose of pills. He offered the book to NAL, which accepted the book without reservation and gave him a $1,000.00 advance. Broke as usual, Himes was forced to take what he considered too small a sum. With the advance he got Willa a ticket to Boston where they hoped she could sell the novel they had written. Once again Himes found himself alone and deeply depressed.

He later managed to return to New York and tried to sell the book himself. Failing at that, he got control of the rights to *If He Hollers,* which he sold to Berkley Books. With this money he returned to Paris. There he remained, broke most of the time and living on the generosity of other writers and the friendship of Frenchmen who knew and admired his earlier work.

At the end of 1957, a meeting at the publishing house of Gallimard with Marcel Duhamel changed his life. Himes had gone in hoping to interest them in an unfinished novel he was writing entitled *Mamie Mason* (eventually to be published in this country as *Pinktoes*). Duhamel was an great admirer of Himes's work, having translated *If He Hollers* into French.

The French had become enthusiastic fans of the hard-boiled school of detective fiction as created by Dashiell Hammett and Raymond Chandler. As early as 1942, Roger Caillois had boldly suggested that the detective story, because of certain characteristics, deserved to be considered as a literary art form. Mainstream fiction, he noted, was constrained by a narrow set of rules that governed its structure. The detective novel was less constrained because of its innate flexibility:

> The detective novel stands out among other works because in writing it, one can create new rules of procedure. When writing other novels, we try to make them stick to very narrow existing rules...We can see at first sight that the detective novel occupies a place of extraordinary originality in the bosom of literature....[31]

One of Gallimard's most famous lines was a series of paperback detective fiction that they called *La Série Noire,* and Duhamel was editor of that series. Perhaps realizing that the tough-guy elements in Himes' fiction must have had their roots in the Hammett style, he asked Himes if he would like to write for the series.

Himes was frank in saying that he knew nothing about writing detective stories and was too short of cash to learn. Duhamel believed in him, however, and insisted that all he had to do was read Chandler, Hammett, or Peter Cheyney in the original English to see how it was done. When Himes was still hesitant, Duhamel explained to him succinctly how it should be done:

> "Get an idea," Marcel said. "Start with action, somebody does something—a man reaches out a hand and opens a door, light shines in his eyes, a body lies on the floor, he turns, looks up and down the hall...Always action in detail. Make pictures. Like motion pictures. Always the scenes are visible. No stream of consciousness at all. We don't give a damn who's thinking what—only what they are doing. Always doing something. From one scene to another. Don't worry about it making sense. That's for the end. Give me 220 typed pages.[32]

Duhamel gave the starving writer a $1,000.00 advance and reeled his victim in.

It is not generally known just how much trouble Himes had getting started in the crime fiction genre. He initially drew on an unpublished short story he called "Spanish Gin" and wrote a 119-page manuscript entitled "The Lunatic Fringe." Set in Spain, "Fringe" is a tale of multiple murders and accidental killings. Apparently it was not what Duhamel wanted, and he sent Himes back to his typewriter.

Himes was stumped until he remembered a story that a friend had told him about a con game called "the blow" that consisted of getting a sucker to put up money for a phony scientific process that would change $10.00 notes to $100.00 bills. During the phony process, an equally phony lawman breaks in and manages to collar only the sucker. The bogus cop allows the sucker to bribe him in order to be let go. In so doing, the sucker loses the money he brought to have raised and the bribe money, as well.

Himes presented the story outline to Duhamel, who was enthusiastic about it. At that point, Himes remembers, he asked a fateful question:

> "You think I should have some police?" I asked, trying to sound intelligent.
> "You can't have a *policier* without police," Marcel said.[33]

And so, as an afterthought, the groundwork for the creation of Gravedigger Jones and Coffin Ed Johnson was haphazardly laid.

Himes named the story after the sucker, Jackson, calling it "The Five Cornered Square," explaining afterwards that a gullible person like Jackson is so square that he has five corners. The French translation of this argot is "queen of the squares" or *La Reine des Pommes* ("apple" meaning "square" in French slang). It was under this title that Chester Himes' first book in many years was published and won the prestigious *Grand prix de la littérature policière* literary award. Overnight he went from starving artist to the talk of Paris.

Over the course of the next 12 years he wrote only seven more stories in the Coffin Ed—Grave Digger series and one other crime thriller set in Black New York. It is through these nine detective novels that he eventually became well known and finally achieved the financial security that had eluded him through most of his writing life.

Many literary critics have tended to dismiss these short novels out of hand. The outlandish violence, the sense of absurdity, and the sexual teasing that make them so memorable have caused many examiners of Himes' work to berate them as commercial potboilers at best and and sheer hatemongering at worst.

Only recently, as critics and scholars have awakened to the subtleties in popular fiction, has there been any realization of what Himes actually accomplished in these books. Himes created a world that was part real and part fantasy and ostensibly used it to entertain. At the same time, he instructed the reader by way of gross exaggeration as to what were the realities of life for the average Black man on the street.

One of Himes' oft-stated theses was that for the American Black life was one vast absurdity. He told his Harlem stories in such a way that this absurdity was emphasized and the dreadfulness laid bare. At the same time, by the story's end, something positive often had occurred. Bad people had been punished or at least circumvented. Lovers had been joined or reunited. Sometimes, two determined detectives were able to establish a modicum of peace in the middle of chaos and hopelessness. Himes used these stories to explain to the white reader that, as bizarre as Black life might seem, the motivations of some Black men and women may not be all that different from his own.

Ultimately, Himes also depicted graphically the plight of the poor urban Black and showed how, in his own way, he had learned to cope with the never-fading shadows of poverty, racism, and hopelessness.

There is much more to Himes than immediately meets the eye. As Fred Pfeil noted in a recent essay on Himes' work, "we know by now, or ought to know, that what gets us off as entertainment is rarely simple and never innocent...when the scene is Harlem and both the criminals and the good guys are black; and when the author is a black man with an analysis of white racism's power to provoke within blacks not only an answering hatred but paranoia, self-doubt, and self-contempts."[34] Pfeil adds that "your reactions to the lurid images, actions, and characters [Himes' Harlem novels] hurl forth reveal as much about you as about Harlem or Himes."

Americans are somewhat fascinated by violence, as modern TV and motion pictures will tell us. Twenty years after Himes wrote his last Harlem story, we note an increasing tendency on the part of movie makers to suggest that difficult problems can only be solved through violence. Stallone, Norris, Schwartzenegger, Eastwood; all of these top-grossing actors have reached their current popularity through a suggestion that might makes right.

However sentimental and generous earlier heroes have been, the quintessential American hero has always been a man with a gun in his fist. It is not altogether clear whether the Harlem stories are as violent as they are because Himes recognized this American obsession and decided to pander to it or whether he used this fiction to work out his own violent fantasies. In an unpublished story called "The Daydream" that Himes wrote in Paris in the 1950s, his first person narrator tells about lapsing into a daydream while reading about the murder trial of a Black in Mississippi.

In his dream, the narrator drives arrogantly into the small southern town and antagonizes the sheriff into a gunfight. After killing the sheriff, he lays waste to the town, killing rednecks one after the other before driving triumphantly out of town. Coming out of his reverie, the narrator addresses himself in the mirror and says, "Son, you are a very sick man."

Himes had very complicated notions of good and bad, of heroism and cowardice. Many are expressed, however obliquely, in the Harlem series. His obsessions with light skin and white women notwithstanding, Himes reveals in these stories an underlying belief that whiteness is inextricably bound up with evil. Most of his worst villains are either white men or light-skinned Negroes. If they do not have light skin, something about them may be white, such as their hair.

Women are the most prone to this. The archetypal Himes woman is a seductive, curvy, amoral sexpot with very light skin. She is a character who has many names but who shows up in virtually every story. At worst she may be a murderess but at best she will be a liar, a cheat, or a faithless lover.

Himes made his most appealing protagonists virile and utterly masculine, but he was not insensitive to the fact that a good man need not be the "badass nigger" of legend. Indeed, many of his protagonists are neither handsome nor courageous. Some are gullible and susceptible to trickery. What they all have in common is a romantic soul and an all-consuming belief in the redeeming power of love.

This belief was deep in Himes, too. Although he portrayed himself in all of his autobiographical writings as a lustful, sex-obsessed male, it is obvious that much of his life was spent in a search for a total and passionate love. It is this side of Himes that leavens the shootings, stabbings, and other mayhem of the Harlem series.

Nothing could keep Himes from feeling depressed over the state of the Black man in America, however. The little victories at the end of each novel are fragile ones, indeed, when compared with the injustices suffered by the Black man at the hands of his native country. Perhaps this is the reason why the final Harlem story, *Blind Man with a Pistol* ends, on such an inconclusive note and why there are no subsequent stories.

Himes was undoubtedly a complex and even a tragic figure. His writing reflects not only his own personal tragedies but also the millions of little tragedies that take place in the Black world every day. It is in the eight novelettes comprising the Harlem Domestic Series that Himes best illustrates this and, at the same time, displays the unique character of Black humor that has helped this race of people survive in the modern world.

The chapters that follow will discuss not only Himes' place as a writer of crime fiction, but also how he used his unique viewpoint to infuse his fiction with qualities that were amusing, compelling, and at times, even electrifying.

Chapter II
The Dark Knights

"Listen, boy," Coffin Ed said. "Brody is a homicide man and solving murders is his business. He goes at it in a routine way like the law prescribes, and if some more people get killed while he's going about it, that's just too bad for the victims. But me and Digger are two country Harlem dicks who live in this village and don't like to see anybody get killed. It might be a friend of ours. So we're trying to head off another killing."

"And there ain't much time," Grave Digger added.

By the late 1950s, the rules that governed the hard-boiled crime story had solidified to the point that most contemporary writers of the genre were mere parodists. Hammett had not written anything in 20 years, Chandler was in a decline from which he could not recover, and Ross Macdonald was essentially still aping the style and manner of Chandler. The only recent innovator in the field, Mickey Spillane, had taken such a drubbing from the critics over his supposed extremes of sex and violence that he had virtually stopped writing.

The rest of this second wave of tough-guy writers ranged from competent practitioners like Thomas B. Dewey and William Campbell Gault to mere pulp artists like Richard Prather. These writers had their loyal following of fans, yet all lacked the fire and color of the fabled "Black Mask Boys." The stage was set for the entrance of a dramatic newcomer.

Since the 1920s, the tough crime story had developed into a kind of mythos. The ingredient that made the genre unique was the fictional detective himself. Typically, this character, in his various guises, was depicted as youthful yet mature, tough but sensitive. Extremely well-read, if not college educated, the private eye could still wield an automatic with authority and throw an explosive punch when necessary. He was always from an Anglo-Saxon Protestant background, probably because of the latent bigotry that has always lived in the bosom of Middle America, but possibly because such a background could also protect him from the feelings of guilt that might assault a Catholic or a Jewish character.

He had a loner mentality that often expressed itself in revenge-motivated vigilante activities, a complete contempt for duly appointed authority, and a penchant for womanizing and excessive drinking. The same mentality also kept him available for whatever romantic interest his creator might throw his way. In the first book-length study written on Dashiell Hammett, biographer and critic William F. Nolan rather dramatically viewed the stories these characters appeared in as:

> ...a new style of detective fiction...: bitter, tough, unsentimental, uncompromisingly realistic, reflecting the violence of its time...Murder bounced from the tea garden to the back alley, and the private gentleman sleuth gave way to the hard-boiled private eye, a man of action who fought crime by his own rules, yet followed a rigid personal code: a knight in a trenchcoat who carried a .38 and knew how to use it, who punished hoods as much as they punished him, who worked outside society for the overall good of Society.[1]

Much of what the detective in this fiction had become was the doing of Dashiell Hammett and Raymond Chandler. Hammett, an ex-Pinkerton detective whose proletarian ideals suggested the idea of a working-class detective, had postulated that the private detective represented the Protestant Work Ethic at its best: a man so devoted to tracking and bringing criminals to justice for his own satisfaction that he preferred detecting to family, creature comforts, sexual pleasure, or financial security.

Chandler, with his Edwardian upbringing and his English public school background, romanticized Hammett's detective. The Chandlerian sleuth idealized women with an almost religious reverence. As disinterested in money as Hammett's hero, Chandler's would place his reputation and even his life on the line to protect the innocent and provide justice when a corrupt bureaucracy could not or would not. In his classic essay, "The Simple Art of Murder," Chandler wrote that his detective hero was "the best man in his world and a good enough man for any world."[2]

In spite of the many imitators and disciples that these two writers spawned, there was still one characteristic that this detective had not had, and that was to be Black. Black characters occasionally appeared in hard-boiled crime fiction of the '20s, '30s, and '40s, but their roles were modest ones. Hammett usually depicted them as pawns of criminals. Jonathan Latimer made them buffoonish. Chandler drew them in fine detail with an uncanny knack for their speech patterns, but they were never more than minor characters off whom Marlowe could play.

There is some irony in the fact that Black writers throughout the 1920s and 1930s also produced lurid tales about tough criminals and detectives for such now forgotten Negro periodicals as *The Pittsburgh Courier, Abbott's Monthly,* and *The Bronzeman.* A writer named Rudolph Fisher published his novel *The Conjure Man Dies* in book form during this era. These stories, viewed in comparison with typical pulp magazine fare of the day, are no worse than much of what was published in *Detective Fiction Weekly, Dime Detective,* or *Black Mask* by white writers. Since only Negroes read these small-circulation weeklies and monthlies, much of this similar output is virtually unknown today.

Chester Himes had not had a great deal of experience writing about detectives when he met Marcel Duhamel in Paris. Criminals were more in his line of understanding. He had been one for a year and consorted with others for more than seven years of his life. Considering the reality from which he sprang, the fictional private eye probably would have appeared as a silly and romantic notion. His personal experience with police detectives was certainly not going to provide him with any heroic notions about them.

However, he did produce one story featuring detectives in his early career. In view of the path his writing took, it makes interesting reading today. "He Knew," published in the December 2, 1933, issue of *Abbott's Monthly*, concerns a pair of tough and uncompromising Black police detectives. The story is much too short for much character development, but Himes created an interesting vignette in which he examined the problems faced by a working-class detective in resolving the conflict brought about by his loyalty to his job and the needs of his family.

Most detective story writers have avoided this conflict by keeping the detective single and unencumbered. Himes met this conflict head-on by spending much of the story inside his protagonist's head as he walked his beat. The detective (coincidentally named Jones), worries about how his children may be growing away from him and the values he has tried to instill in them.

In a somewhat predictable ending, Detective Jones and his partner unwittingly kill Jones' two teenaged sons during a gun battle in a darkened warehouse. Even before Jones realizes that it is his own sons he has killed, he voices some rather emotional and (for a detective hero) uncharacteristic feelings about the brutal realities of his work:

A light, what he'd give for a light, Jones thought. He experienced a sudden distaste for his job—shooting men down in the darkness like rats, rats! For an instant he felt that he was going crazy.[3]

Himes once related in an interview that the real impetus for the creation of Grave Digger Jones and Coffin Ed Johnson came from a pair of black police detectives that he knew in Watts during the 1940s. Himes described the pair as callous and brutal men who used an excess of physical force and emotional terror to keep the people in their precinct under control.[4]

Himes' own first-hand experiences with the police, combined with his remembrance of the two brutal Los Angeles cops, must have been in force when he first conceived of Digger and Ed. Thus he probably did not intend them to be the main focus of his first detective novel. As if to underscore this feeling, his cynicism about policemen (of any color) comes out bluntly in this early description of them:

Grave Digger and Coffin Ed weren't crooked detectives, but they were tough. They had to be tough to work in Harlem. Colored folks didn't respect colored cops. But they respected big shiny pistols and sudden death...They took their tribute, like all real cops, from the established underworld catering to the essential needs of the people—game keepers, madams, streetwalkers, numbers writers, numbers bankers. But they were rough on purse snatchers, muggers, burglars, con men, and all strangers working any racket.

In this unflattering yet sharply worded portrait, Himes is expressing his understanding of not only the detectives but also the world in which they operate. The detectives take bribes and protection money from gangsters and pimps, but their doing so is accepted on both sides of the fence. At the same time, they try not to interfere actively in any activity which the community tacitly supports, regardless of its technical illegality. Perhaps unwittingly, Himes was mimicking the traditional hard-boiled ethic which places justice over law.

While these policemen make up their own rules about upholding the law, they think nothing of terrorizing small-time criminals. Unlike the whores and gamblers, these criminals are prone to hurt someone physically while plying their trade, and the detectives consider this behavior off limits. Perhaps coincidentally, these petty criminals are also the only ones who are unlikely to be able to pay them off.

These attitudes Himes expresses may seem grotesque, but they are attitudes which are accepted in the Black netherworld about which he writes. By white standards, attitudes here are absurd, but it is an absurdity that the Negro inhabitants have lived with for so many years that it has become their reality. These are poor people with little hope. What little hope they have left they have invested in the short-term possibility of hitting the number for big money and the long-term possibility of getting into heaven.

A hero in Harlem is somebody who has beaten the system, risen above his origins, and yet remained a member of the community. A Johnny Perry (*The Crazy Kill*) who has served time on the chain gang for murder and survived to become the owner of a successful gambling club is someone to emulate. This is even more the case for flamboyant evangelists like Reverend Deke O'Malley (*Cotton Comes to Harlem*) and Sweet Prophet Brown (*The Big Gold Dream*). They have taken the Black man's salvation and turned it into a money-making business. They not only have wealth, power, and luxury, but also sit on the right hand of the Almighty.

Along with these flamboyant and, to white eyes, twisted visions of heroism and power, Himes' Black world also is filled with genuine grotesques. Writing in the same tradition as Dickens, Twain, and Faulkner, Himes created grotesque characters who, in their very absurdity, serve as models for certain kinds of human behavior. We may laugh at the tribulations of Jackson, Pinky, Dummy, and Reverend Short, but Himes makes it possible for the reader to understand their motivations and possibly even to recognize himself in their twisted bodies.

In a world like this, it is inevitable that any man who represents the white perspective, i.e. the established order, must be different. This is particularly true for a Black man. In Chandler's words, he must be "a complete man and a common man and yet an unusual man." That he will be considered an outsider is accepted from the outset.

In the classic tradition, the hard-boiled detective was a private agent, usually setting himself against the legally appointed or elected bureaucracy. His lack of status, power, and resources underscored the heroic fight of a lone hero against a corrupt power structure.

Digger and Ed, for all of Himes' attempts to make them seem a part of their grotesque backdrop, are much more outsiders in their world than the classic private eye is in his own. As Black cops in all-Black Harlem, they are worse than outsiders to others of their race: they are traitors, upholders of the white man's law. On the opposite side of the coin, although they represent the law, they are still Black men working within a white-dominated power structure. This is not so obvious when they are working alone, but it immediately becomes apparent whenever they find themselves working with white members of the force. The hostility and suspicion of the white officers is often so strong that they cannot ignore it. Many times they must act physically and violently, simply in order to assert themselves as men. An excellent example occurs in *All Shot Up* as the two Black men join a group of white officers at the scene of Black Beauty's death on Convent Street. A flip cop keeps using the word "nigger," in spite of warnings from Coffin Ed. When he uses the word one time too many, Ed beats the man to the ground.

At the beginning of *The Heat's On,* the two detectives find themselves trying to protect Pinky, an albino Negro who has turned in a false fire alarm, from a group of enraged firemen. When they try to calm the angry firemen down, the group of white men ceases to see them as cops, only as two Negroes trying to protect another one. They are nearly hurt in the melee.

Thus Digger and Ed are separate and apart from their fellow Blacks, the police department they serve, and the white power structure in which they try to work. It is one of the ironies of Digger and Ed's lives that they do not begin to really appreciate this apartness until they are on their last case, *Blind Man With A Pistol.* Here they find that they are completely unable to make any headway in the case because of the hostility and suspicion of their Black brethren (with whom they seem to be out of touch) and the prejudice and venality of their white superiors who actively inhibit their progress.

Like Chandler and Hammett, Himes came to the crime novel from a more traditional literary background. He had read widely in prison and was able to draw on other traditions in the creation of his work. Therefore the Harlem he created was not akin to the realistic California that so many fictional detectives walked in. Rather, it is closer to a Dickensian village that is separated by color and grotesque attitudes from the rest of the world.

Himes was frank in admitting to Maurice Duhamel that he knew nothing about detective stories. As a virtually self-educated man, it is probable that he had read very little of the genre he was about to enter. In some measure, this was to his credit, because it allowed him to start out unencumbered by the baggage of his predecessors.

When Grave Digger and Coffin Ed first make their appearance one-third of the way through *For Love of Imabelle*, the prior actions of the other characters already have prepared us for the bizarre figure that these men cut as they keep order in the Savoy ticket line:

> The famous Harlem detective team of Coffin Ed Johnson and Grave Digger Jones had been assigned to keep order.
> Both were tall, loose-jointed, sloppily-dressed, ordinary-looking dark-brown colored men. But there was nothing ordinary about their pistols. They carried specially made long-barreled nickel-plated .38-caliber revolvers, and at the moment they had them in their hands.

Himes makes a deliberate contradiction in this description. The shabbiness of the two detectives seems to cast them in the same proletarian mold of other detectives, but we can tell already that they are not as ordinary as Himes indicates. Having told us in the same breath that they are the "famous Harlem detective team," Himes deliberately invites us to take another look at them. It is clear that everyone in the Savoy ticket line knows them by sight, and it is equally clear that they command immediate respect by virtue of their presence.

In their tall lankiness there is something, too, of the western lawman who stands loosely in the dusty street with his gun held ready to do battle with evil. It is an image that Himes reinforces on a number of occasions. For example, when the pair arrive at the scene of Val's murder in *The Crazy Kill*, Chink Charlie is heard to say "Jesus Christ. Now we've got those damned Wild West Gunmen here to mess up everything!" Later in the same story this image of the small-town lawman is called up when Coffin Ed tells another character that "...me and Digger are two country Harlem dicks who live in this village...."

So little is different about the two detectives that, in the early stories, they almost seem to be interchangeable. In *The Heat's On* Himes tells us:

> Both of them looked just as red-eyed, greasy-faced, sweaty and evil as all the other colored people gathered about, combatants and spectators alike. They were of a similar size and build to other "working stiffs"—big, broad-shouldered, loose-jointed and flat-footed. Their faces bore marks and scars similar to any colored street fighter. Grave Digger's was full of lumps where felons had hit him from time to time with various weapons; while Coffin Ed's was a patchwork of scars where skin had been grafted over the burns left by acid thrown into his face by Hank.

In many ways, they seem like an inseparable pair of twins. They dress alike, usually in black alpaca suits and battered shapeless hats. Both wear their hair cut short and each speaks in a blunt, profane way.

They are also brothers-in-arms, and as if to prove it each carries an identical long-barrelled .38 special revolver built on a .44 frame.[5] They carry these weapons in identical tan shoulder holsters which the detectives keep smeared on the inside with seal fat in order to facilitate a quick draw.

Himes seems to dwell more on these guns than he does on the lives and habits of detectives themselves. He has endowed these pistols with an almost supernatural aura. Jones and Johnson do not have to draw these weapons; they seem to appear in their owners' hands of their own volition and with miraculous speed. The two men brandish them like the weapons of medieval knights-errant and, indeed, they often seem to give the pair the same kind of invulnerability and invincibility as magic swords.

Significantly whenever one of the pair is *hors de combat*, the still-functioning partner makes a point of taking the fallen brother's revolver with him. Possibly it was Himes' way of allowing the missing partner to remain present in spirit during these crisis situations. In *For Love of Imabelle*, after Coffin Ed has acid thrown in his face by Hank, Grave Digger shoots Hank through the right eye with his own revolver and then through the left with Coffin Ed's before the killer can fall to the ground. Before firing the second shot Digger says "For you, Ed." After Digger is shot from behind in *The Heat's On*, Ed breaks into his friend's home to get his revolver before taking it to set a trap and kill their assailants.

In spite of the many obvious similarities between the two men, Himes eventually revealed subtle differences between them. It is likely that in the beginning Himes saw no need to differentiate between the two men. The briefest of readings of *For Love of Imabelle* reveals that the story could have been written without them. Although Himes gave the two detectives a greater part in his next book, the main emphasis was still on the relationship of Johnny and Dulcy Perry and the secrets kept by the half-mad Reverend Short.

By the time of the third book in the series *(The Real Cool Killers)*, some obvious differences between the two detectives began to appear. The first tension in the story harks back to the time Coffin Ed was splashed with acid in *For Love of Imabelle*. It is clear from the beginning of *Real Cool Killers* that since this traumatic attack, Ed has not been the same man and his fear has made him erratic and dangerous.

Himes made this injury central to Ed's character from then on. Ed is a tough, resilient man who not only has been badly traumatized, but who also is no longer quite sane. His hatred of criminals is now tinged with more than a hint of hysteria, and his partner can no longer completely trust him in a tight spot. On more than one occasion, Digger has to restrain him physically to prevent the murder of someone who has unknowingly tripped Coffin Ed's deadly switch.

This quality is first brought into focus at the beginning of *The Real Cool Killers*. When Ed and Digger are in the street in the aftermath of the Greek's death, they attempt to question a group of teenagers dressed in Arab costumes.

The teenagers, all members of a gang, are disrespectful to the two officers; at one point, one of them breaks wind in their faces. Ed is already angry when one boy attempts to splash him with the contents of a bottle. Wild with fear that the bottle may contain acid, Ed responds with gunfire that kills the boy and wounds an innocent bystander. Digger has to fight his friend to keep him from further violence and is hurt in the bargain. To Ed's chagrin and shame, they later learn that the bottle contained harmless perfume.

One of Ed's trademarks is a facial tic in the scarred side of his face. When the tic starts, it is a signal that he is likely to do anything. In *Cotton Comes to Harlem* he gets so angry during the questioning of Iris O'Malley that he almost chokes her to death before Digger can call him back to sanity.

As disturbed as Ed is, he is not insensitive to his problem. After he realizes he has not only killed the teen gangster in *Cool Killers* for nothing but also has wounded an innocent bystander in the process, he is flushed with embarrassment. After he nearly hurts Chink Charlie during an interrogation in *The Crazy Kill*, he goes out into the hallway and cries with shame.

When Ed's paranoia and hate are combined with guilt, he is at his most terrifying and sadistic. Believing Digger has been killed in *The Heat's On* because of his bad judgment, he launches himself on a mad chase all over town to track the killers. In the process, he threatens and beats a score of people before reaching Red Johnny's house.

Himes' capacity for depicting graphic violence and sadism is at a peak during this scene. When the pain—and guilt—crazed Ed fails to get the answers he wants from the pimp, he bashes the man's teeth in with the barrel of his revolver. Not content with this display of violence, Himes describes in sickening detail how the wounded man coughs up blood and bits of teeth. In an uncharacteristically humane gesture, Ed uses a spoon to grab the man's slippery tongue and keeps him from choking to death.

When Ed finally locates the two-timing Ginny, what little humanity he has left is fast disappearing. He strips the woman and throws her naked body on a couch and ties her down. With a knife he cuts the skin in a thin line six inches across her throat. To make certain she gets the point, he shows her what he has done in a hand mirror. Even her stark terror fails to move this implacable man to pity:

> He knew that he had gone beyond the line; that he had gone outside of human restraint; he knew that what he was doing was unforgivable. But he didn't want any more lies.

Few fictional detectives have ever gone so far. For Ed, the job, his guilt, and his own personal thirst for vengeance have put the solving of the case before anything, even human decency. People whom he has regarded in the past with no more than casual contempt have ceased to rate even the slightest consideration in the face of his rage.

Strangely enough, even in this extreme Ed does not completely lose touch with the ideals that made him become a detective. When Ginny offers to cut him in on the loot if he will kill the members of the gang, Himes writes that:

> He was caught for a moment in a hurt as terrible as any he had ever known.
> "Is everybody crooked on this mother-raping earth?" It came like a cry of agony torn out of him.

In Ed, Himes has created a very complex character. He has been presented to us as a cynical, hard-nosed lawman whose pragmatic outlook on life has made him one of the most feared figures in Harlem. It is ironic that in Ed this pragmatism seems to be balanced with a simplistic belief in right and wrong, a fact that prevents him (and probably all cops) from realizing the ultimate uselessness of law (and lawmen) in a society that is governed completely by corrupt influences. Ginny's proposition is such a shock to him that, possibly for the first time, he realizes just how terrible his world, symbolized by Harlem, has become.

Another important incongruity in Coffin Ed's character is that, as brutal as he is with his enemies, he is at bottom a devoted family man with a boyish sense of humor. For example, when he and Digger visit the Great Man night club for dinner, they decide to have watermelon for dessert just as the floor show commences. The sight of the naked, jiggling bottoms of the four sepia-colored showgirls creates such a temptation in him that he begins spitting watermelon seeds at their backsides. Only the quick thinking of the more dignified Digger saves them from being embroiled in a free-for-all.

Ed owns a home next door to his partner in Astoria, Long Island. He has a teenaged daughter named Evelyn whom we meet only once in *The Real Cool Killers*. It is apparent that he is very fond of her: after he is temporarily suspended for the shooting of the teenaged "Arab," his first thought is to go home and spend some time with her or take her to a movie.

When he and Digger discover later that she is being held hostage by Sheik, the head of the teen gang, Ed has himself suspended by a wire around his ankles over the edge of the apartment building. He hangs there for 20 minutes with the wire cutting into his legs, waiting for the chance to shoot Sheik and save Evelyn. Afterwards, he does not chastise his daughter for her thoughtless rebellion but instead quietly takes her home. Possibly he has the insight to realize that he is partially responsible for her lapse in moral judgment.

We see very little else of Ed's or Digger's family life during the course of their adventures. Ed's wife is named Molly and we see her briefly with Digger's wife, Stella, after Digger is taken to the hospital in *The Heat's On*.

We see Digger's wife only one other time. She awakens him in *Cotton Comes to Harlem* when the word comes that Deke O'Malley has escaped and killed two cops. She fixes him Nescafe and warns him to be careful, although she seems far too wise to believe that he will. Digger has two young daughters whom we never meet. We hear at one point that they are away at summer camp, an experience that was once considered a luxury for the inner-city children of New York.

The fact that Digger and Ed have wives and families is something that sets them apart from most of the rest of the hard-boiled world. The time-honored tough guy ethic mandates that the job must be everything, that a detective doesn't really have the right to a family or the time to indulge one. Himes seems to make it possible for Digger and Ed to have families by placing them on a work shift that lasts from late afternoon through the early morning. These night-owl hours allow them to fight crime in the all-night world of Harlem while the respectable world in Astoria is asleep.

It is clear from the story line of *Real Cool Killers*, however, that Himes realized the strain that police work could place on a policeman's family. The horrors that Ed faces on a day-to-day basis, combined with the physical and emotional wounds that he must cope with, undoubtedly have a negative effect on his personal life and his relationship with his daughter.

Ed shows a spark of real individuality and one of the rare instances of independence from his partner when we discover another woman in his life near the end of *Blind Man With a Pistol*. There we discover that he has had, or is having, an affair with a beautiful light-skinned hooker named Barbara Tyne. The discovery comes as a shock to Digger, who expresses an uncharacteristic irritation with his partner. Peculiarly, Digger's irritation is more like what one would expect from a deceived wife than from a male work partner. His behavior seems to suggest that, to Digger, his relationship with Ed is supposed to enjoy that same sanctity. At the same time, Ed's failure to confide his infidelity to his partner shows a rather provincial embarrassment and shame over his breach of societal rules.

Of the two detectives, Grave Digger Jones comes off as the more reasonable personality and the real brains of the team. Even after he is badly wounded in the line of duty himself, he never becomes as trigger-happy as Ed. Indeed, he takes the responsibility, unbidden, for calming Ed down at those times when he has gone off the deep end. It is equally characteristic of Digger that he does so at great personal risk.

Grave Digger is typically the spokesperson for the team, especially if they are called upon to report their findings or explain their actions to a superior officer. It is perhaps because Digger is the more thoughtful one that he often expresses pity or rage or anguish over the fate of victims or the callous indifference on the part of the authorities to Black suffering. In *The Real Cool Killers* he responds to a white man's criticism with

"I'm just a cop," Grave Digger said thickly. "If you white people insist on coming up to Harlem where you force colored people to live in vice-and-crime-ridden slums, it's my job to see that you are safe."

In *Cotton Comes to Harlem* Digger offers the corrupt precinct captain Brice a chance to crack the case by letting Iris O'Malley escape from jail but the cowardly Brice will not take the risk himself. However, he will allow Digger and Ed to carry out their plan if they are willing to take the heat if the plan goes awry. Digger tells Brice "I wouldn't do this for nobody but my own black people" before he storms out to get Iris.

Digger is something of an amateur sociologist. Possibly better than the professors in their ivory towers, he realizes what the race problem is all about. He sees the young lives corrupted every day by drugs, unemployment, and hopelessness. He sees the jobless turn to crime when there is no other way to put food on the table.

His realizations have turned him bitter, so bitter that he sometimes explodes with pent-up rage:

We got the highest crime rate on earth among the colored people in Harlem. And there ain't but three things to do about it; make the criminals pay for it—you don't want to do that; pay the people enough to live decently—you ain't going to do that; so all that's left is let 'em eat one another up.

Digger's anger is much slower to come to the surface than is Ed's, but the warning signs are distinctive to those who know him. The swelling of his neck until the veins pop and the cottony, dry quality of his voice let the reader and his listener know that dynamite is about to explode.

Because he has a better grip on his emotions, Digger is much more ruthless and calculating than Ed. Never having been traumatized in the way his partner has, Digger has more control over his hatred and instinct for violence.

This control is graphically exemplified in *For Love of Imabelle* when Digger accidentally finds Imabelle (the eponymous heroine of the story) in the Harlem precinct station. He takes advantage of the fact that Imabelle doesn't recognize him and enjoys the preening, whorish performance she puts on for him before he slaps her out of the chair.

Only one time during his career does Grave Digger lose such complete control of himself that he attacks someone in a rage. This instance occurs near the end of *The Real Cool Killers* after he has arrested Ready Belcher and Big Smiley. Discovering that Sheik has barricaded himself in the apartment with hostages, the badly frightened Ready reveals that Coffin Ed's daughter, Evelyn, is in the apartment.

Digger has known for some time that Ready has been holding out a piece of vital information. Upon hearing this startling news, Digger has to be restrained to keep him from beating the craven pimp to death.

Under normal circumstances, however, Digger is capable of subtleties that would be beyond his violent partner. A typical example occurs in *Cotton Comes to Harlem* when Digger threatens to shoot Iris O'Malley through the head unless she reveals the whereabouts of the stolen money. With unquestioning loyalty, Ed immediately covers all of the other police officers in the room.

The other officers know that Digger would never commit murder, but they also realize that the volatile Ed will shoot them if they dare to interfere with him.

As far as is known, Digger is faithful to his wife, Stella, but at least once he is severely tempted. When he meets the voluptuous Lila Holmes in *All Shot Up*, sparks fly between the two. Digger appraises her in an aggressive way that is completely out of character for him. In spite of her obvious sophistication and contempt for Digger's lowly position, Lila feels the heat of the meeting.

After Lila is badly wounded later helping the detectives rescue her husband, Casper, Digger comforts her while they wait for the ambulance and strokes her hair. In his typical fashion, Himes closes the door on his detectives' private lives, and we never find out if Digger and Lila consummate their passion for one another.

Following the tradition of other hard-boiled writers, Himes purposely kept the origins of Digger and Ed shadowy. We discover from Mamie Pullen in *The Crazy Kill* that the two grew up in Harlem and went to public school there. During *Blind Man With a Pistol* they mention having been in the army during World War II and reminisce about service in Paris.

How they got on the police force is less clear. A significant conversation takes place between them and Casper Holmes during *All Shot Up*. As they begin to annoy Casper by asking too many pointed questions regarding his activities, the powerful Black politician reminds them that he got them their jobs on the police force. Unwilling to allow him that power over them, the detectives counter that their high marks on the civil service examination and their military service might have had just as much to do with their subsequent hiring. This assertion seems to indicate that the pair were decorated for distinguished combat experience.

Although they are native New Yorkers, their appetites are those of rural southern Negroes. In *Cotton Comes to Harlem* they twice go to their favorite restaurant, Mammy Louise's, for "soul food." The first time they order double orders of ribs with side dishes of black-eyed peas, rice, okra, collard greens with fresh tomatoes and onions, and deep-dish apple pie and vanilla ice cream. Later they return for a meal of barbecued opossum with candied yams, collard greens, and okra.

In *All Shot Up* they also visit Mammy Louise. They are devouring Mammy's specialty "chicken feetsy" when they get a radio call which brings them into the case. During *The Heat's On* they visit the Great Man night club where they enjoy New Orleans gumbo. The recipe, which is not the recipe used in most New Orleans restaurants, includes a bizarre mix of fresh pork, chicken gizzards, hog testicles, and giant shrimp in a base of okra, sweet potatoes, and twenty-seven varieties of seasonings, spices, and herbs.

Neither detective is a big drinker, but several times during their adventures they stop at bars for a whiskey or beer. When their car heater doesn't work during the terrible winter of *All Shot Up*, the pair drink from a bottle of whiskey to keep warm, and the normally sensible Digger gets rather frisky from it.

Although the detectives associate with any number of underworld characters with whom they are on good terms, the only person in their adventures who can come close to being called a friend is their immediate superior, Lieutenant Anderson. Anderson is a figure whose personality never really develops during the eight stories, although he is normally supportive of their actions. He seems to like the two Black detectives, and in turn they are good-natured and respectful with him. Often we see him trying, unsuccessfully, to use Black slang properly, and the pair either smile tolerantly or kid him good-naturedly about it.

Anderson is much more important to the stories than his position of "good" white man or titular superior would imply. His major function is often to supply an audience for the pair when they rage in frustration against a system that fosters and even encourages the corruption which they must constantly battle.

Anderson also serves as a moderating influence on the detectives. Since he seldom has to go out on the street, the rage and frustration that Digger and Ed feel never develop in his personality. Thus he tries to keep them (and himself) out of trouble with higher authority by reminding them that police, even in a violent society, have to answer to the public:

"I'm on your side. I know what you're up against here in Harlem. I know your beat. It's my beat, too. But the commissioner feels you've killed too many people in this area—" He held up his hand to ward off an interruption. "Hoodlums, I know— dangerous hoodlums—and you've killed in self-defense. But you've been on the carpet a number of times and a short time ago you had three months' suspensions. Newspapers have been yapping about police brutality in Harlem and now various civic bodies have taken up the cry."

Anderson often finds himself the man in the middle. His immediate superior is Captain Brice, a well-fed, white bureaucrat whose noticeable prosperity is the result of graft. Brice is far too interested in his own concerns to be bothered with the demands of justice. Brice comes very close to feeding Digger and Ed to the wolves on a couple of occasions, and Anderson does what he can to prevent his doing so.

Although he is an experienced police officer, Anderson never really gets used to Harlem or the seemingly senseless crimes that make running his precinct such an exercise in frustration. At times, he resembles a Greek Chorus as he describes the bizarre life that continues outside the walls of the station house:

Man kills his wife with an axe for burning his breakfast pork chop...man sees
stranger wearing his own new suit, slashes him with a razor...man dressed as Cherokee
Indian splits white bartender's skull with homemade tomahawk...twenty-five men
arrested for trying to chase all the white people out of Harlem—

"It's Independence Day," Grave Digger interrupted.

Anderson comes off as a believable boss, even though we see very little
of him. He listens to his detectives' reports and gives them their instructions
in a businesslike way. Once, when Coffin Ed shows a characteristic disregard
for a killing, Anderson chews him out and sends him packing. This no-nonsense
side of Anderson is balanced by the number of times we see him drinking
with his men in a friendly atmosphere.

As the series comes to a close, Anderson is shown to be just as human
and, by implication, just as weak as anyone else. During *Blind Man With
A Pistol* it becomes clear that Captain Brice is about to retire and that Anderson
has been promised command of the precinct. In order to win this promotion
and the graft that goes with it, Anderson is forced to help his superiors prevent
Ed and Digger from discovering the clues necessary to solving the crime. To
allow them to succeed will open up a large-scale homosexual scandal which
undoubtedly involves important public figures, possibly of both races.

Blind Man With A Pistol is the final story in the series, and it shows
Himes at his most bitter and mistrustful. Anderson's fall from grace is the
final blow that symbolizes a world so corrupt that even Digger and Ed can't
save it. Their rambunctious zeal and their knowledge of underworld life are
not sufficient weapons in a world where faceless and powerful men can
manipulate both the legal machinery of a city and the emotions and actions
of the common people.

Although Digger and Ed lack the polish of Marlowe and Parker's Spenser,
they can be thinking detectives nonetheless. Although they seem rough and
unlettered, they make it clear that they have read a book and understood what
they have read. During their adventures they draw parallels between their cases
and scenes from books such as Hemingway's *For Whom The Bell Tolls* and
Maxim Gorky's *The Bystander*.

On several occasions they make rather startling deductions from clues other
detectives have missed. The sight of a jacked up car near the scene of Snake
Hip's bizarre death, for example, is enough to convince them that a local tire
thief has probably witnessed the death. Furthermore, they reason, a man out
stealing tires during a blizzard must have a "hot" woman to support. Both
contentions prove to be true.

As Black men trying to lead meaningful lives in a white-dominated society,
they have made as much of a success of their lives as they can. They have
been able to purchase homes in a quiet, middle-class suburb and provide decent
lives for their wives and children. At the end of their adventures, however,
they are visibly aging, and after ten years they still have not been promoted
from the lowest detective grade. Because their salaries have not kept pace with

inflation, they still owe money on their houses, and it seems clear that they will remain in debt.

They have changed significantly from the two detectives who took protection money in *For Love of Imabelle*. Like the Continental Op, Philip Marlowe, and other classic detectives, they have joined what William Marling calls "the round table of parsimonious knights."[6] In the world of the hard-boiled detective, it is necessary for the hero to remain poor if he is going to retain his essential honesty. True to that world, Digger and Ed have remained pure, rejecting the opportunities they are offered over the years to enrich themselves.

They have retained their honesty, often at the cost of their emotional security and the love of their families but they are affected by a tragic flaw. They have let the world in which they must live and work twist them into creatures who are sometimes more like beasts than men. Their success in solving crimes has been overbalanced by the sheer savagery with which they pursue criminals.

In a telling scene near the beginning of *All Shot Up*, Mammy Louise berates them for beating and killing so many people. Hurt by this accusation, Digger and Ed protest that the people they have hurt all have been criminals and that they are not by nature violent men. Suddenly, they have to leave the restaurant to answer a radio call in their car. Their precipitate rush causes Mammy Louise's nervous bulldog to jump at them, and without thinking, Digger nearly shoots the animal. Only Mammy Louise's restraining hand prevents the foolish dog from becoming another of Digger and Ed's victims.

In his now-classic essay on Himes' detective fiction, Raymond Nelson summed up these characters and their saga by saying "if the vehicle itself is small, Himes's accomplishments within it are not, and the residual portrait left by these books—of Coffin Ed and Grave Digger outlined against the dull, lurid light of a criminal city—is one of the compelling images of our time."[7]

It is possible that Nelson allowed himself to be a little too romantic in his assessment of these characters, but it is hard to fault him for it. In the work of the best writers of the hard-boiled detective thriller, the heroes have all been men who, for their own reasons, placed the safety of the innocent and the search for truth over and above their own prosperity and well-being. Himes has created two heroes who fit that mold and, at the same time, heralded the beginning of a third wave of hard-boiled heroes who have reshaped and given new life to one of the few truly American literary genres.

Chapter III
The Mean Streets

It was a street of paradox: unwed young mothers suckling their infants, living on a prayer; fat black racketeers coasting past in big bright-colored convertibles with their solid gold babes, carrying huge sums of money on their person; hard-working men, holding up the buildings with their shoulders, talking in loud voices up there in Harlem where the white bosses couldn't hear them; teen-aged gangsters grouping for a fight, smoking marijuana weed to get up their courage; everybody escaping the hotbox rooms they lived in, seeking respite in a street made hotter by the automobile exhaust and the heat released by the concrete walls and walks.

"Down these mean streets a man must go..." So goes Raymond Chandler's classic ode to the world of the hard-boiled hero. It is a world that we have come to know well from numerous tellings—vital, bustling, and romantic, but possessed of a corrupt, dark soul and the savagery of a jungle.

This dark underbelly of the corrupt American city has become the new frontier that the detective must tread furtively just as his fictional predecessor, Natty Bumppo, roamed the primeval American forests. However, the American city has become a much more frightening and treacherous place than that long-ago frontier. The American penchant for greed and excess has turned it into a dangerous urban swamp, filled with conscienceless killers, drug lords, vicious pimps, amoral prostitutes, and sexual deviates of all persuasions. Thanks to the almost inevitable link between modern civilization and moral degradation, the city remains corrupt and evil through the scheming of crooked cops, political grafters, and bureaucrats.

To this urban mythology, Chester Himes added his own unique touch. A self-made tough guy and a familiar of gamblers, bootleggers, whores, and stick-up artists, Himes spent seven and one half years in one of America's toughest prisons during the 1920s and '30s. This experience provided him with a background unique among American writers of his day.

To add to this, Himes was an habitue of the toughest part of any American town—the ghetto. This was a world unknown to most white writers, a world dominated by characters who were tougher and had less to lose than their white counterparts. They were hard, cruel, and cunning because there was nothing else for them to be, nothing greater to which they could aspire. Lacking the education or religion that inspired some of their brethren to greater heights

38

or to at least hope for better days, these men and women undoubtedly felt that they had nothing to lose by following lives of crime or dissolute behavior.

Besides his unique experience, Himes also brought an interesting philosophy to crime writing. As he told John Williams in an interview, "American violence is public life, it's a public way of life."[1]

As a Black man coming of age in pre-civil rights America, Himes had good reason to know that this fact was, perhaps, more true for the Negro than for anyone else. The gangsterism that arose in Prohibition America made violence a fact of life in many cities. World War I had left a dark pessimism in the American mind, and urban violence became the legacy of that pessimism. This, coupled with a typically American penchant for seeking vengeance for wrongs both real and imagined, often resulted in the Negro finding himself the victim of lynch mobs all over the country.

In Himes' mind, the Black ghetto is a symbol of racial repression and is itself symptomatic of a greater American illness. Here, Blacks are physically and emotionally separated from the wider world. The residents are often jobless, have little money, and consequently have little hope.

As a result of this hopelessness, some of these ghetto dwellers become cruising sharks, preying on the unwary of their own race. A jungle mentality rules, and the gun, the knife, and the club decide who will rule and who will survive.

In Himes' view, whites seldom enter this world, and when they do it is usually to exploit further the people they have imprisoned there. To make matters worse, the white-dominated authorities are seemingly indifferent to what goes on. Himes sees them thinking that the safest thing for society at large is that Blacks should be contained in an area of their own. If they kill and exploit each other, it is of no consequence to the authorities or white society. White authorities will enter this land only if a white man is killed, much as the frontier cavalry would enter Indian territory to exact reprisals for raids on white settlers.

Himes illustrates this point graphically in both *The Real Cool Killers* and *Blind Man With A Pistol*. In each case, white men who enter the ghetto seeking sex with Black prostitutes are murdered. Authority's response to the crimes is large-scale police dragnets which demean and victimize virtually everyone in the quest to uncover the criminals.

These dragnets can be seen more as tools of oppression than real attempts at justice. At the conclusion of *Cool Killers*, several young Black men are killed, and the police leave the scene dusting their hands in satisfaction. When they later discover that they did not actually get the real killer after all, the authorities still choose to act as if the case was closed successfully.

It becomes clear during the course of *Blind Man With A Pistol* that the solution to the killing of a white homosexual will cause a city-wide scandal. Faceless but powerful men in the city power structure put pressure on the police department to obstruct the investigation, and as a result the best efforts of Digger and Ed to solve the crime are stymied.

In Himes' Harlem the mean streets are both a literary creation as well and a reflection of reality. Himes lived through some of the most important literary periods of American history. As he was growing up, the Harlem Renaissance was in full swing. For the first time, Black writers, poets, dramatists, and musicians were making their ideas felt. At the same time, they found the beginnings of an acceptance by the world beyond their own.

As a young man, particularly after his release from prison, Himes lived through the Great Depression, which created its own literary traditions. As Raymond Nelson perceptively pointed out in his important essay on the Harlem series, Himes "recaptures the spirit (without succumbing to the naivete) of the Harlem Renaissance, and manages to mold the substance of two literary eras into a single balanced response to experience."[2]

Like the writers and artists of the Harlem Renaissance, Himes feels no embarrassment about the Black characteristics that whites may find amusing or ridiculous. Indeed, he holds them up to intense scrutiny while indicating his own personal approval of his characters. With utter faithfulness, he records the almost Dickensian names, the outlandish clothing the people wear, the slang they speak, the music they sing and dance to, and the food they eat.

At the same time, Himes' proletarian attitudes and the pragmatism inherent in his own life experience give an edge to the descriptions that earlier writers could not have expressed. These characters whose lives he chronicles may be grotesque, absurd, and even ridiculous at times, but those same lives also have elements of pathos and tragedy. The outlandishness of their behavior cannot hide the fact that some must steal or sell their bodies to live. It cannot change the fact that some must take drugs or drown themselves in raw, homemade whiskey in order to forget the tedious hopelessness of their empty lives.

Earlier critics of Himes' work have tended to suggest that when he turned to the writing of crime stories, he forsook the protest style which first brought him into the public eye. This is a mistake undoubtedly perpetuated by people who have tended to react viscerally to Himes' work, rather than critically. In truth, Himes took a genre (and one that "serious" critics tended to despise in the 1950s and '60s) and used it to send the same message he had been sending since he wrote his first novel in the 1940s. To his misfortune, the subtlety involved in trying to express an essentially sociological theme within the narrow boundaries of the tough crime novel probably contributed to deep misunderstandings by critics. With his actual message thus obscured, Himes drew more critical abuse from American critics while the French applauded him enthusiastically.

The skill with which Himes used the conventions of the crime drama to protest the conditions of Black life deserves to be applauded. For example, his novels are filled with the bleak depictions of ghetto street life that sear the reader's soul with their honesty. Although meticulously detailed descriptions of the backdrop are a traditional part of the tough crime novel, for Himes these descriptions serve a much greater purpose than local color. He is using the crime novel as a means to bring us face-to-face with the bare facts of ghetto life:

Black-eyed whores stood on the street corner swapping obscenities with twitching junkies. Muggers and thieves slouched in the dark doorways waiting for someone to rob; but there wasn't anyone but each other. Children ran down the street, the dirty street littered with rotting vegetables, uncollected garbage, battered garbage cans, broken glass, dog offal—always running, ducking, and dodging. Listless mothers stood in the dark entrances of tenements and swapped talk about their men, their jobs, their poverty, their hunger, their debts, their Gods, their religions, their preachers, their children, their aches and pains, their bad luck with numbers and the evilness of white people.

These carefully-constructed prose/poems that became Himes' trademark are far more than just background. As Jay R. Berry asserts, he is "compiling a naturalistic case study of various aspects of Harlem."[3] In one street, Himes presents all of Harlem's (and by implication, all of Black America's) ills. The decay is pervasive; the good live side-by-side with the wicked. The innocent children cannot help but be tainted by the moral decay, which Himes symbolizes in his descriptions of physical decay. The children run down the street, ducking and dodging, almost in practice for the day when some will do it in earnest.

In depicting his netherworld, Himes is telling part of his own life story. In the first full-length American study of Himes' work, James Lundquist asserted that "his imagination was suddenly and somewhat strangely freed from the burden of autobiography that had, despite the power of his earlier novels, made his range seem limited and his quick-action prose occasionally out of place."[4] This judgment, however, seems ill-considered when one makes detailed comparisons of Himes' life with his work.

Michel Fabre, who is very familiar with the genesis of Himes' writings, insists that Himes *never* stopped writing about his own life; every story he wrote was, to an extent, an exercise in autobiography. To those steeped in the details of Himes' life, this is all too obvious. For example, the names of many of the secondary characters—Bunch Boy, Four-Four, Johnny Perry, Valentine Haines—were the real names of his familiars and teachers when he haunted the tough side of Cleveland. His intimate knowledge of narcotics, prostitution, and gambling all spring from this period of his life.

Although there is never a character in the Harlem series that one can point to and say with certainty, "this is Chester Himes," Himes' personality is present in many of the major characters he created. An obvious case is Sheik, the leader of the teen gang in *The Real Cool Killers*. Like Himes, Sheik is well-built, light-skinned, and intelligent. He is attractive to women, but treats them badly. His insane anger at the white race seems to mimic Himes' own self-destructive hatred during his late teen years.

Johnny Perry of *The Crazy Kill* also possesses certain of Himes' traits, although he is based on an actual character that Himes knew in Cleveland. Like Himes, Perry is adept at gambling. Similarly, Perry has served time in prison, and the experience has tended to strengthen, rather than weaken him. Probably more importantly, Perry's loyalty to a woman he loves is so strong that it borders on self-destructiveness. Himes showed he was capable of such behavior himself in the tragic love affair with Alva that he chronicles in the first volume of his autobiography.

In some way or another, most crime writers create their heroes in their own image, and this is as true of Himes as anyone else. Grave Digger and Coffin Ed actually represent two distinct sides of Himes' character. Grave Digger is much more thoughtful and reasoned in his approach to problem solving than his partner. Of the two detectives, he is clearly the more intelligent and his many observations on Black life, racial problems, and the socio-economic concerns of the urban Black often reflect Himes' own judgments. Digger's restrained bitterness over racial injustice also echoes that of Himes in his later life.

Coffin Ed, on the other hand, is a much more visceral character than Grave Digger. Ed, who is disfigured and nearly blinded by acid in his first adventure, is somewhat mentally unbalanced by the experience. Whenever the two detectives are faced with any kind of danger, Ed becomes as volatile as nitroglycerin. Even Digger eventually becomes a little afraid of his friend after he nearly kills several people in violent rages.

This mindless tendency toward violence coupled with a fierce hatred is much like the mental state that Himes describes in himself during the period before he was sent to prison. Himes describes in his autobiography how he once pistol-whipped a bartender and tore up a bar room when he was refused service. During a time that he worked for a landprop, he often shot at people in a rage when they offered him money for his own girlfriend. In prison, Himes tells us, his capacity for bursting into violence often caused many a larger man to back away from him.

Himes understands violence very well. As with so many other experiences, he has a personal knowledge of things that other writers can only imagine. Himes knows that real violence is nothing like the bloodless violence of television and movies. In real life, blood spurts, bones shatter, and brains are splattered against the wall. Himes uses this knowledge, says Jay Berry, to be as detailed as possible in his descriptions of almost incredible violence in an effort to drive home to the reader the point that reality in Harlem is violence or the threat of violence.[5]

For the suffering, inarticulate masses of Harlem, violence is a way of not just getting even, but also of expressing themselves. In a world where there is often no legal recourse to a wrong, instantaneous retribution provides that recourse. When a prostitute finds her man in bed with another whore, she forces him at pistol point to jump naked out of an apartment window. On his way down, she shoots him in the head. In this way, she takes revenge on the lover's faithlessness and sends a message to others that she will not put up with it in the future.

This kind of violence is not only frightening because it is so pervasive, but also because it is so sudden and hideous. In *The Real Cool Killers*, a wizened old Black man pulls a knife on a white bar customer. When the old man refuses to back down, the bartender chops off his knife arm with an axe. The drunken old man, still bent on violence, gropes on the floor for the knife which is still clutched in the dismembered hand.

In *All Shot Up*, a man fleeing the police on the back of a motorcycle skids on an icy street and runs full tilt into a truck carrying several sheets of thin sheet steel. The steel neatly slices his head from his shoulders and the headless body continues to steer the cycle down the street for several blocks. Later in the same book, gangsters plunge a hunting knife into the head of a bodyguard. Struck deaf, dumb, and blind, he staggers blindly down the street, screaming silently in his own head for help.

In *The Heat's On*, a depraved old drug addict plots to break into his former mistress' safe with nitroglycerin. Suddenly, a goat enters the room and, in spite of the old man's efforts, will not leave. During the struggle, a shotgun precariously leaning against a bureau falls over, goes off, and sets off the nitroglycerin. The explosion is so severe that the investigating officers cannot distinguish the remains of the man from that of the goat. The irony is that the old timer used much more nitro than was necessary and has destroyed not only the safe and its contents, but the entire house as well.

Himes' violence is horrifying, but it also has an absurd edge to it. The absurdity, however, does nothing to mitigate the horror it evokes. Perhaps unknowingly, Himes is echoing Raymond Chandler's determination that:

> It is not a fragrant world, but it is the world you live in...It is not funny that a man should be killed, but it is sometimes funny that he should be killed for so little and that his death should be the coin of what we call civilization.[6]

It is Himes' recognition of this absurdity that seems to underscore the utter futility of the lives of everyone in Harlem. Often the treasure that so many die for in his stories proves to be nonexistent. In *For Love Of Imabelle* for example, five men die over a trunk of gold ore that proves in the end to be fool's gold.

In *The Big Gold Dream* Abie the Jew steals an old sofa that he believes is filled with a numbers payoff. It turns out to be filled with Confederate money instead, but that does not prevent him from being murdered for it.

Two women and seven men die for a cache of narcotics in *The Heat's On*. Not one of them realizes that the heroin was destroyed before the action in the story began.

Always, though, the violence continues to work on two levels. One level is the expectation that a detective story will be violent—there must be death for the detective to avenge. On another level, the violence represents much more. Sometimes the old Chester Himes, the unrepentant protest novelist, slips into the text and uses the savagery to cry out against the plight of the poor urban Negro trapped in this modern Walpurgisnacht:

> Goldy's scream mingled with the scream of the locomotive as the train thundered past overhead, shaking the entire tenement city. Shaking the sleeping black people in their lice-ridden beds. Shaking the ancient bones and the aching muscles and the t.b. lungs and the uneasy foetuses of unwed girls. Shaking the plaster from the ceiling, mortar from between the bricks. Shaking the rats between the walls, the cockroaches crawling over kitchen sinks and left-over food; shaking the sleeping flies hibernating in lumps like bees behind the casings of windows. Shaking the fat, blood-filled bedbugs crawling over black skin. Shaking the fleas, making them hop. Shaking the sleeping dogs in their filthy pallets, the sleeping cats, the clogged toilets, loosening the filth.

It is doubtful that a white writer could have written crime stories with this precise blend of violence, humor, irony, and pathos. Virtually every writer of Black detective stories has been white, and while their work usually succeeds on a purely superficial level, it fails when the writers try actively to produce a feeling of reality about Black ghetto life.

The only white crime writer who has come close was Raymond Chandler in his classic, *Farewell, My Lovely*. Himes himself admitted that Chandler's depiction of Los Angeles' Central Avenue district was an effective one. Chandler also effectively illustrated the isolation of the Black community and the indifference of authorities to what goes on there. His publicity-hungry Lieutenant Nulty complains to Marlowe that even the goriest murders in the Central Avenue area are just "shine killings," unworthy of the attention of the newspapers or the cops themselves.

In spite of this understanding, however, Chandler was a white writer with a strong prejudice against all minorities. His descriptions of Black Los Angeles are not only sinister, but laden with contempt. He revels in the filth and decay he sees and finds no sympathy in himself for the lives of the people trapped there.

Himes was an inhabitant of this world and knew something that Chandler did not, namely that as sinister as this world was, it was not completely without its redeeming aspects. Himes feels an affection for this world that probably no white writer can. He usually refers to the Coffin Ed/Grave Digger stories as his "Harlem Domestic Series," indicating perhaps that the Harlem of his imagination is a kind of racial home for his people. He emphasizes this often with greatly detailed descriptions of the food, music, and night spots, and with references to Harlem's glorious past.

In an affecting essay in the March, 1988, *Esquire* magazine, writer Pete Hamill describes how the ghetto was a home for Black doctors, lawyers, and businessmen, and other successful Blacks. According to Hamill, they were the examples for thousands of kids who eventually found their own success and their way out of the ghetto. As often as the *Amos 'n Andy* television show was vilified for painting Blacks as con artists and buffoons, for years it was the only place where Blacks were routinely shown as police officers, judges, lawyers, doctors, and respectable businessmen. Himes knew this side of the ghetto, too, and he takes pains to let the reader know that his Harlem has more than just criminals. Good people live here, too, as Himes shows in a Sunday morning scene from *Cotton Comes to Harlem:*

> Everything happens in Harlem six days a week, but Sunday morning, people worship God. Those who are not religious stay in bed...But the religious get up and put on their best clothes and go to church... A drunk better not be caught molesting them; he'll get all the black beat off him.

He stresses over and over this Harlem is a totally unique place. It is a place where the rules that govern the rest of society do not apply. When a white cop grabs at an easy answer for a murder during *The Crazy Kill,* Grave Digger is quick to remind him that

> This is Harlem. Ain't no other place like it in the world. You've got to start from scratch here, because these folks in Harlem do things for reasons nobody else in the world would think of.

To emphasize this factor, near the end of *The Real Cool Killers,* Himes has the white police chief demand to know why, when Sonny Pickens was chasing Ulysses Galen through the streets with his revolver, people treated it like a free show, rather than intervening to help the man. The Black detectives explain to him that every day in Harlem Black residents see some white man chasing a Black man with intent to do bodily harm. Suddenly, for the first time, they were seeing a Black chasing a white. This was something different— something, in fact, that many of them had waited their entire lives to see.

The chief does not understand this explanation, but the detectives and the reader realize that for the onlookers this turning of the tables was a symbolic evening of the score.

Himes reminds us on many occasions that there are only two kinds of people in Harlem: the squares and the hustlers, the wolves and the victims. There is only one major difference between the two and that is the path they have chosen. The hustlers will not give in without a fight. They cannot fight the white establishment that put them where they are, but they can prey upon their own kind in order to get a bigger slice of purgatory. Without knowing it, they are still losers. The squares have come to a dumb, acquiescent acceptance of their lot, but the hustlers thrash about, never knowing that they are predestined to meet their end from an overdose, a cut throat, or a slug from the gun of a cop like Digger or Ed.

There are traditional lines of hustling in Harlem, and each of the eight Harlem Domestic stories focuses on one or more of them. In *For Love of Imabelle*, the con game is the focus. In fact, virtually everyone involved in the caper except for Jackson and the two detectives is a con artist of some kind. *The Crazy Kill* is about a murder, but the background is the colorful world of the professional gambler. The teen age gang and rampant juvenile delinquency provide the focus of *The Real Cool Killers*, although prostitution provides a strong second focus.

Sex is both a business and a preoccupation in this world and it is the homosexual *demimonde* of Harlem that figures in the plot of *All Shot Up*. *The Big Gold Dream* surveys the grip that religious charlatanry has over the Black subculture, although organized gambling is an important secondary theme. *Cotton Comes to Harlem* features another religious charlatan fronting an elaborate con which makes use of Marcus Garvey's "Back to Africa" movement.

The Heat's On is totally concerned with the Black community's most pervasive ill, narcotics traffic. Finally, *Blind Man With A Pistol* combines the elements of the homosexual subculture and the rise of the Black Power movement.

Himes often weaves strands of several of these evils into a single story. For example, narcotics is more than an evil in Himes' Harlem—it is a fact of life that cannot be ignored. This is particularly interesting in light of the national problem it has become today.

Intravenous drug use seems to have been an accepted part of Black life even in the 1950s, because in the earliest story, the character of Goldy shoots himself several times with the potent mixture of cocaine and morphine known as a "speedball." Two characters in *The Heat's On* also regularly use this mixture.

Marijuana use is so common that Chink Charlie Dawson in *The Crazy Kill* can admit to Digger and Ed that he has bought and used it without fear of arrest. The two detectives often pass people in the streets smoking it and teenagers in several stories, most notably *The Real Cool Killers*, use it like veterans. Sonny Pickens admits to having smoked it just before he began chasing Ulysses Galen through the street with his blank revolver.

Killers in Himes' Harlem are all drug users. Slim and Jodie in *Imabelle*, Slick and Susie in *The Big Gold Dream*, and the albino gunman in *The Heat's On* all use cocaine, opium, marijuana, or some combination of the three.

Prostitutes, madams, and pimps are also a part of every story, no doubt because Himes, as he wrote in *For Love of Imabelle*, considered the sale of sex to be "catering to the essential needs of the people." Strong-willed madams are characters in several stories and important confrontations take place in bordellos on three different occasions.

Each time Ed and/or Digger enter one, they perpetrate a particularly violent act. In *Imabelle*, Digger shoots the eyes out of a killer's head. In *Heat*, Ed strips and tortures a woman for information in one bordello and later smashes a man's teeth out in another. These instances, combined with the violence that is perpetrated against female characters throughout the story, seem to indicate a link in Himes' mind between promiscuity and violence.

Himes clearly shows his contempt for religion on many occasions. The place of the religious shyster is so strong in the series that it is clear that Himes believes religion is a racket that victimizes almost as many Blacks as narcotics does.

The first preacher we meet in the series is the Reverend Gaines in *Imabelle*. Himes makes it clear that Gaines is a fire-breathing minister with a strong belief in God: at the same time, he presents him as a pompous fool. For all of his strength of conviction, when he is finally confronted with the real sins of assault, theft, and murder, Gaines is shocked to his core by the knowledge. This ultimately useless and naive man is the best preacher in Himes' world.

Reverend Short, the holy rolling storefront preacher of *Crazy Kill* is poor enough to lead one to conclude that he is honest and God-fearing. In reality, he is a particularly wicked preacher. While he preaches abstinence and celibacy, he lusts after a parishioner's wife. His lust, combined with his addiction to a mixture of cherry brandy and opium, drives him to madness and murder.

Himes reserves his worst contempt for the ministers who use the simple faith of the poor Black to bilk him out of his hard-won money. Sweet Prophet Brown is the archetype of this kind of preacher: he is a flamboyant man with a red-lined purple cape, white hair, and nails that have grown unchecked into curled talons. He whips a street revival into such a frenzy that women are climbing over each other to purchase "blessed" bread crumbs with five, 10, and 20 dollar bills.

Brown's power is such that he holds the police and all authority in contempt. When he is nearly killed by Alberta Wright because he has stolen her money, he unashamedly tells reporters he stole it because "it takes a lot of money to be a prophet these days. It's the high cost of living."

The Reverend Deke O'Malley in *Cotton* is a hardened criminal who has served time in prison. He has no religious credentials other than those he has invented for himself. He uses his prison term to convince ignorant Blacks that white authorities fear him and have sent him to prison to shut him up. He makes use of Negro memories of Marcus Garvey's "Back to Africa" movement to bilk Black families out of $87,000.00. Like Sweet Prophet, O'Malley is vain and believes himself to be invulnerable.

The most sinister of Himes' preachers is the hare-lipped Prophet Ham, who runs the Church of the Black Jesus in *Blind Man*. Of all the religious charlatans in the Harlem series, he is the most frightening. An aura of evil hangs over him as he plots violence against both the white race and Black moderates.

Because these characters conceal their real intentions or motives, they also represent another of Himes' favorite themes. In Himes' Harlem, it is rare that anyone is really who he seems to be. Shifting identities often confuse the reader and the detectives as well. In *Imabelle,* for example, a U.S. Marshal turns out to be a murderer and a thief. A Black nun in the same story who sells tickets to heaven is revealed to be a larcenous transvestite. In *Big Gold Dream,* an old Jew who seems to make a precarious living buying and selling second-hand furniture turns out to be a rich conniver. He has made a fortune buying old furniture from poor Blacks, knowing that this is where they hide their money.

Even the respectable often turn out to be disreputable. Casper Holmes, the powerful politician of *All Shot Up,* proves to be a closet homosexual who uses his veneer of respectability to hide his deviancy. To make matters worse, he uses his position to steal large sums of money from his political party.

It is not only the men who lead double lives in this world. When Billie Belle does her nude dance with a cotton bale in *Cotton Comes To Harlem,* her sexuality rises from the page like a mist:

> Spasms caught her from time to time and she flung herself against the bale convulsively. She rubbed her belly against it and she turned and rubbed her buttocks against it, her bare breasts shaking ecstatically...Men stared lustfully...Bodies of women in the audience shook uncontrollably from compulsive motivation. Lust rose in the room like miasma...Billie's smooth voluptuous body was wet with sweat. It gleamed like a lecher's dream of hot flesh. Her breasts were heaving, the nipples pointing like selecting fingers.

But Billie is a confirmed lesbian who hates men with the same passion with which she will seduce a woman.

Himes seems to have negative feelings about homosexuality, because he seldom paints a sympathetic picture of a homosexual in the series. The men usually appear weak and ineffectual, and the women are uniformly vicious and sometimes murderous. Knowing what we know now about life behind bars, it seems clear that Himes must have had some experience with homosexuality while he was in prison. What that experience was, we will probably never know, although the platonic love affair depicted in *Cast the First Stone* may provide a clue.

Himes was a man who believed passionately in his own virility: he pursued women with an almost sexual greed. Whether or not he suffered a lapse in prison, it is abundantly clear that he viewed homosexuality with abhorrence. Indeed, the grotesque girl/boys he depicts in *All Shot Up* and *Blind Man With A Pistol* have a nasty, nauseating quality about them.

If Himes' Harlem is an ugly place, filled with filth and grit and peopled with hustlers, killers, and deviates, it is likely that he saw Black urban life in these terms. Himes started his writing career vehemently protesting the life to which whites had relegated the Black race. The printed page becomes an outlet for the bitterness and hatred of the forces responsible for what the Black experience has become.

When economic necessity placed him in the position of having to write crime fiction in order to live, he did not stop being the same man he always had been. He once told John A. Williams that "when I went into it...I was just imitating all the other American detective story writers...I haven't created anything whatsoever; I just made the faces black, that's all."[7]

Whether or not he made these remarks out of embarrassment, modesty, or just short-sightedness is impossible to know. The fact remains, however, that he *did* create something entirely different and brought new life to a style of writing that had grown stale. Because he was the first Black writer to attempt to write this type of popular fiction, he brought his own unique background, fears, disappointments, and bitterness to it.

Thanks to Himes, white readers were, for the first time, given access to a world that most could not even imagine. In his own time there were those who thought that Himes created some sort of fantasy world for his detectives to roam. Others believed that he was simply venting his hatred on his readers. Yet what he described more than twenty years ago is routine front-page news today.

Himes chronicled a bitter decade during which Blacks stopped allowing whites to ignore their world and forced Black concerns and Black problems into the light so that they became national, rather than simply racial problems. Narcotics traffic and addiction, Black-on-Black crime, and brutal, senseless murder were things that no one in either race wanted to talk about then, but must face together now.

As scholars have become increasingly aware of the work of many writers who devoted themselves to what someone once called "the poetry of violence," it has become obvious that there is much more to this work than cheap thrills and titillation. Though many critics have derided the work of Chester Himes for over 40 years as ugly and hateful or cheap and gaudy, it is an inescapable fact that in these eight short novels he has done something significant. Like Raymond Chandler and a few others, he has written, in fictional blood and crime, a social history of a time and place, and in so doing he told the story of a race of people who lived in the mean streets of Black American at mid-century.

Chapter IV
Color And Character

"Now I've heard everything," Grave Digger said. "Here's a white colored man who puts in a false fire alarm that Riverside Church is on fire, getting half the fire equipment in New York City on the roll and all the police in the neighborhood up here—and why? I ask you why?"

"Because he don't like black colored people," Coffin Ed said.

The use of color to indicate a character's moods and personality traits is a common device among writers, and Chester Himes was no different from many of his peers. Because he was a Black man writing about a fictional Black world, however, the use of colors takes on more subtle meanings in Himes' work than might be readily apparent.

We have noted already that the circumstances of Himes' life had produced in him some rather extreme views on racial matters. He tended to see his world as one contaminated by white-instigated oppression and injustice. These views were candidly verbalized in his fiction, particularly his post-prison short stories and his early novels. The rather negative reaction to his work by the white literary establishment only tended to harden his already bleak outlook on life.

Although he was descended from light-skinned Blacks, Himes had rather negative feelings toward other light-skinned Negroes whom he met. In his early life, he felt insecure about the ones he met at college, and for some unknown reason he felt that they looked down on him. He mentioned, as well, that light-skinned prostitutes were "hard to get" (doubtless cause for some resentment in a young man). Himes began associating with toughs and prostitutes because he felt that it was okay to be a Negro around these less pretentious Black people.

In his early book-length fiction, Himes expressed his ambivalence toward the lighter skinned Negro in no uncertain terms. In *If He Hollers*, for example, Bob Jones' light-complected fiance and her socially prominent family are depicted as mealy-mouthed sell-outs. Their unwillingness to push for greater racial equality is seen by Himes, through Bob, as a basic unwillingness to risk losing the social and financial security that their compromises with the system have gained for them.

By the mid-1950s, when he began to write detective fiction, Himes was a worn-out and badly disappointed man nearing the age of 50. Although he had not found the racial equality in France that he had hoped for, his resentment

50

of his native land had not abated. It was inevitable that these feelings would show themselves in his crime fiction. As a result, white people are often depicted quite negatively. At the same time, Black characters with light skin also are shown in a negative light.

More interesting are the subtleties Himes used that were not evident in the high-minded protest fiction of his early days. The color white is used symbolically over and over in the series to suggest moral failure or outright evil. White is not actually a color. It is, in reality, the absence of color. It is a tradition in western fiction, particularly melodrama, for white to suggest the presence of good or purity. Himes uses it in an ironic fashion to suggest exactly the opposite. It was a convenient device for him to use because by applying it to skin, hair, clothing, etc., it could be used to symbolize an absence of morality in characters of both races.

With white representing evil, it should come as no surprise that taken as a group, white people come off quite badly in the Harlem stories. Usually they are of four types: wealthy white people who enter Harlem to exploit the Blacks who live there, white police and bureaucrats who consider Harlem a problem to be swept under the rug as quickly as possible, white policemen who may be sympathetic but who lack the imagination to really understand the plight of the Black man, and white hired killers who come from out of town to do the bidding of more powerful criminals.

Himes had at least one vicious, knife-wielding killer in almost every story. Like the religious charlatan and the seductive and faithless temptress, the dope-crazed or depraved killer was a Himes archetype. This killer could be of any color, of course, but the Black ones usually possess a lightness of skin that isn't present in a protagonist or victim. Jody, a bronze-skinned killer menaced Imabelle and Jackson in *For Love Of Imabelle* while tan-colored Susie the Mugger hung menacingly in the background of *The Big Gold Dream*.

Just as often, though, this recurring character was white, and he seemed to be more menacing for his whiteness. In *The Heat's On,* Digger and Ed are both nearly done in by a killer who has

...a dead white, death's head face with colorless lips pulled back from small yellow teeth and huge deep-set eyes like targets on a pistol range: black balls rimmed with a thin line of white about which were large, irregular patches of black—a hophead's face.

In *All Shot Up,* the worst of the three killers hired by Casper Holmes to steal the political party's money is a white gunman with a sinister, Mississippi drawl. The sheer viciousness of this character's murders is an early clue that helps Digger and Ed tie the case together. By the time that they send Lila Holmes up to Casper's office, this dangerous cracker has turned on his boss and has used his knife to "slit Casper's eyelids and jab inside his nostrils and slash his tongue." It is the look of this killer, however, that makes even the street-wise Lila's blood run cold:

His coarse black hair was still plastered to his head, but his nostrils had whitened at the corners. He stared at Lila from black eyes that had the bright enameled look of a snake's.

As bad as these killers are, the exploiters are really the worst of the villains who populate Himes' Harlem. However, they usually have very little part in the story. As a symbol of white oppressiveness, they usually appear on stage for a very brief period and then hang menacingly in the background of the story until the case has been resolved.

Possibly the best example of this role is Ulysses Galen of *The Real Cool Killers*. Galen is nicknamed "The Greek," a tip-off to the fact that he indulges in sexual perversion. Described in the story's opening scene as a large man with a "big-featured, sallow face with the blotched skin of dissipation," he sounds like a debauched Roman senator. He is dressed in a gray suit, which is Himes' color for wealth, and his tie is red, the color of sensuality.

We later discover that in his own world Galen is a pillar of the community. A widower with two grown children, he is a successful executive with a soft drink company. He visits Harlem in order to satisfy his urge for sexual excesses. Later, when Digger finds a miniature bull whip in Galen's car, the Greek emerges not only as a sex fiend, but as a symbol of the white slave owners who enforced their desires on their slaves through the use of the lash. The fact that he beats and sexually molests teenaged Black girls only tends to strengthen this image.

In the same category but of less importance to the story is the white manager of the Dew Drop Inn. Although he too has remained in the background, he has made it possible for his bartender, Big Smiley, to sell Galen the use of the tavern basement for his perversions. On a lesser level, he deliberately debases Black teenagers and makes them easy prey to people like Galen by serving them alcoholic beverages.

Somewhat worse than Galen is Benny Mason, the white drug kingpin of *The Heat's On*. Mason is a shadowy presence who hovers over Harlem as he pumps in the plague of narcotics which, even in Himes' era, was fast becoming the bane of the Black community. Mason represents Himes' idea of white society, deliberately debasing and destroying the Black man and, just as he did through slavery, profiting from it monetarily.

Mason is responsible for more than drug running. He has been responsible for corrupting Gus and leading him ultimately to his death. His men have attacked and nearly killed Grave Digger and Coffin Ed. Finally, Mason himself murders Sister Heavenly on the street in broad daylight. As he is taken into custody following this last act, Mason is heard to say, "I want to talk to my lawyer." Ironically this demand is a protection afforded to the Black man under the Constitution but denied him through poverty. Even though the forces of justice have temporarily put an end to Mason's corrupt influences, Himes leaves unsaid the possibility that Mason's constitutionally protected right to a fair trial may put him back on the street to further corrupt Black youth.

Because the heroes of the Harlem series are duly appointed police officers, one might imagine that in Himes' work all police officers are to be trusted invariably. This is far from the truth. Among the worst are the high-ranking officers. The white police chief in *The Real Cool Killers* is an excellent example of police duplicity. At the outset of the story, the Chief tells numerous lies to the press, including the false identification of Sonny Pickens as the killer of Ulysses Galen.

This false identification places Sonny's life at risk because the Chief holds back the information from the cops working on the street. That Sonny could be killed is not as important to the Chief as the capture of the other juvenile delinquents. Later, after Sheik kills a policeman and threatens to kill Evelyn Johnson, the Chief seems much more interested in taking Sheik than in saving Evelyn's life. Grave Digger must disobey the Chief's orders and risk suspension in order to enter the hostage room.

Possibly the worst aspect of the Chief's personality is his callousness at the close of the case. Besides Ulysses Galen, a policeman and three Negro youths have been killed. Two teenaged girls, have been terrorized and the two Black detectives have risked their lives to end the crisis. In the face of all this suffering, the Chief dusts his hands with a satisfied smile and dismisses it all with the remark, "That wasn't too difficult, was it?"

But the Chief is only thoughtless and uncaring. Himes saves his special contempt for the cops who use their authority to extort money from the Black people they are supposed to protect. Angelo, the flashily-dressed white precinct sergeant who is on the take from Sister Heavenly in *Heat's On,* is a prime example.

At a somewhat higher level is the Harlem Precinct's commanding officer, Captain Brice. He is famous for sending Digger and Ed on suicide missions and making them take all the risk when rules must be broken in order to break a case. We notice, however, that he is well dressed and prosperous-looking. The study of detective fiction has taught us that characters who wear expensive clothing are usually suspect.

By the time he appears in *Blind Man With A Pistol,* it is an established fact that Brice has been using his position to enrich himself illegally. The graft has become so much a part of the job that Lieutenant Anderson, who has been promised a promotion and command of the precinct, wants the job for the graft as much as for the increased prestige.

White men exist at every level of Himes' world to exploit and cheat the Black residents of Harlem. Physically frail and white-haired, Abie the Jew in *The Big Gold Dream* seems like an insignificant and harmless presence, but his guise is a sham. Dressed in a black suit and brown felt hat, he seems to fit into the Negro world. When we meet him at Alberta Wright's apartment purchasing her furniture from her husband, Rufus, Abie seems no more than a sharp businessman. Of course, he is Jewish and tradition has prepared us for the idea that a Jewish tradesman, particularly one who deals in castoffs, will be a hard bargainer.

Later, however, we discover that he has a more sinister side. First, he has been running a scan with Rufus. Rufus lets him into the apartments of women with whom he is romantically involved in order to sell Abie all of the furniture. A pretense exists between the two that they are conducting a business transaction, but this facade is simply to protect the Jew. He is actually paying Rufus for the service of letting him in, not for selling him the furniture.

On a higher level, Abie is cheating Black people a second time. His long career in purchasing second-hand furniture has taught him that uneducated Black people often hide their life savings in their furniture. Legend has it that he built the foundations of a considerable fortune on the $30,000.00 he once found in an old sofa. Now he actively seeks out old furniture for the money he inevitably finds therein.

All of these white men who come into Harlem to cheat and exploit are outsiders, but none so much as Colonel Robert L. Calhoun in *Cotton Comes To Harlem*. Calhoun comes from the Deep South, pretending to be the salvation of the Black man. When we first meet him, he is located in an office, outside of which are posters that depict glowingly the jobs, opportunities, and good lives that await northern Negroes who will return to the South. The posters promise the chance for improved income and social standing and depict the Negro being welcomed by a man looking very much like Calhoun.

Calhoun has a "narrow, hawklike face covered by...a mane of snow-white hair." He has a "wide, drooping white mustache" and a "white goatee." His "narrow-set eyes were ice-cold blue and his back was ramrod straight." Himes notes that his eyes prevent him from looking exactly like the colonel in the poster.

Himes gives us numerous tip-offs to the fact that Calhoun, who is essentially a symbolic character anyway, is not on the up-and-up. First of all, his name conjures up images of John C. Calhoun, the fire-breathing secessionist of the Civil War era. Second, when Calhoun remarks to his nephew that "you got to think of niggers with love and charity," his use of the word "nigger" is in direct opposition to the concept of "love and charity." His "Back to the Southland" movement is a sly attempt to trick unwary Negroes back to the origins of their enslavements in order that they again may be subjugated and exploited for their labor.

By the time that Calhoun makes his appearance, we have noticed that the very color of white has come to symbolize evil to Himes. Calhoun, with his white hair, mustache, and beard is the epitome of evil. The whiteness of his hair and beard blends in with the whiteness of the bale of missing cotton which gives the story its name. Cotton, which was the cause of so much Negro suffering in the 19th century, has appeared through some evil magic to cause more suffering in modern Harlem.

White hair, especially, is another classic Himesian tip-off to an evil exploiter. One of the earliest characters to exhibit this characteristic is Reba, the amazonian landprop (or madam) of *The Real Cool Killers*. When Digger first goes to interrogate her, he discovers that "she was as tall as his six feet two, with snow-white hair cut short as a man's and brushed straight back from his forehead."

Even without the foreknowledge that she is in the sex business, her sultry seductiveness is apparent in the knowledge that her "lips were painted carnation red" and that she has "a red rose in the V of her mammoth bosom." Beyond her aggressive sexiness, she is undoubtedly a dangerous woman. We are told that she once caught her man locked in a sexual embrace with another prostitute. She made him jump naked out of a third story window and shot him through the head on the way down. An old man tells Digger that it "warn't nobody but her husband and she didn't get a day."

This information seems to suggest that she has the protection of the law in any endeavor. Her assurance of her safety is manifest in her defiance of Digger when she tells him "you can't close me up and you can't make me talk." When the case is over, and all of the criminals either have been taken to the morgue or to the lockup, Reba is among the latter group. However, we are told that she has called a Negro city councilman with orders to get her out of jail.

The information that she has been involved in the wholesale contribution to the delinquency of minors along with Big Smiley, Ready Belcher, the manager of the Dew Drop Inn, and, for a while at least, Ulysses Galen, proves that she is as bad a person as Harlem has to offer. The fact that she is Black only seems to make her worse.

Digger and Ed meet a similar type in *Cotton Comes to Harlem* when they visit the bordello of Sarah. Sarah is described as "a buxom black woman with snow-white hair done in curls as tight as springs. She had a round face, broad flat nose, thick, dark unpainted lips and a dazzling white-toothed smile. Her dark eyes were stone cold." Dressed in a black satin gown with a high decollete and long sleeves, Sarah lacks the lewd sensuality of Reba. The white hair, coupled with the empty smile and the cold eyes, leaves the reader with only a sense of Sarah's potential danger.

White hair flags our attention elsewhere in the series. Abie the Jew, who works with Rufus Wright to steal furniture in *Big Gold Dream*, has white hair and proves to be a classic exploiter. A white man with white hair, Abie, like Colonel Calhoun, attempts to present a harmless and friendly exterior to Blacks in order to trick them.

In the same story, Himes also provides a black counterpart to Abie in Sweet Prophet Brown. Possibly the most archetypal of all Himes' preachers, he presents an appearance that is both bizarre and regal:

His smooth black face with its big buck teeth and popping eyes was ageless; but his long grizzly hair, on which he wore a black silk cap, was snow-white...

Dressed in a cloak of purple, the color of royal power, Brown is a sight to awe the simple poor of Harlem who place their trust in God and his messengers.

Brown is also Himes' most comical villain. Although Brown is more ridiculous looking than Reverend Short *(Crazy Kill)*, more dramatic than Reverend Gaines *(Imabelle)* and far less attractive than Reverend Deke O'Malley *(Cotton)*, his evil nature is not readily apparent at first sight. Only the white hair signals to us that he is the chief villain in the story. Although Rufus Wright and Abie the Jew both prey on Harlem's squares, they are both eliminated early in the story. Slick Jenkins and Susie the Mugger are both dangerous and violent, but ultimately they do more damage to each other than they do to Alberta Wright and Sugar Stonewall, the story's titular protagonists. Brown is the only villain to survive the story, and Himes' rather ambiguous ending leaves the reader with the feeling that, in spite of his near-fatal knife wound and his exposure to the police, Sweet Prophet will continue to prosper through his exploitation of the poor Black's need to believe in the Hereafter.

White hair is not the only signal for criminality in the series. Himes manages to use the color in a number of other, less expected ways. Nowhere in the series does Himes catch us so completely off guard as he does in *The Heat's On*. The detectives converge on the scene of a false fire alarm where Pinky, "a milk-white albino with pink eyes, battered lips, cauliflowered ears and thick, kinky, cream-colored hair" is about to be set upon by a group of angry firemen.

Pinky tells the detectives a rather convoluted story in which he claims that his father's wife and her African lover are plotting to kill Gus, Pinky's adopted father. With the logic that has become the hallmark of the denizens of Harlem, Pinky has pulled the fire alarm to call attention to Gus' plight.

Like Sweet Prophet Brown, Pinky is too ridiculous looking and too much of a half-wit for anyone to suspect him of anything. Once *Heat* moves on from Pinky's appearance, the story so quickly fills up with genuinely sinister characters that the albino half-wit is nearly forgotten. Only after all of the villainous characters have killed each other does the reader come to realize that white-skinned Pinky is the real murderer. He has killed his own father before the action of the story even takes place.

Ironically, the reason for the murder is skin color. Gus refuses to take Pinky with him to Ghana because "all them black Africans wouldn't like colored people white as [Pinky], and they'd kill [him]."

Himes uses white skin to express his opinion of several other characters in this story: Daddy Haddy, Jake the pusher, and Sister Heavenly. Daddy is "an old man...who had white leprous-looking splotches on his leathery tan skin." Another corrupter of Black youth, the old man runs a tobacco shop that serves as a numbers drop and a connection where pushers sell teenaged school kids sticks of marijuana and doctored-up decks of heroin. Jake is a well-dressed hunch-backed dwarf. A yellow-skinned white man, Jake haunts

Harlem in order to push heroin. The worst of the trio is Sister Heavenly. An old woman who makes a living selling drugs and quack cures, Heavenly previously has been a whore who ran away from her farm family because she was too lazy to chop cotton. When we meet her, she has been using skin lightening creams for so many years that she has bleached her skin to the color of parchment. Like all the other bad guys in *Heat*, Daddy Haddy, Jake, and Heavenly all come to violent ends.

By the time he wrote his last entry in the series, *Blind Man With A Pistol*, Himes seemed to be of the opinion that his Harlem characters are in as much danger from their own kind as from the white man. Although the enslaving presence of the white man continues to hang over Harlem like a dark cloud, it is the disarray caused by the naive Marcus Mackinzie, the Black Power movement of the villainous Dr. Moore, and the sinister madness of the Prophet Ham that seem to pose the greatest danger to the community.

In the very beginning, however, Himes presents a vignette in which the police discover a rundown building filled with black clad "nuns" and dozens of naked, malnourished children presided over by an impossibly old man who calls himself Reverend Sam. Sam, who admits to being the husband of the nuns and father to all the children, seems like a harmless eccentric to the investigating police officers, but Himes tells us that he is dressed in a "spotted long-sleeved white gown." Somehow we are not surprised when three bodies of his former "wives" are discovered buried in the rubble.

When one begins to understand this rather subtle surfacing of Himes' ambivalence about whites in his writings, it comes as no surprise when he expresses negative feelings about the light-skinned members of his own race. A prototypical character in the Harlem series is Imabelle, the eponymous heroine of the first book in the series, *For Love Of Imabelle*. She is part of a group of rather ordinary-looking Negroes on the opening page of the story, but one look at her is enough to tell you that she is anything but ordinary:

She was a cushioned-lipped, hot-bodied, banana-skin chick with the speckled-brown eyes of a teaser and the high-arched, ball-bearing hips of a natural-born *amante*.

Himes tells us in the same breath that Jackson, her man, is "as crazy about her as moose for doe." But Jackson is Imabelle's antithesis. "A short, black fat man with purple-red gums and pearly white teeth made for laughing," Jackson is the picture of a Negro music-hall caricature. Even the least suspicious of Himes' readers is bound to ask why this highly desirable sexpot is hooked up with this short, fat, funny-looking little fellow.

It does not take us long to discover that Imabelle is taking the gullible and trusting Jackson for a ride. The most salient feature of Imabelle's character (aside from her considerable sexuality) is her successful career of manipulating men. During the breakneck pace of this story, Imabelle double-crosses Jackson to help Hank, Jodie, and Slim, double-double-crosses the gang in order to get away from them, and leaves Jackson and his brother to almost certain death in her attempt to escape.

By the end of the story, it is impossible for the authorities to discover the whole truth of Imabelle's involvement in the case. The police and the district attorney are convinced of her duplicity, but without Jackson's testimony they cannot hold her on a single charge.

Like Sweet Prophet Brown and a few other Himesian scoundrels, Imabelle leads a charmed life. Digger tells the frustrated and incredulous district attorney not to worry about Imabelle; one day, he promises, he and Coffin Ed will catch the girl "with her pants down." Perhaps Imabelle knows this or perhaps she is simply tired of being manipulative for a living. For whatever reason, she retires from hustling and settles down with her faithful Jackson, who marries her and makes her as honest a woman as she is capable of being.

Along with her other flaws and faults, Imabelle seems to set herself apart from other members of her race. On several occasions, she addresses other characters in the story as "nigger," which seems to indicate a basic contempt for people with darker skins than her own. This arrogant apartness from other Negroes is a characteristic that will surface in other light-skinned players in Himes' saga.

It would be interesting to know if such a prototypical female ever actually figured in Himes' life, because she shows up quite often in this series. For Himes she is what the blonde who could "make a bishop kick a hole in a stained glass window" was to Raymond Chandler. She seems to have been his ideal of Negro beauty, femininity, and sexuality.

Oddly enough, she was also a symbol of duplicity and faithlessness. She shows up quickly enough in *The Crazy Kill* in the person of Dulcy Perry. Dulcy, who is married to the ultra-virile Johnny Perry, has "round, seductive buttocks...short-cut orange-yellow curls framing the olive-brown complexion of her heart-shaped face." Dressed in a rose-colored dress, she inflames the desires of both Chink Charlie Dawson and the mad Reverend Short. Married to both Valentine Haines and "Four-Ace" Johnny Perry, Dulcy is clearly too much woman for one man.

For all her duplicity, however, Dulcy comes off as a more sympathetic character than Imabelle. When the story is over, it is clear that she has tried to hide her past to prevent Johnny from being hurt. Like all of Himes' seductive tarts, however, lying comes much too easy for Dulcy, and once she starts she cannot stop. Her tragic flaw is that she cannot place her trust in the truth, even with Johnny, whose honor is a byword in Harlem.

The only truly evil seductress in Himes' group of light-skinned hussies is Ginny, the sexpot of *The Heat's On*. Before we even meet her, we know that she is married to an older man and is actively involved in cheating on him with an African. When the detectives see her for the first time dancing a suggestive shuffle with a drink in her hand, even they are startled to see

A high-yellow woman...with the high sharp hips of a cotton chopper and the big loaded breasts of a wet nurse...her breasts poked out...like the snouts of two hungry shoats.

They also note that she has evil-looking slanted cat-like eyes, which prompts Grave Digger to declare that "I wouldn't have one (a cat-eyed woman) for my own for all the tea in China."

Unlike Imabelle and Dulcy, Ginny is aggressive and hostile. When Digger and Ed first meet her and identify themselves as detectives, she scornfully dismisses them as "nigger cops" and demands to know "what you whore-chasers want?" It takes a good deal more than two detectives to frighten this woman. During her interrogation, she adds brazenness to hostility and cheerfully admits to committing adultery. As the story progresses, Ginny constantly plays both ends against the middle and changes her allegiance to go along with anyone whom she sees as possessing the upper hand. This strategy proves to be her undoing, and she becomes the only one of Himes' high-yellow hustlers to suffer a violent death.

Both braver and smarter than Imabelle and Ginny is Iris O'Malley of *Cotton Comes To Harlem.* Coming so near the end of the series, Iris represents Himes' refinement of this particular stock character.

She was a hard-bodied high-yellow woman with a perfect figure. She never wore a girdle and her jiggling buttocks gave all men amorous ideas. She had a heart-shaped face with the high cheekbones, big wide red painted mouth, and long-lashed speckled brown eyes of a sexpot and she was thirty-three years old, which gave her the experience.

Iris has no allegiance to anyone but herself. It is clear from her remarks and actions that she sees herself as an island and has no interest in being confined by any relationship or ideology. When Coffin Ed and Grave Digger confront her in her apartment, they explain that their main interest in the case is the "eighty-seven colored families—like you and me—." But before Digger can complete his sentence, Iris whips back "Not like me!" Apparently she is not interested in being included in the Black world, a fact that is not lost on Grave Digger when he characterizes her as one of "these half-white bitches."

There is something about these women that brings out the worst in Digger and Ed. Digger slaps Imabelle out of her chair when he discovers her at the police station. Ed strips Ginny and tortures her into cooperating with him. Each of these women is cowed by the physicality of these two brutal men, but Iris is tougher than any of her predecessors.

During her confrontation with the pair, her anger and indifference eventually push Ed over the edge, and he nearly chokes her to death. Later, when she has recovered from his attack, she jumps up and hits the tough detective squarely in his nose, making it bleed. Perhaps a little cowed himself by this aggressively unfeminine behavior, Ed allows that he "had that coming."

Her anger and physical toughness come to the fore in other parts of the story. When she finds Deke O'Malley in the apartment of the seductively-dressed Mabel Hill, she attacks the woman and a terrible struggle ensues ending in Mabel's death. Later, when she and O'Malley are tied up in his church hiding place, the fact that Iris is bound hand and foot in a chair does not prevent her from throwing herself at her lover and attempting to kill him.

Iris is unusual from a sexual standpoint as well. We discover late in the story that she is involved in a long-running homosexual affair with the lesbian dancer, Billie Belle. It is clear during their conversation that the affair means more to Billie than it does to Iris. To Iris, it is probably just one more self-indulgence. She has no problem rationalizing this lesbian lover while obviously enjoying a hot-blooded marriage with Deke and feels no remorse over it. Her jealousy over Deke's affair with Mabel and her subsequent lack of guilt over Billie make Iris seem almost masculine in her sexual affairs. Such a sexual double-standard is much more typical of the chauvinistic male personality than of the female.

Iris is also sexually aroused by violence. When she is threatened by the two gunmen who have turned on Deke, "her terror was so intense it became sexual—and she had an orgasm."

This rather unpleasant personality trait is something that Iris shares with Ginny. When Ginny has been stripped and is being tortured by Coffin Ed, Ginny is sexually aroused by Ed's viciousness. Later, she tries to win the big man over with her sex, promising, "you'll want me when you've had me. You won't be able to get enough of me. I can make you scream with joy. I can do it in ways you never dreamed of."

Like Philip Marlowe and the Continental Op before him, Ed rejects the idea of sex with a criminal woman, no matter how wantonly alluring. He responds to her promise with

"you think because I'm a cop I've got a price. But you're making a mistake. You've got only one thing I want. The truth. You're going to give me that. Or I'm going to fix you so that no man will ever want anything you got to give."

Although Digger and Ed never seem to feel any sexual desire for these bad yellow women, they have no trouble hating them and expressing this hatred in physical abuse. Their sadism is the only way these proletarian heroes can allow their arousal to be expressed. To indulge in sexual intercourse with a female criminal would taint them forever.

This sexually inspired sadism probably also has another meaning in Himes' outlook on crime and punishment. Very few of the villains in the Harlem series live to go to trial and thence to jail. Most meet their ends at the hands of Digger and Ed or at the hands of some other criminal. In this way, each story is wrapped up with some finality. Justice is served by a ritualistic killing, although the law may be bent or entirely circumvented.

With the exception of Mike Hammer and a very few other modern crime characters, the tradition of the hard-boiled crime novel has forbidden the killing of women at the hands of the detective. The detective is a knight errant whose creed demands that women be idealized and spared the ultimate cruelty that can be inflicted on a man.

In Himes' Harlem, most bad women usually are spared a violent death. Imabelle, Dulcy, and Sissie are punished with a bad scare and allowed to redeem themselves by becoming good wives to their stories' male protagonists. Lila Holmes is badly wounded by a man, but not by an agent of the law. Iris O'Malley is jailed and will probably be sent to prison, but her testimony against Deke will probably result in a reduced sentence. Only Ginny, of all Himes' bad girls, is violently killed, and not surprisingly, Ginny is killed by Sister Heavenly, herself a light-skinned bad girl grown old.

Inasmuch as the detective's code proscribes the killing of a woman, no matter how evil, a physical beating is probably the only means of administering punishment that is left to Digger and Ed. Himes seems to justify it because, first, they are all "half-white bitches," and second their deceitful beauty and overpowering sexuality very likely will render ineffective any real effort to punish them for their wrongs.

The two detectives are not hindered by the same restraint when it comes to light-skinned male characters. The first one they meet in the series is Chink Charlie Dawson, a big yellow-skinned young man who is running to fat. Chink is one of the most despicable men in the entire Harlem saga.

A sharp dresser, he clearly fancies himself a sport and a ladies' man. He enjoys himself regularly with Doll Baby, while actively chasing after Dulcy Perry. Before the story is over, we discover that he will stoop to blackmail and extortion, on top of the moral sin of adultery. Even before we realize his criminal tendencies, we discover that he has a very good job bartending in a white gentleman's club uptown. The implication is that he is something of a white man's lapdog who enjoys many favors because of his toadying.

Himes expresses his contempt for this character by having Digger and Ed torture him in a manner similar to Himes' own torture at the hands of Chicago detectives years before. When the yellow-skinned scoundrel arouses the detectives' ire, they render him senseless with a terrific blow to the midsection. Handcuffing his ankles together, they hang him from an open door and, with their feet in his armpits, bear down on him. Chink is forced to talk to them.

Chink's worst crime is not listed in the civil statutes. He is a would-be adulterer, and it is not up to Digger and Ed to punish such a crime. Dulcy arranges for him to be caught naked in her house where Johnny Perry kills him in a jealous rage.

A more vicious male character is Sheik, the leader of the teen gang in *The Real Cool Killers*. Sheik "was a tall yellow boy with strange yellow eyes and reddish kinky hair. He had the broad-shouldered, trim-waisted figure of an athlete. His face was broad, his nose flat with wide, flaring nostrils, and his skin freckled." This character, who is somewhat reminiscent of Himes in his younger days, is a truly malignant figure. His madness, assumed by other characters to be sheer viciousness, is the key to the entire story.

By the time the case has been unraveled, Sheik has proven to be guilty of every crime in the book. He has impregnated Sissie and has attempted to seduce Evelyn Johnson. He has been deeply involved in pimping and is initially believed by everyone (including himself) to be the real killer of Ulysses Galen. His death at Coffin Ed's hands ends a spree in which he is responsible for the deaths of two more people and for threatening the lives of both Evelyn and Grave Digger.

It is only in his final story, *Blind Man With A Pistol,* that Himes does not use skin color as a determinant for evil. In this story, written 12 years after *For Love Of Imabelle,* Himes was clearly writing in a kind of despair. Certainly, the menacing evil of white domination hovers over Harlem like a cloud, but the elements that are destroying Harlem from the inside are all black. Marcus MacKenzie is destroying it with his naivete, Dr. Moore is preaching Black power while secretly using the movement to enrich himself, and the sinister Prophet Ham is whipping up racial hatred for his own obscure purposes.

All of these characters are Black, and all lack any identifying whiteness that might signify their inherent evil. Possibly Himes came to realize that all of the Black man's exploiters were not white, after all.

Prior to this, however, blackness (or at least deep brownness) was an indication of a character's intrinsic goodness. Jackson of *Imabelle* fame serves to make this clear. He is trusting, loyal and tenacious in the pursuit of his goals, and he possesses sufficient moral courage to overcome his own terrors when the need arises.

At the same time, however, Jackson also is depicted as an object of ridicule and slapstick buffoonery. Virtually every action Jackson takes tends to make him look dense or foolish at worst. It is tempting to conclude that Himes invested his own ambivalence about being a Black man in his depiction of the only very Black and truly good character in his first story.

Jackson is drawn in rather broad strokes and resembles nothing so much as the cowardly, buffoonish Negro who so often played the valet or chauffeur to "B" movie white heroes during the 1930s and '40s. He can go from sleepy stupidity to wild, wide-eyed terror. As if to emphasize the cheap humor in this wild fear, when Jackson embarks on his bruising, headlong flight from the warehouse, Himes has Jackson remember a rhyme that goes "Run, Nigger, Run, the patteroler get you." Jackson's fear is made all the more ridiculous by his memory of the old street corner rhyme.

Jackson's loyalty to Imabelle and his courage are his finest qualities, but Himes chooses to lampoon even these in the scene where the pair are briefly reunited in the ghetto apartment where she has been staying with Slim:

She held him at arm's length, looked at the pipe still gripped in his hand, then looked at his face and read him like a book. She ran the tip of her red tongue slowly across her full, cushiony, sensuous lips, making them wet-red, and looked him straight in the eyes. . .

The man drowned.

When he came up, he stared back, passion cocked, his whole black being on a live-wire edge. Ready! Solid ready to cut throats, crack skulls, dodge police, steal hearses, drink muddy water, live in a hollow log, and take any rape-fiend chance to be once more in the arms of his high-yellow heart.

Every good intention and all of the sterling characteristics that Jackson possesses are cheapened by the fact that he is too stupid to realize how worthless and scheming the beautiful Imabelle is. He risks his life several times during the story on her behalf, never realizing that Imabelle is using him (and practically everyone else, as well) throughout the story. Himes' romantic nature takes hold in the end when he finally reunites the pair and allows them to go off into the sunset together. In terms of everything that has already happened, however, it is an unbelievable and unsatisfying fairy tale conclusion to a story with a theme of treachery and deceit.

The character of Jackson was obviously a gross exaggeration, invented as much for comic relief as to provide a sympathetic Negro protagonist. But Himes must have seen how useful such a character could be because he made a Jackson-like character part of the formula that he was inventing for himself. In virtually every story, there is a protagonist who is dark-skinned, trusting, and gullible. These characters act as catalysts for the action, and the individual stories tend to revolve around them.

In *The Crazy Kill*, for example, Himes gives us Aesop "Sonny" Pickens. In keeping with his namesake, Sonny invents a fable in which a cuckold is confronted by his paramour's husband. Unfortunately, his joke backfires and he finds himself accused of murder and in danger of being killed by both the police and the teen gang that "liberated" him. Neither as black nor as gullible as Jackson, Sonny is nevertheless a lackluster young man where intuitive thinking is concerned. A mature, responsible person would never chase someone else through the streets with a gun, but this is what he does, thereby setting the entire adventure in motion.

As the story progresses, Sonny never seems to realize the madness lurking behind Sheik's handsome and dynamic exterior. This inability puts him at greater risk and nearly results in his own murder at Sheik's hands.

Like Jackson, however, Sonny is possessed of a romantic nature. When he is faced with Sissie's loneliness and her pregnancy, he unselfishly takes the feckless and irresponsible girl's hand in marriage. This willingness to love and honor a person less worthy than himself is a hallmark of Himes' sucker/ protagonist.

Although Johnny Perry is a far cry from the foolishly gullible Jackson and Sonny, he is victimized by a duplicitous female and is made to look just as foolish. We tend not to place Johnny in the same category as Himes' other titular protagonists because he is so virile and masculine and, seemingly, so much in control of his world.

In truth, however, his entire situation is in jeopardy because of his love for Dulcy. She has used his trusting and honorable nature to conceal from him the facts of her continuing marriage to Val Haines. Even when Johnny, acting in the role of detective, uncovers the truth of her past life, the sucker in him cannot resist the gesture of betting $10,000.00 on her love and fidelity. Later, after he has risked his future life and freedom by killing Chink Charlie, his only thought is for his lost love. It is implicit in his character (and in that of the other dark-skinned suckers) that, given the chance, he will take back his wife and continue to love her in spite of her past trickery.

In *The Big Gold Dream*, Himes switches the sex of his sucker. Here, it is Alberta Wright who is led astray by a compelling member of the opposite sex. Ironically, it is not romantic love that proves her undoing, but rather her belief in God and Sweet Prophet Brown. Brown hypnotizes her in order to make her give up all the money she won playing the numbers, never realizing that the trusting and sweet-natured woman plans to give him all the money anyway.

Alberta, like Jackson and Johnny Perry, has a scheming and unscrupulous lover in the form of Sugar Stonewall. Although Sugar shares many traits with Imabelle, Dulcy, and other female characters of their ilk, he lacks their cunning and intelligence. Unlike her male counterparts in the series, Alberta recognizes this part of his personality but does not hold it against him. When her troubles with Sweet Prophet and the law are all over, it is clear that she still loves Sugar in spite of his flaws and plans to continue playing house with him.

There are occasions when the motif of skin color and character seems to break down. In *Imabelle,* for example, Grave Digger finds Hank and Jodie holed up in the home of Billie, a voluptuous, light-skinned madam. Although Billie is guilty of harboring fugitives from the law and is clearly in the habit of paying graft and protection money to cops, she cooperates with Digger and helps him in the fight with the two criminals by disabling Jodie with an axe.

In the same story, Himes also provides us with the character of Jackson's twin brother, Goldy. The exact opposite of Jackson in every way, Goldy is as suspicious and duplicitous as Jackson is trusting and honest. He makes his living pretending to be a nun who sells tickets to heaven. At the same time, he acts as a stool pigeon for Digger and Ed and consorts with madams, con artists, and other underworld types. He is willing to kill to get the gold ore from Imabelle, and he resorts to other dirty tricks, such as slipping a mickey finn to his brother to keep him quiet.

Although Goldy is a bad Black person, and Billie is an almost-good light-skinned Negro, this ambiguity in their characters is explained by the ambiguity in their sexualities. Goldy, for example, is a transvestite whom all of Harlem believes is a woman. When he is brutally murdered by Hank and Jodie, the murder is perpetrated largely because of Jodie's outrage that Goldy has been masquerading as a woman.

Billie, whose masculine name provides an early indication of her secret, is even more ambiguous than Goldy. In spite of her feminine exterior, Billie is an hermaphrodite who is just as much male as female. Her ambiguity of character is matched by her ambiguity of action. Although she is a consort of criminals she sides with Digger in the fight with Jodie and Hank.

This ambiguity factor takes over again in *All Shot Up*. Casper Holmes, the forceful and masculine Harlem political boss, is a dark-skinned Negro, but he turns out to be a homosexual. Everything in his life, including his beautiful wife, is no more than a cover for his sexual secret.

Casper's sexual ambiguity is shared by his wife, Lila. Lila is so sexy that the normally celibate Digger starts to make a play for her. However, Lila is not as light-skinned as other Harlem sexpots. Lila "had the type of beauty made fashionable in the 1930s by an all colored musical called *Brownskin Models*," but possesses a bounty of Himes' favorite sexual attributes:

She was rather short and busty, with a pear-shaped bottom and slender legs. She had short wavy hair, a heart-shaped face, and long-lashed, expressive brown eyes...Her breasts stuck out from a turtleneck blue jersey-silk pullover as though taking dead aim at any man in front of her.

In spite of this abundance of pulchritude, Lila goes about Harlem masquerading as a man (and somehow pulling it off). Her sexual ambiguity is more than matched by the ambiguity of her actions. It is never made completely clear why she indulges in the masquerade or why the wife of a powerful Black politician is out engaging in petty larceny.

It is doubtful that any aspect of Himes' writing career provided as much grist for discussion as his use of color and skin shade to indicate a character's moral persuasion. It is very likely that much of this meaning of color grew out of his experiences with his mother and father, who represented many of the characteristics related here. His mother was very light-skinned, beautiful, and haughty. Her disdain for darker-skinned Blacks was one of her most outstanding characteristics and her undoubted belief that she was superior to dark Blacks is certainly the basis for the haughtiness expressed by Imabelle, Ginny, Dulcy, and Iris. Certainly her self-made isolation from others of her own race has a bearing on the tendency of these characters to dismiss other Harlemites as "niggers."

Himes' father, of course, was short, muscular, and squat. He was very black and possessed of extremely negroid features. Hard-working and pedestrian in his ways, he must have looked very foolish to his elitist wife and his son,

Chester. Himes referred to his father as an "Uncle Tom" because of his tendency to accept the life to which he was relegated. Himes' contempt for his father's honesty and his relative unconcern for that which he could not have must certainly be closely related to the contempt that Himes expresses for the dark-skinned suckers who populate his Harlem. One can only guess at how he used this device to mitigate his own pain and frustration with the inescapable fact of his race.

Chapter V
Rage And Love

She was a cushioned-lipped, hot-bodied, banana-skin chick with the speckled-brown eyes of a teaser and the high-arched, ball-bearing hips of a natural-born *amante*. Jackson was as crazy for her as moose for doe.

Chester Himes felt that he was woefully unprepared for the task of writing a detective story. Although he certainly harbored romantic fantasies about himself, the romantic, chivalric world of the classic private eye had nothing to do with the world he had inhabited.

On the other hand, crime and the life of the ghetto hustler were things he was well acquainted with.

His first book was published as *La Reine des Pommes* by Gallimard in 1958 and was renamed *For Love Of Imabelle* when it appeared as a paperback original in America. The story was revised slightly and reissued later under the title of *A Rage in Harlem.*

The story opens in an apartment in Harlem. A young man named Jodie, a sexy, light-skinned woman named Imabelle, and Jackson, a fat, comical-looking Negro are all watching a man named Hank perform an experiment. The air is thick with tension because Jackson has given Hank $1,500.00 in $10.00 bills for the purpose of changing them into hundreds.

After Hank places the money into Jackson's oven, the stove suddenly explodes. Smoke fills the room and all is confusion. Simultaneously, another Black man bursts into the room and identifies himself as a U.S. Marshal. A mad scramble ensues, during which only Jackson is caught.

Faced with ten years in prison, Jackson offers the lawman $200.00 to let him go. After some hesitation, the cop agrees and Jackson takes him to his place of employment, the mortuary of H. Exodus Clay. There, he manages to get into the safe and steals $500.00. Jackson pays off the marshal who drives away.

Jackson is left on the street with the knowledge that he must find $200.00 to replace what he has stolen. Believing that if he can find Hank again he can get him to change the remaining $300.00 into $3,000.00, he goes to the home of Imabelle's sister. We discover through Jackson's interchange with the sister that he believes Imabelle met Jodie at the sister's house.

The sister claims not to know Jodie, however. Furthermore, she denies having seen Imabelle in days and tells Jackson that her sister is a liar. Enraged at this calumny, Jackson visits his pastor, Reverend Gaines. After spending some moments in prayer, Jackson decides to spend the rest of the night attempting to win back his lost money gambling with the remaining $300.00.

The next morning finds him flat broke, however. When he calls his apartment, his landlady tells him that the U.S. Marshal has taken Imabelle and her trunk away. Jackson is stunned by this news and is worried about Imabelle and her mysterious trunk. Against his better judgment he decides to visit his disreputable twin brother Goldy.

Goldy, a transvestite masquerading as a nun, sells tickets to heaven on the street for a living. When Jackson tells Goldy his story, he immediately recognizes "the blow" from Jackson's description and is suspicious that Imabelle is in league with the con men. Jackson vociferously denies the charge, but Goldy is not convinced.

The information about the trunk particularly interests Goldy. When Jackson refuses to talk about it, Goldy surmises that the trunk must contain something valuable. He agrees to help Jackson find Imabelle and, to keep him out of the way, slips Jackson a doped drink.

Later, in a house he shares with two other crooked transvestites, Goldy tells them the story and enlists their aid. Afterwards Goldy visits the post office where he inspects the wanted posters. He soon finds one with three Black men wanted for murder in Mississippi and surmises they are the men he is after. Committing the faces to memory, he spends the rest of the day searching for news of the criminals.

For three days Goldy scours Harlem looking for the three con men. Finally, his roommate, Big Kathy, informs him that a man named Morgan has been in Kathy's whorehouse bragging to a hooker about a lost-gold-mine pitch. Morgan's description matches that of Hank.

When Goldy tells Jackson this news, Jackson eventually confesses that Imabelle's trunk contains gold ore that originally belonged to her husband. She has been keeping it in order to force him to divorce her. Goldy decides that there must be at least two hundred pounds of gold in the trunk. They begin to plan how they will get Imabelle and the trunk back.

Goldy goes to Kathy's whorehouse where he finds Hank and Jodie being entertained by a young prostitute. Soon the whore excuses herself and talks to Kathy and Goldy. She explains what she has found out, including the news that the gang has another man named Gus Parsons circulating through the Black community looking for suckers.

Goldy leaves the bordello to find Grave Digger Jones and Coffin Ed Johnson, a pair of tough Black police detectives. He fills them in on the Mississippi murderers and their gold mine scam. He convinces the detectives not to take Hank and Jodie until he brings them together with Parsons.

The following afternoon Goldy fixes Jackson up with a roll of stage money and sends him to a seedy bar. Once in the bar, Jackson buys a drink and pays for it with his large roll of bills. A drunken ex-fighter tries to take the money away from Jackson but a well-dressed brown man stops him.

After the bar quiets down, the well-dressed man takes Jackson aside and buys him a drink. Jackson quickly realizes that this man must be the Gus Parsons he is seeking. Parsons simultaneously recognizes in Jackson the perfect mark. They go out to dinner where Parsons tells Jackson the story of the gold mine. Jackson pretends to fall for it.

Gus and Jackson leave for the gang's hideout. Goldy, along with Grave Digger and Coffin Ed, follows at a safe distance. A short way down the street, Parsons attempts to overpower Jackson but the two detectives intervene and beat Parsons up. The helpless Parsons quickly agrees to take them to the hideout in order to avoid further punishment.

They arrive at a building in the warehouse section down by the river. Jackson is sent ahead to get the door open. To his surprise, the door is answered by Imabelle, who invites him in. Inside, Jackson finds Hank and Jodie, along with Slim, who is now pretending to be an assayer. The gangsters freeze at the sight of Jackson, which gives the two detectives time to come in and get the drop on them.

Before Coffin Ed and Grave Digger can take complete control of the situation, however, a scuffle ensues between Jackson and Jodie, who draws a knife. Imabelle gives a piercing scream and in the confusion, Digger accidentally shoots Parsons, and Hank throws a beaker of acid into Coffin Ed's face. Some of the acid splashes onto Slim, burning him badly.

In a frenzy of pain and rage, Ed sprays the room with bullets, scattering the crowd and knocking out all the lights. As Grave Digger moves to cut off their retreat, he is accidentally knocked out as Ed flails about with his gun.

Slim and Imabelle come out, grab a taxi, and order the driver to take them to the hospital. Goldy, lurking nearby, spots the acid burns on Slim's neck and insinuates himself into the same taxi. The trio manages to make it to the hospital without further incident.

After Slim and Imabelle alight from the cab, Goldy remains inside and orders the taxi driver to wait for their emergence. When they finally come out, Goldy follows them to a tenement on Upper Park Avenue. He stays close enough to discover which apartment they have gone to before returning to his secret hideout. There he waits for Jackson to turn up.

After numerous near-misses with the law, Jackson eventually makes his way to his brother's hideout. The pair arm themselves with an antique revolver and a piece of lead pipe before repairing to Clay's funeral parlor. There Jackson dresses in his chauffeur's uniform and steals Clay's hearse.

They drive back to the tenement where Goldy left Imabelle and Slim. Primed for danger they go up to the apartment where, to Jackson's relief, they find only Imabelle. She warns them that Slim will return very shortly and urges the pair to get her trunk downstairs as quickly as possible. She promises to wait for them, but once downstairs, Imabelle runs away as fast as she can.

By the time the two brothers have wrestled the heavy trunk down the stairs, Imabelle has vanished. Jackson goes back upstairs to look for her. Goldy comes close to shooting his brother for his stupidity but decides to wait inside the hearse for him.

When Jackson gets back upstairs he is so overcome with exhaustion and despair, he falls asleep. Meanwhile, Hank and Jodie drive up in a truck that they have stolen. As they drive abreast of the hearse, they see the trunk of gold ore inside and stop to get it.

As Hank opens the rear door to the hearse, Goldy covers him with his revolver. Unfortunately Jodie grabs him from behind and overpowers him. They now realize that Goldy is a stool pigeon. Goldy begs for his life until Jodie slaps him so hard that the slap dislodges Goldy's headdress, revealing him as a man. This discovery so enrages Jodie that he cuts Goldy's throat as an elevated train rushes by.

The noise of the train awakens Jackson, who decides to go back downstairs. He almost runs right into the two killers but manages to hide in a stairwell closet just in time, unaware that they are placing Goldy's corpse in the back of the hearse. After he hears them go upstairs, Jackson wastes no time in leaving the neighborhood.

Meanwhile, Imabelle has been racing to the railroad station in order to get out of town on the first train. A middle-aged garbage worker, inflamed by her looks, attempts to proposition her. Not bothering to stop, Imabelle slashes the huge man with a knife. He in turn chases her into the station and creates a huge commotion. Eventually a pair of detectives takes her into custody and removes her to the Harlem precinct station for questioning.

At the same moment, Jackson is pulling up in the lot of the same train station where Imabelle has been. As he attempts to remove the trunk from the hearse so he can hide it in the baggage room, he discovers the corpse of his brother lying in the back of the vehicle. This draws the attention of nearby police, and soon he is off again on a wild chase through Harlem. Finally he goes to the home of his preacher and tells him the whole story. The preacher advises Jackson that he must turn himself into the police.

The scene shifts back to the Harlem precinct station where Digger has arrived and recognized Imabelle. She does not recognize him and attempts to enlist his interest by putting on a preening sexual display. Digger slaps Imabelle right out of her chair. With the permission of the night watch commander, he drags the woman out in handcuffs, telling her she will either cooperate or he will pistol-whip her until no man will look at her again. Imabelle reluctantly agrees to help.

Just before daylight, Imabelle guides Grave Digger to a whorehouse run by Billie, an hermaphrodite in her middle forties. Only Hank and Jodie are there, being entertained by two teenaged whores. Billie tries to keep Digger from making trouble in her house, offering him everything from other wanted criminals to $5,000.00 cash. Digger wants only revenge, however.

In the other room, both Jodie and Hank are intoxicated from smoking opium and are playing the Victrola. When Imabelle enters the room Digger steps into the room behind her and demands that they give themselves up. Jodie attempts to back out while using his whore as a shield. Billie nearly decapitates him with an axe. Hank tries to outshoot Digger and is shot through both eyes.

As Imabelle cowers on the floor in terror, Digger demands to know where Slim is. She confesses to him that Slim has been in the ore trunk, dead, all of the time.

As the scene changes, the few remaining characters are sitting on the twenty-second floor of the county office building. Presiding over the meeting is an assistant district attorney named Lawrence. He has just finished reading Digger's report which concludes with the discovery of Slim's body in the ore trunk. The ore, as it turns out, was nothing but fool's gold.

The bodies of the gangsters and Goldy have been removed to the morgue. Coffin Ed is in the hospital recovering, and his eyesight has been saved. Unfortunately he will never look quite the same again.

Lawrence is incredulous after hearing the story. Jackson continues to swear to Imabelle's innocence when all available evidence and common sense points to the contrary. To add to the unreality of the story, all of the charges against Jackson have turned out to be misdemeanors, and H. Exodus Clay refuses to press any charges.

Finally, Imabelle is brought in. She explains that Slim was, in reality, her common-law husband whom she has not seen in a year. She claims to have met him by accident at Billie's where she often went to "visit." Slim and the others coerced her into attempting to bilk Jackson. She complied because she was afraid of them. She had stolen the trunk of fool's gold from them the year before when she found out that Slim was cheating on her. She did not go to the police, she says, because the gang has committed no crimes in New York prior to bilking Jackson, and she was unaware of the Mississippi murder charge.

She further explains that after the fight at the warehouse hideout, the three remaining crooks had a falling out when it was decided that the acid-burned Slim was too conspicuous to travel with them. When he refused to remain behind, Jodie killed him.

Deciding that they could get more fool's gold in California, Hank and Jodie then took enough ore out of the trunk to make room for Slim and placed him inside. Their intention was to throw the trunk into the river but when Jackson drove off with it, their plans were spoiled.

When Lawrence asks Imabelle how she got involved in the altercation at the railroad station, Imabelle begins to tell what the reader can see are outrageous lies. She claims that when she left Goldy and Jackson at the apartment house, she was actually on her way to the police. She also claims that she had nothing to do with the brothers' removal of the trunk from the Park Avenue tenement. She insists that they were so bent on doing it that she was afraid that arguing with them would only result in all of them being caught by Hank and Jodie.

Digger and the district attorney know she is lying, but they have no charges on her without Jackson's help, and he believes in her implicitly. The district attorney decides to hold her, but only because he is afraid of what Digger might do to her once she is back on the street.

The scene shifts to Clay's office. Jackson enters and finds Clay in a forgiving mood. We discover the reason for his heartiness is that he will make a nice profit from burying the four gangsters. Clay even offers to bury Goldy for free and agrees to have his lawyer bail Imabelle out of jail.

As the book closes, Jackson and Imabelle are reunited and Imabelle, probably relieved to have someone as reliable (if gullible) as Jackson taking care of her, happily enfolds him in her arms.

In the truest sense of the word, *For Love Of Imabelle* is not a detective story. The plot is much more concerned with character development and dialogue than mystery, and, although there are mysterious elements to the story, there are no startling secrets revealed at the conclusion.

The book has much less in common with the work of Hammett, Chandler, or Ross Macdonald than it does with the hard-boiled crime stories of a writer like W.R. Burnett. Burnett and other writers such as James M. Cain wrote fiction that viewed life strictly from the criminal's point of view and in consequence their work tended to be grimmer and much more violent that the private eye tale.

Certainly the detectives, Grave Digger and Coffin Ed, make a colorful appearance, but their place in the story is very much subordinate to that of Jackson and Imabelle. According to Himes, they were created almost as an afterthought, and it is clear that the story could have been resolved without their intervention.

Himes' lack of expertise in writing detective stories was more than made up by his consummate skill as a creator of characters, a describer of rich background, and as a master of low-life dialogue. Himes cleverly concealed the fact that he didn't know how to create a mystery by eschewing the first-person objective realism that is so much a part of the Hammett/Chandler style. In *Imabelle,* Himes allows the reader to selectively see the actions of everyone in the story. The selectivity, however, is the key. The reader seems to be seeing everything, yet confusion is all that emerges from the rapid flow of action.

Instead of having a detective uncover clues that gradually unravel the mystery for the reader, Himes gently peels back layers until key pieces of information come to light. For example, when the story begins, we believe that Jackson is only worried about the disappearance of Imabelle. Only somewhat later do we discover that he is also worried about the disappearance of Imabelle's trunk. Still later, we discover that the worry over the trunk is because of the gold ore that it contains.

It is interesting that, although Himes rejected the use of the lone-wolf private eye and the first person narrative style, he did (intentionally or accidentally) make use of the chivalric code that made Chandler's work so unique. Chandler likened his detective heroes to the romantic knight errant who lived by a strict code of behavior. Among his traits was a disdain for material gain, a penchant for placing himself in danger in order to protect the innocent, and a deep reverence for women.

In *Imabelle*, the buffoonish Jackson takes up the knight's lance, rather than the detectives. Although he is a foolish and gullible character, Jackson is the only honest and noble person in the story. Like the medieval knight, Jackson has a deep reverence for and belief in the power of God. On several occasions he prays to God for strength, and twice he visits a minister for spiritual guidance.

Although he is often afraid, his major concern, throughout the story, is for the safety and welfare of Imabelle, his damsel in distress. After Jackson is taken into custody by the phoney marshal, Jackson places his own honor and safety in jeopardy by stealing money from H. Exodus Clay. Even then, his major impetus is to save Imabelle. When he sees her, apparently in the custody of the phoney marshal, his first thought is that the marshal has violated his own bond of trust and taken Imabelle to jail.

Imabelle's considerable sexual allure has a great deal to do with Jackson's courage and strength. When his strength and courage are at their lowest ebb, a look from her charges him with indomitability and strengthens his flagging resolve:

"Where's Slim? I'm going to bash that bastard's brains to a raspberry pulp, may the Lord forgive me," he said.

It is important to note that, in spite of his apparent stupidity and his comic-opera Negro fright, Jackson is a virile male with the strength and courage to defend himself. When the criminals, Imabelle, Jackson, and the detectives converge on the warehouse hideout, Jodie attacks Jackson, and the two trade punches with Jackson giving no ground. Earlier in the story, when he discovers that his brother, Goldy, has played him false and fed him a mickey finn, Jackson attacks him and nearly beats him up.

Ignoring the elements of the story that play up the ridiculous aspects of his character, one can see that many of Jackson's personality traits are not as silly as they may seem. Jackson only looks stupid in relation to the trickery and deceit that surround him. In reality, he is only naive and unpracticed where lying, robbery, and murder are concerned. As an honest, hard-working man, he gets along fine in his normal world. When he finds himself thrown, much like an Alfred Hitchcock hero, into a world he doesn't understand, he is naturally confused and frightened much of the time.

Even the traditional hard-boiled hero was not immune to fright in the face of physical danger. Philip Marlowe, the Continental Op, and other, more contemporary tough-guys often are eloquent in the descriptions of their fright when confronted with death.

Other characters in the story also fall in with the concept of the medieval epic. Goldy, for example, resembles the wizard who is capable of helping the hero, but most often is as evil as the hero's enemies. Goldy uses what may be described as magical talents to disguise himself as a woman and he uses strange incantations to confuse all around him. With his skills he is able to safely travel the underworld and part the darkness in his quest to discover the identities and whereabouts of the criminals.

An irony of Goldy's career is that once he abandons his wizardry and picks up the tools of the man of arms (i.e., his antique Colt revolver), he loses his powers over the forces of darkness. In his confrontation with Hank and Jodie he is easily overpowered. When his gun flies across the street to disappear into a pile of slush, it presages his own ghastly end. His murder by Jodie isn't simply a gangland throat-cutting, it is an exorcism. As in an ancient myth, his head is almost severed from his body and his life force gushes in a great gout onto the dark and hellish street. His scream of rage and fear merges with the shriek of the steam engine overhead to create an unearthly cry which symbolizes not only his own hopelessness and pain but that of all the Black people who live in the dark forest that is Harlem.

Imabelle makes a strange damsel in distress because she lacks the major element that such a heroine must have: purity of the soul. She lies and double-deals and attempts to use every man in the story. It is the strength of Jackson's belief in and love for her that makes up for her weakness. She may, in reality, be a deceitful and dishonorable tramp, but Jackson's reverence for her lifts her above all that. While everyone else in the story is chasing the "grail," represented by the trunk of gold ore, Imabelle is Jackson's grail. In the true style of the naturalistic hero, Jackson is interested only in the intangibles of life and Imabelle symbolizes for him all that is worthwhile and worth having. He comes close to sacrificing everything for her. In a way, it is a heaven-sent reward that he never realizes how badly she has betrayed his trust and love.

Hank, Jodie, Slim, and Gus Parsons all have no trouble symbolizing the dark knights of legend. They are always in shadow. Like many of the evil villains of mythology, they change their identities several times in an effort to confuse the hero or to thwart good. They pretend to be businessmen, gold miners, federal assayers, and U.S. Marshals in order to perpetrate disorder.

Jodie is particularly evil, and the relentlessness with which he plays with and uses his knife symbolizes the barely repressed violence that bubbles under his honest, "working stiff" appearance. The gruesome murders of Goldy and Slim attest to the fact that he is the darkest force of all. Jodie is also somewhat prototypical for Himes because, throughout the Harlem series, the most fearful killers are always drug-crazed switchblade knife users.

A number of other things are also particularly evident in this first story that would show up over and over in the Harlem Domestic series. The most important factor is the utter futility of life. The grail that all of the characters seek throughout the story, the trunk of gold ore, turns out to be completely worthless. It is particularly appropriate that it should be "fool's gold." The irony of so much death and misery resulting from an entirely futile search is in its own way symbolic of the futility of the Black man's search for equality and a better life.

The futility is evident in many other ways, too. The hapless Jackson seems to fall from the frying pan into the fire over and over again. Each time he embarks on a new plan to rescue himself and Imabelle, he finds himself in worse trouble.

Imabelle, though much more cunning than Jackson, is no better off than he is. Even though she lies, connives, and commits assault in order to escape her troubles, she, too, is continually tripped up by circumstances. One of Imabelle's worst problems is that she is too cunning and not trusting enough. Doubtless her experience with men has taught her to place little faith in them.

Instead, she relies on her sex to get her what she wants. Ironically, her sexiness is so cheap and sluttish that it has little effect on anyone but Jackson. At various times she tries her sex appeal out on the killers, the cops at the railroad station, and on the vengeful Grave Digger. At no time does it really help her.

The one time that she wants least to be alluring is when she is accosted by the garbage worker outside the railroad station. Possibly for the only time in her round-heeled life, she genuinely does not want a man's help or attention. She responds to his overtures with a knife instead of a calculating smile. In so doing, she brings about her own downfall.

It is interesting that, with all the talk about sex in this story, there are no scenes of lovemaking in the entire book. Imabelle uses her sex as a defense and as a weapon, but there is little suggestion that it is ever used for pleasure. There is some possibility that, for all her allure, Imabelle may be sexually unattainable. Her true, chaste, love seems to be reserved for the fat, eunuch-like Jackson, who regards her as a love object, rather than a sexual one.

Himes wrote in his autobiography that he was very prudish about sex, and we get some indication of that in the Harlem series. In all eight novels there are only two scenes in which characters engage in sex, and those are so understated that one could almost miss them.

A sexual theme that Himes used in this story and was to use over again in the series is that of sexual ambiguity. As was mentioned before, Goldy makes his way about Harlem disguised as a nun. Everyone, including Digger and Ed, believes Goldy to be a female. His fat, sexless body shrouded in the nun's habit and even his name suggest a femininity of a sort, even though we are told that he has a wife with whom he spends weekends.

A greatly similar example is displayed in the case of Billie, the mistress of the whorehouse where Hank and Jodie hole up. She is hermaphroditic and is at least half male and half female. This is emphasized by her voluptuous bosom and the dark hair growing on her face. She is involved in a frankly feminine business, and yet, when called upon, she attacks Jodie like a man and vanquishes him.

A character who deserves special mention in any discussion of *For Love of Imabelle* is H. Exodus Clay, the premier mortician of Harlem. Clay is introduced primarily as a comic character, with his name symbolizing both the eventual exodus from the earth by all men and the clay to which they will be interred and with which they will become one.

On a somewhat more serious note, Clay is also a prototypical character. Described as an overdressed old man with parchment-like skin, Clay is the first of what we may think of as light-skinned exploiters. Imabelle, herself, belongs to this group, but Clay is actually worse. He literally makes his living from death, and it is clear from his dress and his other circumstances that he is doing very well at his trade. At the same time, he is a tyrannical boss who does not pay his help particularly well, nor feel any affection for them.

One may be confused by Clay's generosity at the end of the story. He drops all charges against Jackson, helps him bury his brother, and reunites him with Imabelle. Clay's kindness has little to do with his fondness for Jackson and much more to do with the happiness he feels for all the business that Jackson has inadvertently brought him. He not only collects from the city for burying all the gangsters, but he gets to keep the money found on their persons. He keeps Jackson on because he knows that he can milk Jackson's guilt and childish gratitude for his job and keep him on at substandard wages for years thereafter.

Himes must have felt some affection for Clay, for he continued to bring him into subsequent stories. In almost every case, the tight-fisted old undertaker reaps the rewards of his proximity to Grave Digger and Coffin Ed. Other such light-skinned exploiters and manipulators would not be so humorously depicted.

Grave Digger and Coffin Ed are a genuine peculiarity in this first story because Himes pays so little attention to them. When we first catch sight of them outside of the Savoy, we are told that they are "the famous Harlem detective team." This causes us to take a close look at them and we wait, somewhat in vain, to discover just why they are famous. It would seem that in Harlem, their fame is based chiefly on their violent response to the least provocation.

Unlike most other hard-boiled heroes, they do not seem motivated to perform good works. In fact, they are initially depicted as strictly inward-directed cops. We are told that they take bribes and protection money from pimps, whores, and gamblers but that they react with horrible violence when they catch up with a street criminal of any kind. Their violence seems to be their most important characteristic. Our attention is continually drawn to the obsolete long-barreled revolvers that they carry and the legendary speed with which they will bring them into play. Himes tells us that:

Colored folks didn't respect colored cops. But they respected big shiny pistols and sudden death. It was said in Harlem that Coffin Ed's pistol would kill a rock and that Grave Digger's would bury it.

Himes makes it clear that these men are outsiders and that, in order to make themselves felt in their dark world, they have had to be twice as violent and deadly as anyone around them. They have, to some extent, lost touch with reality because violence is their sole means of expressing themselves. This is particularly well-illustrated when they stop an incipient riot in the precinct station by firing a fusillade into the ceiling. That the ceiling is already filled with holes from similar incidents attests to the fact that their means of communication with the rest of the world has degenerated. They no longer bother to attempt to keep the peace with words—a brutal response to any deviation has become their trademark.

In some ways, they remind us of parents who do not have the patience to deal with their children on an intelligent basis. Such parents generally reward any kind of misbehavior with a slap rather than a remonstrance. Himes may have been likening his characters to unruly children and the detectives to stern, unforgiving parents.

They seem to feel very little compassion for their fellow Blacks, particularly in this first story. They are men alone and feel no kinship with anyone else in Harlem. They know all along that Jackson is a helpless square who has been pushed into a corner, but all they are really interested in is taking the criminals. If Jackson is with them, he will suffer the consequences.

Even in this first outing, however, they are not without redeeming features. When Coffin Ed is temporarily blinded by acid in the warehouse fight, his first thought is for his partner. Almost driven crazy by the pain and the personal fear he feels, he cries out over and over for his partner. This comradeship for a brother-in-arms is another throwback to the chivalric imagery in the story.

It is noteworthy that very few other hard-boiled writers have ever written about two detectives. By creating two detective heroes instead of one, Himes broke away from the tradition of the lone-wolf hero but may have been attempting to express two sides of the same personality in two distinctly different characters.

Later, when Ed is in the hospital and Grave Digger has recovered from his clout on the head, he becomes a man with a mission. The other crimes Hank and Jodie and Slim have committed mean nothing to him now. He embarks on a trail of vengeance and, in typical hard-boiled style, he breaks every rule in the book in his quest to track the killers down. It is clear in his final confrontation with Hank and Jodie that he has no intention of bringing them in alive. He forces Hank to draw against him, then deliberately shoots out both of his eyes.

Possibly Himes' greatest accomplishment in this first story is his startling use of Harlem as an imaginative and realistic backdrop to his story. Himes calls attention to the glorious past of his city with references to musicians and writers and the glittery night spots like the Savoy, but he contrasts that world starkly with the seething nastiness that may lie a block away from the glamor.

His ability to create poetry out of his descriptions of the horrible conditions in Harlem was to become a trademark of his work and is something to look for in each succeeding novel. It is in these odes to Black ghetto life that the protest in his writing stands out so clearly:

> Looking eastward from the towers of Riverside Church, perched among the university buildings on the high banks of the Hudson River, in a valley far below, waves of gray rooftops distort the perspective like the surface of a sea. Below the surface, in the murky waters of fetid tenements, a city of black people who are convulsed in desperate living, like the voracious churning of millions of hungry cannibal fish. Blind mouths eating their own guts. Stick in a hand and draw back a nub...East of Seventh Avenue to the Harlem River is called the Valley. Tenements thick with teeming life spread with with dismal squalor. Rats and cockroaches compete with the mangy dogs and cats for the man-gnawed bones.

In these vivid poems, Himes conjured up in his readers a real feeling for the hopelessness of the urban Black. The valley of despair is presided over by Riverside Church and Columbia University, twin bastions of white domination over religion and education. Far below, completely cut off from the healing solace of education, religion, and respectability, live Imabelle, Hank, Jodie, Slim, Gus, and all the other gangsters. These characters are those hungry cannibal fish that Himes is talking about. In their desperation to steal a better life for themselves, they literally lead themselves into a destruction that is self-made, yet is also abetted by the ambivalence of the white community.

As if to emphasize the darkness that lies in the crumbling tenements and in the minds of the muggers and prostitutes that ply their trades there, much of the action in Himes' Harlem takes place at night. The tension that is so much a part of Jackson's flight from the warehouse and Imabelle's fearful entrance into the bordello are heightened by Himes' emphasis on the dark mystery of Harlem's unknown corners.

Himes also used American Negro traditions in the production of this story. On several occasions he harks back to what we might think of as nostalgia but what were, to him, reminders of the Negro's lowly place in society. For example, we learn from Goldy that his nickname came from the resemblance that he and Jackson bore to the pickaninny characters on the Gold Dust Twins soap powder box.

Later, when Jackson is running fearfully through the night in his headlong flight from death, he remembers a childish rhyme that goes "Run, nigger, run; the pateroller (patrol or patroller) get you." In this instance, Himes reminds us through Jackson's experience that the Black man's lot has often been as the prey of relentless pursuers. As Jackson is bruised and torn by the urban obstacles in his path, we also remember those Blacks who were battered and torn by undergrowth and tree limbs as they ran from slave catchers over one hundred years earlier.

Himes used very few white characters in this story. In fact, the only substantive white character is the assistant district attorney who appears near the end. What is particularly interesting about Himes's use of white characters is how they accentuate the foreignness of Harlem and the Black race to the average white world. The district attorney can not understand how Jackson can fail to see Imabelle's complicity in the con game. Furthermore, when H. Exodus Clay refuses to press charges against Jackson and even goes out of his way to help the young man, the d.a. is convinced that Jackson has something on the old mortician.

It is a foreignness that Harlemites understand, however. Midway through Jackson's flight from the warehouse, he comes upon a drunken old Negro rag picker. The old man is suspicious of Jackson, but when police arrive and begin questioning Jackson, the old man bands together with him and pretends to be his father. This unquestioning allegiance to each other in the face of a threat by white police is a hallmark of Himes' Harlem, and it is something that readers will see in the series again.

One of Himes' major dictums was that Harlem and, indeed, the entire Black world, was turned upside down from that of the whites. White rules of conduct, logic, and morals did not apply here. The white characters not only do not understand this, they never learn otherwise. As a rule this is somewhat to the benefit of the Black characters who not only do understand it, but consistently use it against white intruders into their world.

With this first novel, Himes rejuvenated his already strong reputation with the French reading public. His colorful prose and his gift for protest glibly cloaked in dark humor and violent action brought his career back to life. Strangely enough, the American public, which had almost universally condemned his early work, expressed some guarded enthusiasm for this strange new turn in his career. It would be over ten years and his last novel before some critics would begin to sing his praises. Even then, other American critics would still castigate his work and accuse him of reverse racism.

At any rate, Himes was transformed overnight from a desperate and hopeless man into a successful author with a bright future. It was a foregone conclusion that he would write more stories about Harlem and he did not disappoint.

Chapter VI
Cops Have Lives, Too

"I'll kill him!" Sugartit raved in a choked voice. "I'll kill him for that!"

"Kill who?" Sheik asked, scowling at her.

"My father. I hate him. The ugly bastard. I'll steal his pistol and shoot him...I hate him the dirty cop!"

With his new career firmly in the groove, Himes left Paris for Scandinavia. As he relates in his autobiography:

> I began writing...on the first day of our arrival to the accompaniment of children's voices playing below in the street. As before, I entered the world which I created. I believed in it. It moved me, troubled me. But I could control it, which I have never been able to do to the world in which I really live...I could think like the teen-aged gangsters, the black multitude of Harlem, the black detectives, who were no more creations of mine than any of the others; in fact my mind was theirs...[1]

Himes' new story revolved around a gang of teenagers for whom breaking the law was a kind of child's game. The fact that his own career as a criminal began when he was a teenager once again leads the investigator to suggest that he was using parts of his own life as the basis for his fiction.

His second entry in the Harlem series (which he originally called *If Trouble Was Money*) was released by Gallimard in 1958 under the title of *Il pleut des coups durs* and is something of a landmark in the series because, for the first time, his detectives take center stage and begin to develop as separate personalities.

The story begins on a warm October night in a bar called the Dew Drop Inn. Rollicking music is blaring from the juke box, and the female patrons are cavorting about the floor in wild, suggestive gyrations. Curiously out of place in this Negro establishment is a big, well-dressed white man who is becoming excited by the dancing. Several of the women are obviously flirting with him.

Suddenly a scrawny old Negro pulls a switchblade knife and attacks the white man. The bartender intervenes and, with a fireman's axe, slices off the old man's arm. He soon faints from blood loss.

By this time, the white man has fled the bar and is looking through the window when a young man named Sonny Pickens happens by with two friends. All three are high on marijuana. Sonny pulls a revolver from his pocket, accuses the white man of fooling around with his wife, and chases him down the street.

At the corner the white man runs past a group of eight boys dressed as Arabs. They, too, are high on marijuana. As the white man leaps to avoid a speeding car, Sonny fires his gun, and the white man falls to the ground. Sonny and his friends crowd around the prostrate man, laughing hysterically.

A radio call about the disturbance brings Coffin Ed Johnson and Grave Digger Jones to the scene. The Arabs recognize the pair and attempt to escape, but the two detectives surround the group. Sonny is quickly disarmed and handcuffed.

Sonny insists that the man isn't dead; only fainted. An examination of his body, however, shows a bullet hole in the white man's forehead.

As sirens herald the arrival of more police, Digger decides to frisk the Arabs. During the frisk, one of the teen Arabs flings liquid at Ed from a small bottle. Remembering the acid throwing incident, Ed reacts instinctively and fires twice. His shots kill the Arab and wound a female bypasser.

Digger grapples with Ed to keep him from going completely out of control, and in the confusion the Arabs, Sonny, and Sonny's friends escape. When the other police arrive they find Digger fighting desperately for control of Ed's gun as Ed raves and weeps uncontrollably. Finally another cop steps in and knocks Ed out.

As Digger brings his partner back to consciousness, he explains to a police sergeant what has happened and provides a description of Sonny. Confident that a handcuffed man can't be too hard to find, the sergeant sends his men out on a search.

Meanwhile, Ed has come to and is chagrined to learn that he has shot two people over a bottle of perfume. Digger chastises his partner and warns him that he has to keep himself under control as Lieutenant Anderson and detectives from the Homicide Squad arrive.

As all the detectives discuss the difficulties of the case, the lieutenant in charge of the Homicide Squad comes up and provides the startling information that Sonny is innocent because his revolver is a harmless blank pistol.

Meanwhile, the remaining members of the Moslem gang, Sheik, Choo-Choo, and Inkey, have taken Sonny away from the police dragnet. In spite of the fact that Sonny continues to protest his innocence, the leader of the gang (Sheik) insists that they are going to hide him anyway. As they pause in a basement to remove their Arab costumes, Choo-Choo notices for the first time that Sheik does not have his zip gun. Asking his leader where it is, Sheik replies offhandedly that he gave it to Bones, a member of the gang who split off during the escape.

At the entrance to a top-floor apartment in the same building, the boys are met by an old colored woman. She asks them where Caleb, her grandson, is. Since Caleb is the one who was shot, they invent a story about him working late in a bowling alley. Before she can become more inquisitive, Sheik takes everyone back to the room he rents from Granny.

After locking their disguises in a trunk, he leads them out onto a fire escape to watch the police below. Sheik realizes that they are conducting a house-to-house search to find Sonny.

For the first time since the escape, Sonny explains that he couldn't have killed the white man because his gun was a harmless toy. Sheik takes on a brutal, dangerous look at this news and tells Sonny that the cops are undoubtedly trying to frame him. He sets the other two boys to work getting Sonny' handcuffs off.

Presently a voice at the door exchanges a secret password with Sheik, and, in response, the door is opened. A teenaged Black girl named Sissie enters, breathless with excitement. She has come in response to the news about the shooting, and it seems clear that she hoped Sheik was one of the victims. Before long, another teenaged girl called Sugartit comes into the room. She is grief-stricken over Caleb's death, and it becomes obvious that she also harbors bad feelings for Sheik. A great deal of arguing and crying goes on until Sheik brutally tells Sugartit that the man who killed Caleb was her father. Sugartit is Coffin Ed's daughter.

Back at the scene of the shootings, the chief of police and numerous other police officials have gathered to face the numerous reporters who have arrived. The chief identifies the dead man as one Ulysses Galen, sales manager for a beverage company. Harlem, it appears, was his sales district.

It quickly becomes apparent that, once the general facts about the killing are made available, everything else the chief tells the reporters is a half-truth or an outright lie. The chief falsely identifies Sonny Pickens as the killer and reports that he was snatched from the police by a juvenile gang called the Real Cool Moslems. The chief also reports that one of the gang was shot trying to throw acid in the face of a detective.

After the doubtful reporters are dismissed, some of the police officers begin to wonder if the Moslems weren't involved in Galen's death and if Sonny is connected to them. Digger is skeptical and believes that anyone could have put the bullet in the white man. He goes off to investigate that angle while the chief suspends Coffin Ed pending an investigation. Ironically, Ed laments the fact that he couldn't have been sent home earlier so he could have taken his daughter to a movie.

The other two boys finally succeed in cutting the chain between Sonny's handcuffs. In spite of the summer heat, they dress him in a baggy sweater and a pair of driving gloves in order to cover the cuffs. Anticipating the arrival of the police, Sheik sends Sonny and Inky up to the roof where the deceased Caleb kept a pigeon coop. Sonny is to pretend to be Caleb and tell the police that he is teaching pigeons to fly at night. Sheik figures that since the cops think all Negroes are crazy, they will swallow this story if the two boys act simple-minded enough. After they are gone, Sheik reveals that he actually intends to kill Sonny and dispose of his body.

Back at the Dew Drop Inn Digger begins to question the bartender, Big Smiley, about how the fracas began. Smiley talks freely, off-handedly suggesting that Galen was really too important to kill. Digger picks up on this instantly and forces Smiley to explain his remark. Smiley explains that Galen had been seen recently with a pimp named Ready Belcher.

Smiley sends Digger to Bucky's, a high-class Black joint in Washington Heights. Digger arrives to find a sedate restaurant populated with racially mixed couples, homosexuals, and high-class Black prostitutes. Bucky, a chubby, well-dressed Negro pianist, manages to evade Digger's questions even when Digger bullies him. The detective gets no substantive information from the man, but he gets an indication from one of the prostitutes at the bar that she has some information, and he leaves with her.

Swearing him to secrecy, she tells him to see a madam named Reba. It is obvious that the prostitute knows things about Galen, but she refuses to tell what she knows. Reba, a voluptuous six-foot Negress with a shock of snow-white hair, greets Digger with an easy familiarity. When pressed, she admits that Galen used to come there, but she finally barred him from the premises. She won't tell why, but indicates Ready will tell him. When she brings Ready out he tries to act tough with Digger, but the detective beats him half senseless and drags him out.

Back at the crime scene, the police finally arrive at Granny's apartment. Granny knows nothing about the shooting or the reason for the search and sends them into the room where the teenagers are waiting. The sergeant gets nothing from Sheik and eventually decides to visit the roof to talk to "Caleb." The sergeant and his men find Inkey and Sonny on the roof. In spite of the sergeant's efforts to trip them up, Sonny's pretense of stupidity finally allays the old cop's suspicions. The police carelessly search the two boys and finding nothing, take them downstairs to the apartment.

As the police officers discuss what to do with the five young people, they are thunderstruck by Sugartit's announcement that she is Coffin Ed's daughter, Evelyn. She produces a special police identification card to prove it.

The sergeant is so shocked at this turn of events that when Sheik makes the mistake of joking about his engagement to Evelyn, the old cop loses control of himself and beats the boy unconscious. Before leaving to continue his search, the sergeant makes arrangements for the two girls to be allowed through the police dragnet. As he leaves the apartment, he apologizes to Granny for the commotion. In return, he gets only a fiercely disapproving glance from the silent old woman.

After the police leave, the five young people feel pretty proud of themselves for putting a fast one over on the police. Sheik regains his confidence quickly and offers marijuana around to everyone. When the drug starts to take effect, Sheik begins to encourage Evelyn to take off her clothes to have a little fun. When she starts to comply, Sissie intervenes and tells her to go home.

Sheik reacts violently to this interference and throws Sissie onto the bed. When Sonny adds his opinion that messing with Coffin Ed's daughter is dangerous and foolish, Sheik chokes Sonny senseless and ties him up inside a canvas sack.

Meanwhile, Grave Digger has dragged Ready Belcher out to his car and forced him to talk.

Ready supplies the information that the Greek was a sadist who delighted in beating women with a leather whip. His style was to pick up school girls in his car and drive them to Reba's. This went on until Reba got suspicious about the noise and caught him in the act. Reba threatened to shoot him and barred him from her premises.

Ready explains that the reason Galen had so much success in getting women to go with him was his willingness to pay $100.00 for a session. Few would return for a second session, however, and at least one girl was hospitalized as a result of the beatings.

Ready had been helping Galen to find girls. They had recently been in the Dew Drop Inn together looking for a particular girl. The girl was the friend of another girl named Sissie, whom the Greek had already had. At Digger's insistence, Ready identifies the second girl only as Sugartit. The Greek had seen them together in Harlem after he had whipped Sissie. All Ready claims to know about the two girls is that they belong to a teen gang called the Real Cool Moslems. Instantly, Digger sees the connection between the dead man and the gang of teenagers.

Digger demands to know the name of Sugartit's father, thinking that it might be the old man killed in the bar fight. Ready swears that he doesn't know, but Digger doesn't believe it.

Digger takes Ready down to Harlem Hospital to find out what he can about the old man. When he speaks to the doctor on the case, the surgeon explains that the old man died without regaining consciousness. Digger examines the dead man's clothing and discovers a scrap of paper with a message. The note says:

GB, you want to know something. The Big John hangs out in the Inn. How about that. Just like those old Romans. Bee.

This means nothing to Digger or to Ready, so they leave.

Ready has told Digger that the Greek drove an expensive green Cadillac when he was on the prowl. When Digger finds it, he notices that the car has a prestige license plate number, suggesting that someone important in Harlem must be covering for the Greek's activities.

After breaking into the car, Digger finds a miniature bull whip and a manila envelope full of pornographic photographs of nude, teenaged girls. Ready claims not to recognize any of the girls depicted in them, though Digger remains skeptical.

Digger returns to the Dew Drop Inn carrying the bull whip in his hand. In the last booth in the joint are seated a group of three teenaged boys and four girls. At the sight of the whip, all four girls give a start and look frightened.

Digger advances on Big Smiley, the bartender and informs the man that he knows Smiley has been holding out on him. The man finally admits that Sissie and Sugartit come into the Dew Drop sometimes. At this admission Ready begins to wilt, confirming Digger's earlier guess that he, too, has been lying.

When Smiley admits that Galen had met Sissie there with Sheik, the four teenaged girls attempt to escape the bar. Digger heads them off and makes them sit back down. Putting more pressure on Big Smiley, he forces the man to admit that Galen took Sissie and many other girls into the basement of the bar for whippings. When Digger shows him the nude photos, Smiley admits that he knows two of them: a pair of girls known around the bar as Good Booty and Honey Bee. Smiley admits further that the whippings have been going on in the basement for about two months and that Galen has paid him $25.00 each time.

Digger produces the note he took from the old man's clothing and, with Smiley's reluctant help, realizes that the old man must have been a relative of GB, probably Good Booty. The frightened bartender swears he doesn't know who is covering for Galen in Harlem. He also claims not to know who Sugartit's father is. He does know, however, that one of the Read Cool Moslems lives in an apartment down the street where he raises pigeons.

The climax to the interrogation comes when Digger asks Smiley if Galen has had any of the girls sitting in the bar. Smiley identifies one girl in the group as Good Booty.

In quick succession Digger closes the bar and has both Smiley and his white manager arrested for contributing to the delinquency of minors. Moving to the table full of teenagers, the detective dismisses all of them to the waiting patrol wagon except for a haughty girl who has identified herself as Gertrude B. Richardson. Digger begins to question her about her father, then quickly switches to the subject of the bar fight and the subsequent death of the old Negro. Gertrude realizes that the dead man was her father and nearly shoots herself in her grief before she is wrestled to the floor and disarmed.

On the rooftop of the apartment building, several policemen are talking about finding Sonny. The talk turns to the handcuffs Sonny was wearing and one officer opines that by now Sonny must surely have cut the chain of the cuffs. Another mentions that gloves would have hidden the separated manacles. The officers quickly realize where they have seen a Black youth wearing gloves and quickly descend the fire escape.

Inside the apartment, Sheik is on the verge of attempting to leave in order to throw Sonny into the river when the cops enter the room. When the half-conscious Sonny sneezes, the cops open the sack and find their man.

Down on the street several officers are questioning a boy named Bones about a zip gun with which he was found. The questioning is interrupted by the arrival of Digger, Ready, Big Smiley, and Gertrude. Digger recognizes Bones as one of the Moslems and has him arrested.

At the chief's insistence, Digger explains all about Galen's sadism and the activities of Ready, Big Smiley, and Good Booty. He concludes that, while he doesn't know who Sugartit is, he has discovered that the Moslems hang out in a nearby apartment where there is a pigeon loft. This news excites the police sergeant, who reports that he has been in that very apartment.

Digger, realizing that the two girls in the apartment must be Sissie and Sugartit, makes Big Smiley describe Sheik for the sergeant, who quickly recognizes his man. As the chief begins to upbraid the sergeant for not bringing the kids in, the hapless officer attempts to defend himself by explaining that since Coffin Ed's daughter, Evelyn, was there, he thought they were all right.

Digger, realizing that Ready knew Evelyn was Sugartit, beats Ready unconscious in a rage. He is being restrained when Coffin Ed comes up, explaining that he has been out looking for Evelyn. As Digger and the chief try to get him to go home and save him from the embarrassment of his daughter's misbehavior, gunshots erupt from the apartment building.

As searchlights are focused on the front of the building, the officers see Choo-Choo stagger to the fire escape landing and plunge over the rail. Immediately after, a cop emerges from the same window. He reports that after they found Pickens, one of the Moslems grabbed an officer's gun, and a fight erupted in which a policeman and a teenager were killed. The Moslem escapes into the rear of the apartment, threatening to kill Evelyn unless he can talk to Grave Digger and the chief.

Against the chief's orders, Coffin Ed works his way to the back of the building while Digger and the chief go to the apartment door. The chief offers every promise to Sheik, who refuses to believe the assurances. He tells them that he knows that they have had him tagged as Ulysses Galen's killer ever since they realized that Sonny didn't do it. He admits that when he saw the Greek running down the street, he shot him with his zip gun just for fun.

Sheik demands that the street be cleared of cops, that an ambulance be driven up to the door of the building, and that Grave Digger come through the door and lay his pistol on the table. Digger agrees, even though the chief promises to suspend him for it.

After all the other cops retreat down the stairs, Digger enters the room with Sheik and Evelyn where Granny still sits quietly in her rocker. Following Sheik's instructions, Digger places his gun on the table and stands to one side.

Holding a knife to Evelyn's throat, Sheik reaches for the revolver, not knowing that behind him, Coffin Ed is hanging head downward from the roof waiting for his chance. When Sheik releases Evelyn, Ed dispatches him with a single shot.

The chief, his bad humor all gone now that the crisis is over, raises Digger's suspension and sends everyone else home. Ed quietly takes his wayward daughter away with him.

Granny, who everyone thought was asleep, is found to be dead in her chair, still wearing her look of disapproval.

By the next morning Inkey and Bones have spilled everything they know. The police discover that all of their stories tally with Sheik's final confession. The case seems to be closed, although Sonny Pickens is still being held for disturbing the peace.

Just when it seems that everything is wrapped up, the homicide lieutenant in charge of the case reports that ballistics studies prove that Sheik couldn't have been Galen's killer. The zip gun was a .22, and Galen was killed with a .32 revolver. This creates a lot of consternation at headquarters, but Digger insists that justice has been done. The commissioner agrees and orders Digger to throw the death bullet away.

The scene changes to an apartment in the San Juan Hill district of Harlem. Digger rings the bell of an apartment and asks to see Sissie. Once inside, Digger questions Sissie gently until she admits that she stole her uncle's .32 revolver. She stole it, she says, because Galen was after Evelyn, and Sissie was afraid for the other girl after what had happened to her.

She explains that she made a date to see Galen at the Dew Drop. Her plan was to get Galen to drive her around in the car, during which time she would shoot him and run away. When she got to Lenox Avenue and saw Sonny Pickens chasing Galen down the street, she took advantage of the confusion and shot Galen. She escaped unseen and threw the gun down a storm drain.

The final scene takes place in the Centre Street jail where Sissie has gone to visit Sonny. Sonny asks her what she plans to do now that Sheik is dead. She admits to Sonny that she has done a lot to be ashamed of. She is pregnant with Sheik's child. At this news, Sonny tells her that he will make immediate arrangements for them to be married.

This novel is the first in the series that can really be called a true "detective story." It is the first one in which the story is as much about the detectives as it is about the criminals. It is particularly of interest to students of the series because, for the first time, Himes goes to some lengths to show how the two detectives differ in their behavior and outlook. Even more importantly, Himes shows graphically how the violence and corruption inherent in their jobs have emotionally affected his two heroes.

It is very clear that the acid throwing in *For Love of Imabelle* has had an irrevocable effect on Coffin Ed. He has been so badly scarred emotionally from the experience that it is amazing that he has been allowed to remain on active street duty. His temper begins to fray when a teenaged Moslem farts at him, and he becomes a wild man when the bottle of liquid is thrown at him. Formerly a cool hand with his revolver, he sprays shots all over the street, wounding an innocent bystander in the process. Even worse, he so loses touch with reality that he has to be knocked unconscious by a fellow officer to prevent him from perpetrating even more mindless violence.

The fact that this same man has a teenaged daughter comes as a something of a surprise to the reader. Heretofore, the private lives of the two detectives have been kept firmly in the background of the stories. It is interesting that, far in advance of a time when the family and marital problems of cops were common knowledge, Himes produced this convincing scenario in which a working detective's relationship with his family could be damaged by the consequences of his work.

When we first realize that Evelyn is Ed's daughter, we are stunned to realize that she hates him and wishes him dead. Although Himes has never allowed us a glimpse of the detectives at home, we can only imagine that a sensitive teenaged girl with a father who is gone all the time might feel ignored by him. At the same time, the horrible wounding he experienced in his earlier adventures would certainly have affected his family members and their feelings for and about him.

Ed seems to realize this when, after being sent home by the chief, he expresses the wish that he could have been sent home earlier in order to spend some time with his daughter. As emotionally battered and withdrawn as he has become, even he realizes that they are growing apart.

Ed's later actions are of interest, too. At the point that Digger and the others discover that Evelyn is being held hostage, Ed reappears on the scene, explaining that he has been looking all over Harlem for his child. When he realizes the situation, he acts instantly on her behalf, placing himself in grave jeopardy. Risking further suspension for interfering in the crisis against the chief's order, he risks death by having himself suspended head down from the top of the building. For twenty minutes he hangs from wire wrapped around his legs waiting for the chance to make the shot that will save his child.

In one respect Himes fails us in this slice of life story. When Evelyn is freed from Sheik's clutches, her father takes her quietly home where she is treated for shock. We do not, however, get any insights into whether or not Ed and his daughter resolve the differences that drove her to join a teen gang, smoke marijuana, and at least consider the possibility of illicit sex with Sheik.

For the first time in the series, Grave Digger emerges both as the brains of the detective team and also as the more sensitive hero. By the end of the story, we sense that Digger really bleeds for the Negro race. As opposed to Coffin Ed, who has been physically hurt to the point that he is no longer rational, Digger proves to be the partner who has become more emotionally hurt by the violence, hatred, and corruption he sees every day.

The differences in these two men become apparent almost from the beginning of the story. When Ed momentarily goes berserk and begins shooting people, Digger risks his own life to bring his frightened partner under control. When another officer has to intervene and club Coffin Ed unconscious, we realize just what a frightful risk Digger has taken in interfering with his fear-maddened partner.

Digger continually places himself at risk in the course of this story. When Sheik demands that Digger enter the room where Evelyn is being held and give up his gun, Digger risks both his life and the chief's wrath for disobeying orders.

Later, Digger risks a further suspension when the discovery is made that Sheik was not the killer of Ulysses Galen. Standing on his moral outrage at what the white pervert has done to the Harlem community, Digger states that he would rather lose his job than follow the case another step. As far as he is concerned, justice was really served when Galen was shot dead in the street.

Digger also puts on a remarkable display of detective work as he follows the trail. In a very short time, he follows a trail that leads from Big Smiley at the Dew Drop Inn to Bucky's club, Reba's whorehouse, Harlem Hospital, and finally back to the Dew Drop where everything comes to resolution. Only once during his investigation does Digger fall back on actual violence to get information. With everyone but Ready Belcher he is able to uncover key items of information through the skill of his questioning and the force of his considerable personality. One gets the feeling that, but for Sheik's belief that he killed Ulysses Galen, the case could have been resolved without further bloodshed.

Digger's finest moment in the story and in the series comes when he finally interviews Sissie at her uncle's house. It is plain to the reader and to Digger that Sissie, obviously an orphan who was taken in by distant relatives, lives in a loveless household. Her aunt's contempt and hatred for her serves as an explanation as to why Sissie would seek out the comforts of a teen gang to gain the acceptance she has not found at home.

Digger seems to know before she confesses that Sissie is Galen's killer. When he understands that Sissie has risked her life and freedom in order to save her friend Evelyn from Galen's perversions, Digger is overcome. Sissie's willingness to risk everything for her friend is something that Digger, himself, can understand all too well.

The bonds of friendship provide a pivotal meaning to this story and help to lift it from the surrounding squalor. The willingness of a few Black people to risk everything to save a brother or sister alleviates the tawdriness of the prostitutes, pimps, perverts, and others who prey on the innocent.

As is often the case in the Harlem series, white or light-colored skin and hair provide a clue to the morality of the characters. Sheik is a handsome, light-skinned youth who could possibly be an analog of Himes. He is dynamic, well-built, and, as his nickname attests, attractive to the ladies. He is quick to exert his authority over others and has a knack for bouncing back quickly from a setback. When the police sergeant beats him senseless for pretending that he and Evelyn are engaged, he makes an amazing recovery and seems not to have been chastened by the experience.

His viciousness seems a complete contrast to his handsome features. It is plain that he enjoys inflicting pain on others because he does not miss an opportunity to do it. He slaps Sissie around, bullies members of his gang, and chokes Sonny unconscious. Murder clearly means nothing to him because he intended to kill Galen just for the fun of it.

Reba, the Black madam, has a luxuriant shock of white hair. Standing six foot two with her hair cut short, there is some sexual ambiguity about Reba, especially when one remembers her aggressive past. We are told early on that Reba caught her lover in bed with another woman, made him jump out of a window, and shot him. Her masculinity is allayed somewhat by the swell of her voluptuous bosom, her red lips, and the red rose that she wears in the cleavage of her breasts.

Reba panders to the rich and the well-connected and has no fear of the law. When Digger enters her house, she greets him with an almost comradely air. Later we discover that she provided Ulysses Galen with a room to work out his perversions. Only when she discovered that the Greek was beating young girls with a whip to obtain his sexual gratification did she turn him out at gunpoint. Even someone as depraved as Reba has limits it seems.

The worst evil in the story is represented by the notorious Greek, Ulysses Galen. His nickname symbolizes the sexual perversity that has traditionally been assigned to the Greek people. His first name conjures up the Odyssey of Homer. A wealthy pillar of his own community, Galen has embarked on a perilous voyage through strange and uncharted territory. While on the voyage he is constantly tempted by the sexual allure of the strange creatures he meets.

His last name is drawn from that of Galen, the ancient Greek physician. Galen is remembered for, among other things, his interest in human anatomy. The Greek's interest in pornographic photographs seems to mock the nobler interests of his namesake.

Galen is far worse than either Reba or Ready Belcher. They at least do not pretend to be other than what they are. Galen masquerades as a respectable businessman and comes to Harlem to commit illegal and immoral acts with young Black girls. With his money, he subverts the youth of the Black community and taints the city with his evil. The image of Galen, especially with his miniature bullwhip, suggests a link to the overseers of bygone plantation days who beat their slaves to achieve peaceful compliance and used young Black girls for their own sexual pleasure. Even though Galen is killed at the beginning of the story, his memory hangs over the Black community as a symbol of white decadence and Black subjugation.

An interesting aspect of the Greek's exploitation of Black women is Himes' assertion, through Big Smiley, that certain members of the Black community actually want to be exploited for the social prestige it brings. Smiley insists that even high-class Black women will sleep with white men for this reason and will do it with the knowledge and connivance of their husbands. Himes seems to suggest that this attitude exists and may be a hold-over from the days when slaveholders would take willing Black women into concubinage. It is also worth noting that he had satirized bi-racial sexuality in the book that would eventually be published as *Mamie Mason* and *Pinktoes*.

Galen's disguise of innocence is so good that the casual onlooker feels a certain pity for him when he is first threatened by the drunken old Negro. Only later, after the case is over, do we realize the significance of his fear and horror when he is accused by first the old man and then Sonny of molesting Black women. His worst fear has come true, and his money and prestige cannot protect him from the vengeance of outraged Harlemites.

Himes has some fun with two other ancient historical names in this story. Sonny Pickens' real name is Aesop and, for him, it is an appropriate one. His involvement in the adventure is completely the result of his having concocted a fable with which to frighten the white man he sees outside the Dew Drop. Aesop himself could not have produced a greater exercise in irony. Galen's flight is ridiculous because, although he is truly innocent, he actually believes himself to be guilty. He never realizes that his accuser is an imposter or that his gun is a harmless toy. His guilt literally drives him to his death.

Sheik's real name is Samson. Like his namesake, Sheik is physically strong, yet he is unwise in his choice of female companions. Both Sissie and Evelyn hate him and wish him harm. His lust for them is a contributory cause to his demise.

Himes skillfully manipulates his audience into the discovery of the only real victim of tragedy when he brings Digger to the Dew Drop Inn for the denouncement. There, he uncovers the identity of Gertrude B. Richardson, a wayward teenager who has haughtily called herself "Good Booty." She is disdainful of the drunken old Negro killed in the bar until she realizes that it was her own father who died defending her soiled honor. This revelation is the ultimate plot twist in this convoluted story.

Although Himes may have felt that he had left the world of serious literature far behind as he developed this series, time and again he displayed the imagination of a skilled novelist at work. His use of Granny as a silent angel of death, for example, is probably one of the most imaginative aspects of this novel.

Granny, unbeknown to the other characters, dies quietly in her rocking chair soon after the police enter the apartment looking for Sonny. Her fierce, disapproving stare bears witness to the evil that has been and is being perpetrated in her shabby apartment. She keeps a death watch for her already dead grandson and for Choo-Choo, Sheik, and the policeman who will later be shot there.

At the same time, Granny's corpse bears witness to the running sore that Harlem has become. People have been horribly manipulated by an evil white man, unknown police or city bureaucrats have protected him as he debased Black teenagers, and other people have been viciously and mindlessly killed.

To emphasize how bad Harlem has become, Himes shows the white chief of police manipulating the press when he wrongly marks Sonny Pickens as a murderer in order to get the killers of what he thinks was a respected white businessman. When the case has been satisfactorily explained and the bodies have been carted away, the chief dusts off his hands in a self-satisfied way, as if to suggest an attitude of "good riddance to bad rubbish."

To underscore the injustices that have been done, Ulysses Galen's body is turned over to his family, and the world is allowed to continue thinking that he was a decent, upright man. Sonny Pickens, the quintessential Himes square, has been proven innocent of murder but is still jailed on a trumped-up charge of disturbing the peace.

Himes was no doubt a cynic, but even he believed in the regenerating power of love. Sonny has been unfairly jailed and has lost his shoe-shine stand, but he and Sissie will find a new life and love married to each other. The bastard child that Sissie carries from her affair with Sheik will be born with a name and some hope for the future.

With that, *The Real Cool Killers* ends on a more hopeful note than any of the other Harlem stories. Sonny lacks the romantic power of Johnny Perry, but he is more intelligent, attractive, and steady than Jackson. Sissie, although she has been a foolish and headstrong child, shows a real maturity and loyalty that bodes a happy ending for the pair.

Himes once again took a very simple story and, by concealing some things and gradually uncovering relevant facts, he created an aura of mystery and confusion. He made much better use of his detective characters here, allowing them to share center stage with Sheik, Sissie, and Sonny, rather than lurk in the background until time for the story's resolution.

The detectives were both strengthened and humanized in this particular story. While they seem conscienceless, indomitable, and slightly crooked in *Imabelle*, Himes allows them to emerge as separate personalities with individual strengths and weaknesses. Ed appears as a brave and resolute hero who can exhibit nerves of steel when the chips are down, but who is traumatized and plagued with emotional doubts.

Digger proves himself to be the brains of the pair, unraveling a complex mystery on the basis of detective work rather than relying on physical violence. His sadness at Sissie's revelations about herself and Evelyn Johnson at the end of the story suggests a man who can feel real grief for his friends and for his race, in spite of his daily contact with horrors that would dehumanize other men.

All in all, *The Real Cool Killers* emerges as the best of the first six Harlem novels. Himes provides a strong plot without inconsistencies along with his usual masterful control of characterization and dialog.

Chapter VII
Lying In The "Bread"

Men and women wrestled and rolled. Benches were splintered. The church rocked. The coffin shook. A big stink of sweating bodies arose. "Fornication... fornication..." the religious, mad people screamed.

"I'm getting out of here," Dulcy said, getting to his feet.

"Sit down," Johnny said. "These religious folks are dangerous."

The stunning success of his first two crime novels spurred Himes on to greater activity. Nineteen-fifty-nine was a landmark year for him in that he published three novels during one twelve-month period.

His past life continued to provide much of the grist for his mill, but very often conversations with friends were still the impetus for a plot. For this third entry in the Harlem Domestic Series, he recalled a story told by a friend:

I had begun it by using one of Ollie's [Harrington] cafe stories about a man falling out of a window in Harlem in the early morning hours during a wake and landing unhurt in a basket of American bread.[1]

Because jealousy was the major theme of his new effort, Himes originally titled the story *A Jealous Man Can't Win*. The French title was, of course, much more enigmatic; *Couché dans le pain*, or *Lying in the Bread*. As is the case in English, *pain*, or bread, is French slang for money.

The story opens at four A.M. on a July morning. The manager of an A & P grocery has double-parked his car in front of the store while he opens up, leaving inside a canvas bag full of change. Even though a uniformed policeman is standing guard, a sneak thief manages to creep up, steal the coins, and run down the street. The manager comes out in time to see him and, accompanied by the officer, takes off in pursuit.

Meanwhile, a man standing in a window on the third floor of a nearby building leans out to see the action and falls out, landing unhurt in a big basket of white bread sitting in front of the store. After getting up, he returns upstairs where a wild party is in full swing. The party is a wake being held in honor of Big Joe Pullen, a retired dining car waiter and solid Harlem citizen. The room is full of jazz musicians, Holy Rollers, whorehouse madams, gamblers, and other friends.

94

Of particular importance to the story are Dulcy Perry, present wife of Big Joe's godson, Johnny; Alamena, Johnny's first wife; Doll Baby, a chorus girl who carries a torch for Dulcy's brother, Val; and Chink Charlie Dawson, a young stud who lusts for Dulcy. Before much time passes, Big Joe's widow, Mamie, pulls Dulcy out of the crowd and into the bathroom. Simultaneously, Chink Charlie leaves the wake.

Inside the bathroom, Mamie reproves Dulcy for encouraging Chink Charlie's attentions. Dulcy denies that she is doing this, but her flashy and whorish appearance suggests otherwise. Mamie is sure that Johnny will kill Chink over Dulcy eventually.

Out in the living room, the loud music and laughter are interrupted by a furious hammering on the door. Eventually the door is opened to admit Reverend Short, a bad-tempered Holy Roller minister who upbraids the group for indulging in sacrilege when they should be behaving with reverence. He also claims that Chink Charlie pushed him out of the window.

Without much warning, Short and Dulcy get into a violent argument, during which Short accuses Dulcy of being responsible for Big Joe's death. Mamie denies this, but Dulcy leaves the room, announcing her intention of going home.

As everyone begins to discuss the preacher's fall, the story about the basket of bread comes out. Alamena and Mamie go to the bedroom window and see the basket below which now has the missing Val lying in it with a knife in his chest. Everyone rushes out except Mamie, who stays behind to answer the phone. The voice on the phone makes some confusing remarks about Reverend Short being in the bread basket. Mamie, not understanding, answers that the body in the bread is Valentine Haines, who has been murdered. Mamie's remarks strike the caller dumb and he hangs up the phone.

Down in the street, Dulcy and Chink stand over Val's body. Dulcy accuses Chink of the killing, which Chink denies. As everyone else clusters around, Dulcy flings herself across Val's body sobbing that she will get revenge. At that moment, a police detail headed by a white sergeant comes up and begins to herd everyone into the A & P for questioning.

At this point, Grave Digger Jones and Coffin Ed Johnson show up and help bring the crowd under control. Hard on their heels comes a cream-colored Cadillac convertible driven by Johnny Perry, a big, masculine professional gambler. Everyone, including the detectives, recognizes and respects Johnny and way is made for him. At his request, Digger and Ed release Dulcy into his custody. Everyone else is loaded into a patrol wagon and carted to the Harlem Precinct Station.

At the station, Digger, Ed, and the white sergeant begin the tedious job of questioning all of the mourners. Eventually they bring in Mamie Pullen who has known the two Black detectives since they were little boys. She explains that the reason for Reverend Short's accusations against Chink Charlie stem from an argument they had previously about the morals of the people attending the wake. She also explains that Short's animosity towards Dulcy undoubtedly comes from his own poorly disguised lust for the young woman.

Mamie's interrogation brings several other things to light. She relates the story of the strange phone call, but neither of the detectives can make much sense out of it. In response to their questions about her meeting with Dulcy in the bathroom, Mamie explains about Chink's dangerous interest in Dulcy and her fears that it will lead to violence with Johnny Perry.

The next person to be interrogated is Reverend Short. The preacher claims that Dulcy committed the murder with a knife that he saw Chink give her just after Christmas. This piques the interest of Sergeant Brody, who questions him closely about the murder. Short eventually admits that he saw the murder in a vision and adds that he sees visions all the time. To prove it, Short goes into a convulsion and has to be carried out.

Alamena, Johnny's former wife, comes in next. She explains that Dulcy came to Harlem to sing in a cabaret, and six months prior to the beginning of the story took Johnny away from her. Dulcy's brother Val came to the wedding and never left. He never had a job or any other means of support, but Johnny allowed him to stay around. Alamena claims that Val had no enemies and insists that she has never seen the knife before.

Brodie is puzzled by the knife, which is a hand-tooled English spring-blade hunting knife sold only at Abercrombie & Fitch's. He doubts that anyone would purchase such an expensive knife and then leave it in his victim.

Alamena is followed by Chink Charlie Dawson. He accounts for his time before the wake with a stud poker party at his own apartment which lasted until one-thirty A.M. He got to the wake at two A.M. and left at three-fifty-five to keep a date with Doll Baby. He says that the policeman in front of the A & P was the only person to see him leave.

Chink explains that when he and Doll Baby got together, she wasn't in the mood for sex, so he went down the street to get some marijuana from a friend. Just as he got down on the street, he saw Dulcy come out and also saw Val's body. He insists he has never seen the knife and denies vehemently Short's accusation that he gave it to Dulcy at Christmas.

The detectives decide to hold Chink for further questioning and bring in Doll Baby. She substantiates much of Chink's story. When the detectives bring up the fact that she was supposed to be engaged to Val and yet was entertaining Chink in her room, she dismisses it by saying that since Val cheated on her she could do it to him. Both the A & P manager and the cop saw her leave Mamie's apartment.

Doll Baby explains that the last time she had seen Val was ten-thirty P.M. the previous night. Val dropped her at the wake and went alone to Johnny's club. They planned to meet at the wake in an hour. She insists that Val had no enemies but that perhaps Johnny had gotten tired of him hanging around all the time. There could have been no bad blood between Val and Chink because Val didn't know she was seeing Chink on the side.

Dulcy finally comes in, accompanied by Ben Williams, Johnny's attorney. She denies vehemently that Val and Doll Baby were engaged to be married and calls her a slut. She tells Brodie that Val had left home at ten P.M. the previous evening to go to the Apollo Theatre while she was at the hairdressers. Val had planned to drop by Johnny's club and come to the wake with Johnny. Dulcie left for the wake at midnight with Alamena, who lived in the same apartment building.

When Brodie asks Dulcy about Chink having given her the murder knife, she tells the cop that Reverend Short has driven himself crazy with his unfulfilled sexual desires and that his stories are nonsense. Brodie orders her held on $5,000.00 bond but her lawyer is there to get her out again.

When Johnny comes in, Williams provides affidavits stating that he was at his club until four-forty-five A.M. and that Val had not been seen there all evening. Johnny adds that he had not seen Val since he left Johnny's at nine the previous evening.

Johnny also supplies that he has not minded supporting his brother-in-law. He took Val in, he says, to keep Dulcy from having to slip him money under the table. Val was too stupid to gamble or be a pimp, but Johnny found it amusing to keep him around. Johnny denies any knowledge of the knife.

Out in the street, Dulcy insists that Chink is responsible for Val's death. When Johnny points out that she must also know why Chink did the killing, she backs down.

After lunch at Fat's Down Home Restaurant, the group leaves for Big Joe's funeral. They arrive at the storefront church of the Holy Rollers to find a veritable circus in progress as huge crowds gather to see the funeral. As Johnny and the two women take their places with Mamie near the front of the church, Reverend Short goes into a fire-and-brimstone sermon during which he denounces Dulcy from the pulpit as an adulteress and a murderer. Despite Dulcy's and Mamie's objections, the preacher carries on until, at the mention of "fornication," the church erupts with pent-up passion. Nearly everyone begins rolling about the floor and embracing each other in frantic, erotic embraces. Benches are upset and splintered in the melee.

Finally, order is restored, and the pall bearers take the casket out to the hearse. At the graveside, Johnny and Chink get into a brawl after Dulcie faints, and Chink makes the mistake of carrying her out of the crowd. After the funeral Johnny, Dulcy, Alamena, and Mamie leave for home.

Dropping the other two women off at his apartment, Johnny takes Mamie home alone. During the drive Mamie pleads with Johnny not to kill Chink and to ease up on Dulcy. Johnny counters that he has plenty of reasons to be hostile and suspicious. Mamie lets slip the suspicion that maybe Johnny killed Val. Before Johnny can react to this Mamie changes the subject and urges him to get Short to preach Val's funeral.

After dropping Mamie off, Johnny visits Short's room in the back of the church. During the visit, Short nearly shoots Johnny in the back with a shotgun. Johnny disarms him and is astounded to hear Short accuse him of coming there to kill him to protect Dulcy. The confused Johnny asks why she should have killed her own brother, to which Short replies that only Johnny or Dulcy could have done the deed. More puzzled than ever, Johnny leaves.

Meanwhile Grave Digger and Coffin Ed meet a stool pigeon named Gigolo who tells them that the two people responsible for the A & P theft are Poor Boy and Iron Jaw. They easily find Poor Boy and take him into custody. When they ask him who was in the car with Johnny Perry he swears that he doesn't know but that perhaps his partner saw something.

Soon Digger and Ed have found Iron Jaw and take him into custody. The boy admits that he saw Johnny Perry drive up with another man just before the preacher fell out of the window. He also denies knowing who the other man was.

The scene shifts back to Johnny's apartment where the atmosphere is thick with tension. Johnny demands to know why Short thinks Dulcy is the killer. The more he questions, the more evasive and defensive Dulcy becomes. As they eat dinner, Doll Baby comes in and announces that since she was Val's fiance, she is entitled to the $10,000.00 Johnny was going to give him to open a liquor store. Johnny clearly knows nothing about this, but before he can react, Dulcy attacks the other woman. Doll Baby runs away, leaving Johnny with another mystery.

At ten-fifteen that evening the two detectives go to Chink's apartment and find him together with Doll Baby. The detectives accidentally scare Doll Baby into talking about the $10,000.00 that Johnny was supposed to give Val. Digger and Ed hide their surprise at this news and pretend that they have heard this from her earlier. Shortly thereafter, they leave the apartment.

After the detectives leave, Chink and Doll Baby get into a vicious argument, each one accusing the other of holding out information. Outside the apartment door, Digger and Ed listen with satisfaction. They know the pot is boiling, and something is about to float to the top.

The scene changes to later in the evening at Johnny's apartment just as Chink arrives. Alamena warns him to go away if he values his life, but he insists on talking to Dulcy. He claims that he can send Johnny to the electric chair and that if he doesn't get the $10,000.00 meant for Val, he will tell the cops he gave the murder weapon to Dulcy.

Dulcy, who has been drinking heavily, resists Chink at first but eventually weakens and agrees to give him the money. To get him out, Dulcy gives him $700.00 of her own. Before he can pick it up, however, she vomits all over the money. Before he can wash the money off he hears Alamena say that Johnny is about to arrive, and he bolts out the back.

Fortunately, Digger and Ed are waiting outside for Johnny, and, before he can get his key in the lock, they ask him to come in and answer a few questions. When Johnny refuses to go with them, they back off and let him go. Inside, Johnny finds Dulcy passed out from drunkenness and Alamena cleaning up the vomit. He sends her home and puts Dulcy to bed.

Outside the apartment building, Digger and Ed find a badly shaken Chink. They take him down to the precinct where they grill him with intensity. Having eavesdropped on his conversation with Doll Baby, they know about the knife and the possibility that somebody has something on Johnny. When Chink fails to open up, they torture him until he talks.

Chink admits that he got the knife from a member of the club where he tends bar. He subsequently gave it to Dulcy. With this information in hand, they book him on suspicion of murder and return to Johnny's apartment. They fear that Johnny might kill Dulcy if he finds out that she got the knife from Chink.

They find the apartment deserted except for Dulcy, whom they discover passed out drunk in bed. They go around town searching for Johnny until the end of their shift.

The next morning Mamie Pullen receives a telephone call from Johnny who informs her that he is in Chicago. Mamie, frightened by this turn of events, begs him to trust Dulcy. He responds that he has trusted her but that now he has to know what is going on behind his back. He tells Mamie about Dulcy's condition and asks her to go over and feed her.

Mamie wakens Dulcy while cleaning the apartment. When she tells the younger woman about Johnny's trip to Chicago, Dulcy goes into a violent fit of trembling and takes to bed with a bottle of brandy. In the bedroom she confesses to Mamie that Chink had given her a knife like the one that killed Val. She believes Chink killed Val with one like it but has no way to prove it. Her own knife disappeared shortly before the murder. Dulcy confides to Mamie the fear that Johnny must have killed Val.

As the day wears on, both women remain frozen with fear and indecision. Finally, in the late afternoon, Johnny returns from Chicago. Sending Mamie home, he undresses and gets into bed, telling Dulcy that there is $10,000.00 in his coat pocket. He offers her the chance to take it and be gone when he awakens.

Meanwhile Chink has managed to get himself bailed out of jail and has returned to his apartment. Just as he arrives, he gets a phone call from Dulcy. She tells him that she has the money he demanded. Chink suspects some kind of trap, but he is so overcome with greed that he is willing to do anything to get the money.

Dulcy promises him the money, but only on the condition that he brings his knife in exchange for it. Chink resists coming there and risking Johnny's wrath until Dulcy agrees to have sex with him. At this news, Chink is on his way.

Dulcy greets him in a bathrobe under which she is obviously naked. Chink is nearly incoherent with lust and greed. He lays the knife down, and while he is rooting like a hog in the money she has laid on the bed, she palms the knife and puts it in the pocket of her robe.

She tells him to get undressed and wait for her in that room while she showers. While Chink is lying naked on the bed rubbing the money all over his body, Dulcy slips into the room where Johnny is sleeping. She sets the clock radio alarm to go off in five minutes and dressing hurriedly bolts from the apartment.

In the bedroom, the alarm goes off with a blast, shocking Johnny out of sleep. He grabs for the .38 automatic under his pillow instinctively and looks around for Dulcy. When he sees her gone, he sadly assumes that she has played him false.

With the radio playing so loudly he doesn't hear the door latch clink when Chink comes through the door. For a moment the two naked men look at each other. Then, in a mad rage, Johnny empties his automatic into Chink's body. Not satisfied with that, he then clubs and stomps the corpse. His next realization is of being held in check by two police officers.

Down at the station Johnny begins to shed light on the case. He found Dulcy's knife in a drawer two weeks earlier. He assumed that she had bought it to protect herself from him. Big Joe saw him handling it at the club and admired it so much that Johnny gave it to him. He didn't see it again until after the murder.

Sergeant Brodie shows him still another knife but says it was not the one found in Val. He produces a third knife that did the killing. Johnny is dumbfounded. He explains that the last time he saw Val was at ten minutes before four A.M. on the morning of the wake. He came out of the club and found Val waiting in the car for him, which was a usual occurrence. Val told Johnny that he had been talking to Reverend Short and had something to tell him about the conversation. Because they were late for the wake, Johnny didn't wait to hear what it was before they left.

Just before arriving at Mamie's, Val confided that he was going to catch an early train to Chicago but didn't know where he was going from there. Insisting that Johnny listen to his story, they parked. Before he could speak further, however, they spotted the theft of the A & P money and Short's fall.

After they watched Short return upstairs, Johnny got the idea for a gag. He told Val to go and lie down in the bread while he went around the corner to phone Mamie. He was going to tell her about a dead man in the bread who had fallen out of her window. However, when Johnny got to the phone booth, he found someone using it and was delayed in the execution of his joke by about five minutes. When he finally got Mamie and heard that Val was dead, he hung up and returned to the scene of the crime.

Johnny explains that he went to Chicago after Doll Baby asked him for the $10,000.00. He discovered there that Val and Dulcy were married and that Val probably wanted the money in order to go away with Doll Baby. Brodie books him for manslaughter and puts him in jail.

It is Brodie's theory that Dulcy killed Val to keep him from fouling up her gravy train with Johnny. She then set Chink up to be killed by Johnny in order to save herself from the electric chair. The extra knife puzzles them deeply, however, and Digger and Ed decide to bring Dulcy in.

They visit Mamie and tell her the news of Chink's death, Johnny's jailing, and Dulcy's disappearance. Upset by the news, Mamie suggests that Dulcy must have gone to see Reverend Short. When the detectives register surprise at this news, she explains that Dulcy is really a very religious girl and has gone looking for God in order to soothe her conscience.

When Digger and Ed eventually reach the church, they identify themselves and order Short to come out. The crazed preacher refuses to come out or to give Dulcy up.

While Digger keeps Short busy, Ed sneaks around to the rear of the building. When Short shoots at Digger through the door with his shotgun, he is shot from behind by Ed. Bursting into the room, Digger finds Dulcy tied to the bed with a knife sticking out from between her naked breasts. They take both to the hospital, where Short is confined to the psychiatric ward.

At the hospital the now-lucid Short agrees to talk to Brodie, Digger, and Ed. They discover from him that Big Joe Pullen was the first to discover Val and Dulcy's marriage. Joe had intended to make Val go back to Chicago and get a quiet divorce, but his untimely death prevented it.

However, Joe had told Mamie, and Mamie, in turn, had told Short when he came to arrange Joe's funeral. Short called Val into his church and ordered him to leave town in twenty-four hours or he would tell Johnny the whole story. Val agreed to go and Short had believed him. However, Short claims that during the wake, God had directed him to kill Val.

He relates that while he was in the room with the coffin, he had gotten an overwhelming urge to go into the front bedroom. He knew that God was sending him on some kind of mission. There he went through Big Joe's things and discovered the knife, which he placed in his own pocket. After he fell out of the window, he believed that God was responsible for the action, even though he later blamed Chink.

Once he recovered from the fall, he went into the downstairs hall to wait. While he waited, Val came along and got into the basket of bread. He then walked up and stabbed Val in the heart with Joe's knife before the younger man could react.

Dulcy is not badly hurt since her sternum stopped the knife from penetrating deeply enough to do any damage. She explains to Mamie that the reason she didn't send Val away was because she felt too sorry for him. She never told Johnny because he would have hated her for the deception. She is heartbroken over the way things have turned out and despairs of finding any way to make things right with Johnny again.

At the police station lawyer Ben Williams has just gotten Johnny out of jail and assures him that none of the charges will stick. Johnny's mind is on Dulcy, He is also heartsick over his marriage. When he asks "how can a jealous man win?" Williams advises him to trust his luck. Cautiously, Johnny agrees, closing the story on a hopeful note.

In a 1986 essay on Himes' work, critic Fred Pfeil noted that the opening sequence of this book "flaunts its energy and virtuosity as brazenly as the first long take of any Orson Wells film," and the wake scene is "attended by a cast of characters with enough lust for power, money and sex to fuel the next five seasons of *Dynasty*."[2] These remarks are worth repeating because the scene that Pfeil highlights is one that illustrates the major strengths of this third Harlem story.

By refraining from the use of the traditional first-person narrative, Himes uses the omniscient narrator effectively. The details of the scene and the careful description of the events leading up to and just after the theft of the coin bag are, in a way, a red herring. The previous stories have led us to half-expect another hell-for-leather chase through the streets of Harlem. When the scene shifts abruptly from the chase to the raucous wake, we have no idea that a murder and a genuine mystery are about to claim our attention.

At the same time, this story includes many more characters than the first book, and each is a finely drawn portrait. Himes' trick of following all the characters, describing their personalities and flaws, and playing each off against the other has the effect of making the reader suspect virtually all of them of Val's murder.

These facets immediately mark *Crazy Kill* as a totally different kind of story from the earlier ones. Instead of gangsters and con men, we see a number of more-or-less respectable Harlem citizens. We are not prepared for the kind of mystery that the murder presents. There is no sucker, no obvious villain, only a corpse and the question "why."

Of all the Harlem stories, *Crazy Kill* is certainly the most sexually charged. It is fair to say that coveting "thy neighbor's wife" is the keynote of the story. With the exception of old Mamie and the detectives, all of the other characters are sexually oriented. Dulcy, who is the object of almost everyone's affections, is one of Himes' most blatantly sexual women. She exudes a raw sensuality that even she cannot control. Through the entire book she is naked or half-naked, driving every functioning male in the neighborhood wild with desire. Even Johnny Perry, the character most in charge of his emotions, breaks down at one point and kisses her passionately.

Both Chink Charlie Dawson and Reverend Short have a purely sexual orientation. Each devotes all of his energies to pursuing Dulcy or to controlling the fatal sexual attraction they have for her. Lust proves ultimately to be the downfall of each character.

Himes equates religious fervor here with sexual passion. Short, like the fundamentalist ministers of our own day, tries so hard to lead a sexually blameless life that he has become obsessed with sex. It becomes such a force in his life that it drives him insane. It is interesting to note that, when he finally has the object of his passion stripped and tied to his bed, he symbolically penetrates her with a phallic device (the knife) rather than with his own sexual organ. This would seem to suggest that his struggle between lust and religion has made him physically impotent.

Digger and Ed find themselves faced with naked and near-naked women throughout this case, but they seem curiously detached from the eroticism they find on every side. While the job of being a detective traditionally demands an enforced celibacy, their attitude seems to border on contempt for sex. When Digger and Ed rescue Dulcy from Reverend Short, her first question to them is "I bad hurt?" Digger sneers "I doubt it...you're too pretty to be bad hurt. Only ugly women ever get hurt bad."

Digger clearly holds Dulcy responsible for much of the mayhem that has taken place. His unconcern for her fright and injuries is in the same vein as the brutality he showed to Imabelle and is a precursor to an attitude he will express later in the series when he dismisses women like Dulcy as "these half-white bitches."

In *Crazy Kill,* Himes offers us in Johnny Perry his most heroic and virile protagonist. It is plain that Perry represents an ideal for Himes because he gives such a detailed picture of Perry's arrival on the scene:

He was a big man but, standing, his six-foot height lost impressiveness in his slanting shoulders and long arms. He was wearing a powder blue suit of shantung silk; a pale yellow crepe silk shirt; a hand-painted tie depicting an orange sun rising on a dark blue morning; highly glossed light tan rubber-soled shoes; a miniature ten-of-hearts tie pin with opal hearts; three rings, including a heavy gold signet ring of his lodge, a yellow diamond set in a heavy gold band and a big mottled stone of a nameless variety, also set in a heavy gold band. His cuff links were heavy gold squares with diamond eyes...He was bareheaded. His kinky hair, powdered with gray, was cut as short as a three-days growth of whiskers, with a part shaved on one side. In the dim light of morning his big-featured, knotty face showed it had taken its lumps. In the center of his forehead was a puffed, bluish scar with ridges pronging off like immobilized octopus tentacles. It gave him an expression of perpetual rage, which was accentuated by the smoldering fire that lay always just beneath the surface of his muddy brown eyes, ready to flame into a blaze...He looked hard, strong, tough, and unafraid.

Johnny Perry is a traditional naturalistic, hard-boiled hero and, at the same time, is typical of many of Himes' earlier protagonists. He has suffered persecution in his life, having served time in prison for killing the man who was beating his mother. At the time of the story, he is 46 years old.

Perry, who is named for an actual gentleman-gambler Himes knew in his youth, is really an idealized version of Himes himself. Perry is about the age that Himes was when he left for Europe. His overwhelming masculinity is a caricature of Himes' own virility. Perry is tough, blunt, and completely uncowed by authority or the time he spent in prison.

It is clear that Himes feels that Johnny's imprisonment for defending his mother was a societal injustice against a Black man. Himes may have tried to liken this to the injustice he felt in his own imprisonment. Himes, however, was already a two-time loser when he was brought to trial for robbery. On a subconscious level, he must have realized that to make Johnny appear noble and heroic, he must make the reasons for his incarceration more acceptable than his own had been.

Johnny carries a smoldering rage inside, perhaps because of the injustice that was done him, but it takes much more provocation for that rage to assert itself than was the case with Himes himself, or his detective-alter ego, Coffin Ed. Johnny is too genuinely tough for such theatrics. Even when Reverend Short attempts to kill him, Johnny displays an enviable control. Instead of hurting or killing Short, he only disarms and questions him.

The only times Johnny actually displays his rage is when his jealousy over Dulcy springs to the surface. It is interesting to note that the horrible scar that is on Johnny's forehead pulsates and seems to come alive when his temper reaches the boiling point. This is a characteristic that Himes would later attribute to Coffin Ed.

As was the case in *Imabelle*, the mysteries in *Crazy Kill* could conceivably have been resolved without a detective protagonist. Johnny solves the mystery behind Dulcy and Val's relationship and, having easily handled Reverend Short once, could well have gone on to rescue Dulcy and solve the murder. Johnny behaves in the traditional manner of the proletarian tough guy, moving through the underworld discovering facts until everything has been revealed. He also echoes the Chandlerian hero by loving and trusting to the end a woman who has betrayed him. By using money to test Dulcy's loyalty, he is willing to sacrifice the tangible for the intangible.

Perhaps to keep Johnny from being too perfect and to add an extra hint of danger to him, Himes tells us that he was married to Alamena when he met Dulcy. When he wanted to marry Dulcy, Alamena wouldn't let him go. She persisted until he cut her throat and nearly killed her. It is a strange quirk in both Johnny's character and Alamena's that, even after this violent end to their marriage, she still remains in his life and seems to have his tacit approval to do so.

Alamena is described early in the story as a woman who had once been just like Doll Baby—that is a hustler with no other thought than having fun. Himes' obvious contempt for this type of woman and the sadism to which he continually subjects this character type explains why Johnny is not diminished for this throat-cutting episode in his past. That the sadism has sexual overtones is implicit in the fact that although Alamena has been rejected in favor of Dulcy, Johnny's sexual hold over her is too great for her to drop out of his life.

As if to add to Johnny's already well-established aura, Himes has made him the epitome of the successful Harlemite. As a professional gambler with his own club, he has proven himself in one of the ghetto's traditional areas of endeavor. He is known to almost everyone, and when he drives up in his flashy Cadillac convertible, children run out to greet him and receive the largess he spreads. His equally flashy appearance is not, as one might suppose, the cheap flash of the pimp but a walking advertisement of his success and a source of fall-back wealth if the cards should take a bad turn for him.

Although Coffin Ed and Grave Digger still do not dominate the story, Himes has given them a substantial role in the case and allows their personalities to grow further. In their meeting with Mamie Pullen at the precinct station, we discover that they grew up in Harlem. Mamie's remembrance of them as "Eddie Johnson" and "Little Digger" Jones humanizes them and makes them seem less like the implacable automatons they once appeared to be.

Himes depicts in them genuine sense of humor when he sends them after Iron Jaw, one of the boys involved in the coin theft. When the muscular young man nearly eludes them because of a stolen chicken, the two detectives become so overcome with the foolishness of the situation that they are incapacitated with laughter for a moment. Their good humor is even more evident when, after apprehending the boy, they do not rough him up. Their rather gentle and good-humored interrogation of Iron Jaw is in direct contrast to the brutality that was so much a part of their technique in *Imabelle*.

As detectives they do not win high marks. The only mystery they solve is the theft of the A & P manager's coins, and that is effected with the help of a stool pigeon. This helps place Johnny Perry at the murder scene, but they are plainly working in the dark up until the end of the story. Johnny solves the mystery of Dulcy's secret and it is sheer happenstance that Digger and Ed are able to rescue Dulcy and discover Short is Val's murderer.

Their major importance to the story is reflected in their role as definers and explainers of Harlem mores. Even though they are the ace detectives of the Harlem precinct, the death of Valentine Haines places the case under the jurisdiction of the Homicide Squad, in the person of the white Sergeant Brodie. His whiteness makes it impossible for him to understand much of what he sees and hears. Ed and Digger have to act as interpreters.

As one of the first white characters of any importance to appear in the Harlem series, Brodie symbolizes white contempt for Blacks and the inability of the white world to truly come to an understanding of what Black life is all about.

This first comes to light at the precinct station before they begin interrogating the witnesses. Brodie expresses incredulity over the story about Short's fall from the window. Ed takes this opportunity to inform the sergeant that "This is Harlem, where anything can happen." Later, leaning on his many years of experience as a murder expert, Brodie theorizes that Valentine

Haines had to have been killed over money or a woman. Here, Grave Digger instructs him:

"This is Harlem. Ain't no other place like it in the world. You've got to start from scratch here, because these folks in Harlem do things for reasons nobody else in the world would think of."

What Grave Digger leaves unsaid is that Black people do things for reasons no white person would think of. This is an important moment in the series because, in a subtle way, it prepares the reader for the many bizarre things that will come later. It also is a quiet articulation of Himes' belief that the world of the urban Black is completely different from that of the white.

Digger and Ed's understanding of this will make them much more effective as problem solvers as the series goes on. Their skill as detectives is always based more on their understanding of Black psychology than textbook criminology. Thus, when Reverend Short admits to killing Valentine Haines, they understand much more easily than does Brodie that Short's insanity is of a peculiar, though no less real, kind:

Depends on what you mean by crazy. He was just sexually frustrated and lusting after a married woman. When you get to mixing sex and religion it will make anyone crazy.

This story is also something of a landmark in that, for the first time, Digger and Ed articulate a feeling that is akin to affection for Harlem and a deep concern for its inhabitants. When they have difficulty in getting information from Chink, Coffin Ed reminds him that:

...me and Digger are two country Harlem dicks who live in this village and don't like to see anybody get killed. It might be a friend of ours.

The Crazy Kill is a much more subtle story than most in the Harlem canon. Unlike the others, the story depends much more on plot and characterization than it does on violence. Digger and Ed are particularly restrained in this outing, using their guns only to wound Reverend Short at the end of the story.

They are especially lenient on the people they question. The only character to feel the full weight of their wrath is the arrogant Chink. When he refuses to answer any of their questions, they handcuff his feet together, hang him from a door, and using their feet in his armpits, bear down on him until he gives in. This, by the way, is another example of Himes' use of autobiography in the course of his writing. This particular form of torture is very similar to a kind that Himes himself was subjected to by the Chicago Police after he was picked up there in the 1920s.

Another interesting facet of *Crazy Kill* is how much more inviting this Harlem appears than the one in *Imabelle*. Here we are on the better side of town. The apartments are well-appointed, the women beautiful and well-dressed, and the men materially successful. At no time does Himes stress the degradation of the Black with scenes of squalor or decay. Nothing of his protest style comes through in this story. This is something that will not happen again in the other six books of the series.

In spite of the many differences in this story from *Imabelle,* Himes managed to retain certain themes that were to remain constant in this series. The most obvious is his use of beautiful, unfaithful women. In this story he created two, Dulcy and Doll Baby.

Doll Baby is, in many ways, more reminiscent of Imabelle than is Dulcy. Himes describes her in the opening scenes as "a brownskin model type, slim, tan, and cute." She is dressed in the flashiest manner possible and, according to Himes, "looked strictly on the make." She is a sometime chorus girl which, as Himes tells us in another of his books, can mean anything. She is childish, utterly faithless, and more than a bit ruthless. She claims to be engaged to Valentine Haines, but on several occasions during *Crazy Kill* she seems to be just about to have sex with Chink Dawson or has just finished.

Her ruthlessness shows up again after Big Joe Pullen's funeral. Val Haines has been dead only a few hours when she comes to Johnny's apartment demanding $10,000.00. She arrogantly claims it as her right since she was Val's fiance.

Unlike most of her sisters in the Harlem canon she is rather stupid. Even though she is in the thick of everything from the beginning, she rarely seems to know what is going on. Digger and Ed recognize this about her and use it to trick information out of her.

She is also troublesome in the extreme. She causes a brawl between Johnny and Chink in Fat's restaurant and gets into a fight with Dulcy in her own apartment. Later she gets into a violent argument with Chink.

Dulcy, on the other hand, is neither stupid nor bad. She is as complex a character as Johnny. By the end of the story it is clear that in marrying Val she was saddled with a husband who, while a nice enough guy, was neither bright nor particularly helpful. When she meets and falls in love with the dynamic Johnny Perry, she makes a complicated deal with Val to pose as his sister and provide for his living while he hangs around.

Unfortunately the deal puts her in a self-made trap. Although she deeply loves the dangerous gambler, she is afraid of what he might do if he finds out about her duplicity. Considering how he dealt with Alamena, this fear seems justified.

Her childish petulance and the whorish coquettishness that she often displays covers up a mass of conflicting emotions. Her fear of discovery is complicated by her own jealousy of Johnny's gambling career and the pressure she feels from Chink Dawson's threats to pin Val's murder on Johnny.

Dulcy is very much in the tradition of Himes' other female connivers. She skillfully keeps Johnny off balance with a combination of stubbornness, cunning, and sex appeal. Towards the end, she uses a clever ruse to trick Chink into giving up the evidence that could hurt Johnny and at the same time sets him up to be killed so he can't talk.

Chink Dawson is a particularly fine-drawn character and continues in the tradition of Sheik in *Real Cool Killers*. Like Sheik, Chink is light-complected, oversexed, vicious, and selfish. Unlike Sheik, he is a schemer and a coward rather than a cold-blooded murderer. Chink is a "sport" who likes flashy clothes, nice apartments, and fast chicks. He is already making time with Doll Baby but expends a lot of energy panting after Dulcy. His greed and his lust give him the drive to risk death, beatings, and incarceration by the cops, but ultimately those same motives lead him to a horrible end. Chink is the ultimate sucker of this story.

Valentine Haines, who is never seen alive in this story, exerts a powerful influence. He is somewhat reminiscent of Terry Lennox in Raymond Chandler's *The Long Goodbye*. It is plain that although he was a weak character, he had some quality that men and women liked, since he had both Dulcy's love and Johnny's financial support. In spite of his weaknesses and relative lack of intelligence, he possessed enough personal honor and love for Dulcy to be on the point of departing Harlem when he was killed by Short.

In spite of the skillful construction of the mystery and the relative plausibility of the resolution, the story is not without its inconsistencies. For example, Johnny Perry is presented throughout the story as a businesslike, no-nonsense guy. Yet Himes has him perpetrating a practical joke on Mamie, a behavior that is not at all in keeping with his humorless demeanor.

Just as inconsistent is Dulcy's behavior after she has engineered Chink Charlie's murder. Here is a woman who is a bigamist and who has connived at murder, yet we are expected to believe near the end that she is actually a very religious girl who could consult a preacher for solace and guidance. The fact that she would seek out Reverend Short, for whom she has had nothing but contempt and revulsion, makes the explanation even more ridiculous.

Himes' skill at humor particularly stands out in this story. It is filled with sight gags and funny dialogue. It is interesting to note that Himes does not shrink from drawing his humor from Black stereotype. The raucous wake, complete with drunken jazzmen singing parodies of gospel tunes, is a skillfully constructed scene of comic madness, as is the scene at Reverend Short's Holy Roller church where the congregation goes into a fit of erotic hysteria at the sound of the word "fornication."

Himes follows this up with more subtle digs at Black heritage when he takes his group of mourners to Fat's Down Home Restaurant where the specialty of the day is alligator tail. Even Johnny Perry's uptown Negro attorney cannot suppress a smile at the soul food menu.

One of the most ridiculous jokes happens before the story begins. Big Joe Pullen, who is really the catalyst to all the action, has choked to death on a cigar he was smoking when he went to sleep.

For many reasons, this was one of the best stories in the series. Himes' reliance on plot and character development rather than excitement and violence have much to do with this superiority. It was further proof that he could write formula fiction without resorting to formula and that continuing characters and elements in the series could develop and improve with each outing.

Chapter VIII
A Rain Of Money

"Faith is a rock! It's like a solid gold dream!"

The voice of the Sweet Prophet Brown issued from the amplifiers atop a sound truck and reverberated from the shabby brick faces of the tenement houses flanking 117th Street.

"Amen!" Alberta Wright said fervently.

After the publication of *The Crazy Kill*, Himes interrupted the series with the publication, in 1959, of *Dare-Dare* (published in America in 1966 as *Run, Man, Run*). Because this particular story does not feature Coffin Ed or Grave Digger, there is some possibility that it was written before he began the Harlem Domestic Series and remained unsold prior to the appearance of *For Love of Imabelle*. Certainly, the popularity of the Coffin Ed/Grave Digger stories would have made any thriller set in Harlem a very hot item to Himes' French audience.

Whatever the circumstances, the year 1959 also saw the publication of his second title for that year and his fourth in the Harlem series. It was published as *Tout pour plaire* by Gallimard and appeared as The *Big Gold Dream* in the United States in 1960.

In this story, Himes introduces one of his favorite themes, that of the crooked street preacher who manages through the power of his charisma to charm a fortune out of the ever-hopeful religious poor of Harlem. Other Himesian themes in the story include the honest but gullible sucker who is cheated by everyone and a mysterious fortune that virtually everyone in the story is willing to kill to get.

The story opens as Sweet Prophet Brown, a charismatic but none-too-honest revival minister, is standing atop a sound truck surrounded by a crowd of passionate and fervently religious Blacks.

In this group is the most fervent believer of all, a pretty domestic named Alberta Brown. Alberta is accompanied by her boyfriend, Sugar Stonewall, who shares neither her religious ecstasy nor her passion for Sweet Prophet Brown.

As Brown preaches that faith will turn rocks into gold, Alberta shouts out that, because of her faith, God has sent her a dream in which she baked three pies that burst open to reveal a cascade of $100.00 bills. This is a dream that Brown and his assembled flock can relate to, and they shout encouragement. Brown uses the opportunity to "baptize" the group with fire hoses. The wet but faithful throng crowds around the preacher in order to trade money for the "blessed bread crumbs" he is giving out.

Sugar Stonewall gives Alberta a bottle of drinking water from the lunch basket he is carrying and asks her to get Sweet Prophet to bless it for them. After the blessing takes place, Alberta drinks the water and begins to dance with ecstasy until she falls senseless to the pavement.

Brown's henchman Elder Jones discovers that Alberta is apparently dead. This discovery brings on a panic which turns into a stampede, during which Sugar Stonewall takes off purposefully with some mission in mind.

An inexperienced hearse driver arrives before the police do and soon is driving the body all over the city of New York trying to get a death certificate. The police arrive to find the body gone and no one left from the huge assemblage on the street.

Some time thereafter, a dilapidated moving van draws up in front of a four-story brick tenement on 118th Street. Two big Black men accompanied by a small, white-haired Jew alight and ask for the apartment of Rufus Wright. The trio are met by Rufus on the top floor, and it is soon clear that he is selling Alberta's furniture in some sort of unscrupulous transaction. It is also clear that this is a game that Rufus and the Jew have played before.

After reaching an agreement on a payment, the two laborers begin taking the furniture down to their truck where they are observed only by a muscular but seemingly harmless moron. When the laborers go back upstairs after another load, the young man casually walks away with Alberta's mattress. The laborers quickly notice the missing mattress and somewhat belatedly report it to the Jew, who receives the news without worry.

After the Jew and his men leave, Rufus makes one more fruitless search of the apartment before locking the door with the key we are told that he got from Sugar earlier that day. When Sugar meets Rufus later in the day, we discover that they have been in league to steal Alberta's furniture in the hopes of finding a large sum of cash.

At ten o'clock that evening, the Jew is in his warehouse in the Bronx where he is systematically dismantling Alberta's furniture. As he mumbles to himself, the reader understands that he has made a considerable fortune through his knowledge of antiques and his realization that poor Negroes often hid their life savings in their furniture. Just as he uncovers a stash of $100.00 notes, he is interrupted by a noise inside the building. He is soon killed in a struggle with the intruder who takes the money. As the intruder attempts to escape, he is himself beset by a knife-wielding attacker. Each wounds the other in the fight before the first intruder escapes.

Just past midnight that same evening, a group of police and bystanders surround the body of a man identified as George Clayborne. A little girl informs the cops that she saw a woman dressed in white stab Clayborne before she ran down the street. With her help, they find and overpower the woman nearby. She is armed with a bloodstained knife.

While studying the body, however, the medical examiner discovers that Clayborne was bludgeoned at least a half hour after the stabbing. He doubts a woman is responsible for all the damage and suspects two attackers.

At the Harlem police precinct station, the woman, who turns out to be Alberta Brown, tells Ed and Digger that a premonition sent her after the patrol car as it approached the murder scene. There she stepped on the bloody knife which she claims God instructed her conceal in order to save an innocent man.

Digger believes that Alberta knows who the murderer is but all they can get her to admit is that she hasn't seen Rufus in a year and that "her man," Sugar, left for Detroit.

They book her on suspicion and visit her apartment. There, a fat Black woman occupying a ground-floor apartment, tells them about the Jew and his business with Rufus Wright.

On an impulse they call the morgue for a description of the corpse and realize that the dead man is Rufus Wright. Calling the Bronx to get a line on the Jew's warehouse, they discover from the Bronx precinct that the Jew has been murdered, too.

By two-thirty A.M. the following morning, Sugar has discovered that Alberta has been arrested for Rufus' murder. He is puzzled by this, since he knows that she couldn't have done it.

Returning briefly to his apartment, he hears from the fat woman downstairs that Digger and Ed have been there looking for him. He quickly runs away, only to be stopped by Dummy, a short, muscular deaf-mute. Dummy, who communicates with a pad and pencil, instructs Sugar to go to Mammy Stormy, who will hide him from the cops. Sugar agrees to the plan but, on impulse, follows Dummy to Sweet Prophet's Temple of Wonderful Prayer, which just happens to be across the street from Mammy's.

Repairing to Mammy Stormy's building, Sugar meets a young prostitute coming down the stairs. The girl is in tears because a john has just cheated her out of her pay. Dummy unexpectedly reappears and, through his actions, makes it clear that he is the girl's pimp. This makes Sugar suspicious about Dummy. He reasons that if Dummy had been looking out for the whore all night, he couldn't have been around to know about the cops who were looking for Sugar.

Dummy sticks to his story, insisting that the cops will soon be there. He explains that they have the knife that killed Rufus and know that it is Sugar's. When Digger and Ed pull up outside, Sugar runs upstairs while Dummy scuttles across to the Temple.

Himes drops the story back slightly in time to the point where Digger and Ed have dropped Alberta off at the jail. Reasoning that money must be the motive in the Jew's death, they take off on their "stool pigeon" route and begin looking for someone flashing a roll of new money. They are rewarded in their search by the news that a tough-looking man was seen showing money to girls at a burlesque house.

At the end of their route, they pick Dummy up just as he and Sugar part company at Mammy Stormy's. Dummy insists that a mugger ambushed Rufus and knifed him to death when Rufus tried to escape. Dummy tells them that the killer was a big man.

Dummy also tells them that Alberta Wright had visited his woman the previous night. Alberta explained to them that Rufus had stolen everything while she was in a religious trance. This was not the first time that Rufus had rooked her. They had been married for five years when he ran away with all of her money. She hoped that Dummy could tell her where Rufus was staying.

Dummy explained to Alberta about Rufus' furniture-stealing scam and told her how she could get her furniture back. Alberta rejected this and insisted on seeing Rufus, personally. Dummy offered to find him for her and during his search saw Rufus being murdered. He claims to know nothing about Sugar Stonewall or anything about anyone flashing a roll of money.

Ed and Digger decide to roust Sweet Prophet. They surprise him with the news that Alberta is alive, but he can offer them no explanation as to what happened during the baptism. Sweet Prophet also appears surprised by the story of the furniture theft and the two murders. He can see no connection between these events and Alberta's "death."

Himes jumps the story back in time again to the point where Sugar and Dummy parted company at Mammy Stormy's. Sugar, becoming increasingly suspicious, begins to think that "too much was happening for Alberta's money to have been a secret." The usually dull-witted Sugar begins to piece things together. He recognizes that whoever was watching the moving van from the street knew that somebody had already found the money. After the watcher killed the Jew and discovered that he didn't have it, the watcher would have realized that Rufus had outsmarted him. By then, Rufus would have been warned of the killer's approach and probably stashed the money in his apartment. Sugar figures that Rufus undoubtedly found the money early on and sold the furniture to the Jew to keep him from realizing that Rufus had it.

Leaving the whore for a moment, Sugar goes up to ask Mammy for sweet oil as an earache remedy for Dummy. While there on this pretense, he steals one of her enormous rose-colored nylon nightgowns and a yellow, orange, and white striped bath towel.

Down on the street, Sugar dresses himself in the gown and wraps the towel about his head. Thus dressed and accompanied by the whore, he goes to Rufus' apartment building and passes himself off to the janitor as an African doctor. His mission, he explains, is to treat George Clayborne (Rufus) for impotence. The janitor, who admits to having a young wife, expresses interest in this mysterious treatment.

Ordering the janitor to take off his clothes in his basement storeroom, Sugar starts a massage with the oil he got from Mammy Stormy. Soon, however, he turns the massage over to the young whore, whom he introduces as his assistant. While this is going on, Sugar steals the janitor's keys and breaks into Rufus' apartment and begins his search.

Before long, Dummy also enters the apartment and is attacked by Sugar. Dummy quickly overpowers Sugar and each is surprised to see the other there. Each admits that he is there looking for Alberta's money, so they decide to help each other and go their separate ways.

Meanwhile, Alberta is visited at the jail by a shyster lawyer who tells her he was sent by someone named Slick. He explains that if she will make a fifty-fifty split of her money with Slick, he will get her out of jail. Alberta, figuring that this Slick must know who the killer really is, answers that she will agree to the bargain if Slick will identify the killer to her. The shyster rejects this, and after an exchange of hard words he leaves her.

That same morning Dummy watches a big, flamboyantly-dressed young man emerge from the apartment house across from Sweet Prophet's temple. Dummy recognizes him as Rufus' killer. He follows him down to the ornate Roger Morris Apartment House. Here, the young man meets a well-dressed man whom Dummy identifies as Slick. After a brief meeting the two split up.

Dummy runs ahead and gets back to his starting point in time to see the killer reenter the apartment house just as Slick approaches the Temple. Dummy watches as Slick pulls a con on a pious-looking fat woman coming out of the Temple. He drops an envelope for her to find and, after she picks it up, he comes up and asks her if she found it.

After some bargaining, they count the money in the envelope, and discover $20,000.00, which Slick suggests that they divide equally. After some argument, the fat woman offers to let Slick hold the money in her attache case as collateral, since it contains Sweet Phophet's weekend take of only $3,000.00.

As soon as she enters the Temple, Slick and the killer pile into Slick's car and drive off. Dummy goes around to the rear of the Temple in time to see the woman ducking out the back door. He follows her to the bank where she attempts to deposit three thousand out of the twenty into Sweet Prophet's account. At the window, she becomes hysterical when she discovers that all she has is Confederate money.

Meanwhile, Alberta is arraigned and bound over to the Grand Jury on a $2,500.00 bond. In her cell, she tells a shoplifter that she needs to talk to Sweet Prophet. The shoplifter agrees to get a message to him and, faking a set of cramps, gets herself taken to the jail infirmary.

Sugar is in the courtroom when Alberta is arraigned. Lacking anywhere else to go, he returns to their empty apartment where he makes a final fruitless search. There he falls into an exhausted sleep.

At the same time, Dummy enters the young killer's rooms and searches them. Finding nothing, he leaves the apartment and goes around the corner. There, he sees the pick-up man for a numbers house. Writing a note, Dummy asks where the ever-moving numbers house is located that particular evening.

After hearing that it is at the Woodbine Hotel, Dummy taxis over and waits for Slick.

When Slick appears, Dummy informs him that the young killer is double-crossing him. Without hesitation, Slick takes Dummy along with him on his numbers-running rounds. On the drive, Slick questions the deaf-mute closely. Dummy explains that since even Alberta doesn't know where the money is, only the young killer can have it. Dummy believes that the killer is trying to con Slick into believing he doesn't have it, either. The pair continue to drive around collecting numbers receipts until the mid-afternoon. Finally Slick picks up the killer, named Susie, and they return to Slick's apartment.

Once there, Slick shows Susie the notes that Dummy has written to him. Susie attempts to kill the deaf-mute until Slick stops the fight at pistol point. He questions Susie, who insists on his innocence and accuses them of trying to frame him.

Susie admits to stealing Alberta's mattress from the back of the Jew's truck, but he swears that he found nothing. After awhile, the three men lapse into silence as they try to reason out what has happened.

At eight P.M., Alberta Wright gains entrance to Sweet Prophet's private apartment where she thanks the preacher for bailing her out of jail and asks for his help. She explains that when she had the dream about the exploding pies, she believed that the Lord was sending her a message. She played $20.00 on the money row in the three biggest numbers houses in Harlem. The dream came true and her $60.00 investment paid off for $36,000.00.

When Sweet Prophet chides the young woman for not sharing it with the Lord, Alberta explains that she had always intended to bring the money in, but felt that she should be baptized first. She had hidden the money in her mattress while Sugar was out of the apartment. On Sunday morning she had brought $500.00 to Sweet Prophet to pay for the baptism. The rest of the money was stolen, she insists, while she was unconscious.

She further confides to Sweet Prophet that she has not told the police about the money. Sweet Prophet advises her not to because they will be convinced of her guilt.

Sweet Prophet realizes that the only men in Harlem who knew anything about the money at all are the three payoff men who brought her the money from each of the numbers houses. Slick Jenkins was the last to show up at her apartment.

Sweet Prophet reasons that Slick must be the guilty man. He insists that Alberta go to Slick's place and demand the money from him, using threats of Sweet Prophet's vengeance to back the demand up. Alberta agrees to go.

At almost this same moment, Digger and Ed have come to some realizations of their own and they arrive at Sweet Prophet's right after Alberta's departure. They are curious about why Sweet Prophet went Alberta's bail. They are stunned to discover that he was not involved in the bailout and realize that they must find Alberta quickly. Their misgivings and fears are further confirmed when

Prophet admits knowledge of her numbers winnings and admits sending her to Slick to get the money back.

Angered by his callousness, they race to the Roger Morris Apartments only to find Slick's apartment empty except for his girlfriend. The doorman supplies the information that Slick is accompanied by Susie, the killer. As they stop long enough to put out an all points bulletin on Slick and Susie, they hear from Lieutenant Anderson that Sweet Prophet has reported Sugar Stonewall at the Temple.

They take him into custody, and he explains how Alberta threw him out after he got home late on the previous Saturday night. He became suspicious that Alberta may have taken a new boyfriend. As he went to spy through the bedroom window, he saw Susie already looking through the window.

Sugar watched Alberta all night and saw her visit Sweet Prophet the next day. He realized that she must have come into money but imagined at the time that any she might have was going to go to the Prophet. Later he discovered her getting ready for the baptism and went with her because he had nothing else to do.

When he heard Alberta tell her dream at the baptism, Sugar realized that she had hit the jackpot at all three of the big numbers houses. He could tell from the astonished look on Sweet Prophet's face that he didn't know anything about it. Sugar figured that the money must have been hidden somewhere in her apartment, so he spiked her water with a mickey finn that he always carried. When she fell unconscious, he took the opportunity to rush home and search the apartment.

Following his search, he called the Jew and Rufus, having made a deal that only her television would be stolen. His idea was that when Alberta found the television gone, she would be so frightened by the "robbery" that she would rush to wherever she had the money hidden, thus enlightening him to its whereabouts.

Sugar had left after making his calls to go get Alberta from the revival meeting. Discovering that she had been taken away in a hearse, he returned to the apartment, only to find that it had been cleaned out. He immediately went looking for Rufus, who denied having any knowledge of the furniture or the money. The detectives figure at this point that Rufus must have been the man who went to the warehouse and killed the Jew. Sugar vociferously denies that he was the other man who subsequently killed Rufus. He only admits to running away and being hidden by Dummy.

With all this information in hand, the detectives realize that Sugar must have teamed up with Dummy in order to steal Alberta's money. They immediately set out after Alberta in the hopes of preventing her death. Fortunately, they find her in her empty apartment, unconscious but still alive. After sending her to the hospital, they return to Slick Jenkins' apartment.

They use a trick that gets them in the apartment past Slick's girlfriend. The apartment is dark and quiet as they enter until Dummy bursts forth with blood running out of his mouth. Shots are fired on both sides, and Susie is killed in the exchange. Slick surrenders and claims not to know anything about anyone in the apartment.

Homicide Sergeant Frick arrives with the ambulance, and he immediately begins to question Slick's woman, who turns out to be blind. She informs them that it was actually Slick who killed the Jew. Slick knew of Alberta's big win through his connections and arranged for Susie to rob her in return for a fifty-fifty split. Susie had seen her hide the money in her mattress but because Sugar had been hanging around, the young killer had been unable to effect the robbery. Upon his return the next day, Susie had found Rufus and the Jew there.

From this Slick reasoned that either Rufus or the Jew had found the money. Slick had followed Rufus to the warehouse and had attacked Rufus after he had killed the Jew. Rufus stabbed Slick in the shoulder during the fight and got away. Later, Slick sent Susie after Rufus to get the money away from him. When Susie returned, he related to Slick that Rufus had only Confederate money. Slick, however, had not believed his ally. The Confederate money was subsequently used to cheat Sweet Prophet out of some of his own money.

Still later, Slick had met Dummy on his numbers payoff rounds and had confronted Susie with Dummy's accusations. Following that meeting, Slick had arranged for a bail bondsman to get Alberta out of jail. After Alberta got out, the trio had kidnapped and tortured her. They had only just returned when the detectives arrived.

Frick is still doubtful about her story until she tells them where to find Slick's bloodstained clothing and a wallet filled with the Jew's identification cards. Her motive for turning Slick in is revenge for his having blinded her and turned her into a drug addict.

Alberta stays in the hospital for six days recovering from her torture. On the seventh day, however, she gets her clothing back and sneaks out of her hospital room. On the way, she stops off in the kitchen where she peels potatoes for several hours. Afterwards, she leaves for Sweet Prophet's temple, taking the knife with her.

When Sweet Prophet comes out he expects Alberta to give him some money for a blessing. Instead she stabs him in the chest with her paring knife, nearly killing the charlatan.

Under police questioning she explains that after recovering from Slick's beating, she remembered that early the previous Sunday morning Sweet Prophet had hypnotized her into giving him all the money. After she did his bidding, he had ordered her to forget everything. The blow on the head made her realize that Sweet Prophet had been playing her for a sucker all along. The irony is that he needn't have hypnotized her. She had planned all along to give him all of the money if only he had asked her for it.

They jail her, but it is clear that she will be let out soon since Sweet Prophet was not killed. Sweet Prophet is unrepentant to the end, explaining to the Negro press that he took the money because he needed it to run his temple.

Of the eight Harlem novels, *The Big Gold Dream* stands out as both the most comic and the most inconsistent. The story contains most of the usual Himesian elements: a valuable missing object which is eagerly sought by several groups of desperate characters, a crooked street evangelist, a dope-crazed, knife-wielding killer, and a simple, sweet-natured sucker.

Himes keeps us deliberately off-balance all through this story. We never really understand just what is happening with anyone up until the very end. It seems that he deliberately obscured everything because so much of the story called for a willing suspension of disbelief.

For example, when Alberta suddenly collapses at the street revival, everyone believes she is dead. When she reappears later in the story, we get no explanation as to how she could have been believed dead by so many people, including the hearse driver and the attendants at the morgue where she awakens. Near the end of the story we are given the incomplete explanation that she was simply fed knockout drops. As far as is known, there is no such thing as a knockout drop that creates a state approaching suspended animation.

Himes also cheats the audience badly with the explanation he contrives for the ending. Sweet Prophet has had the missing money all the time, and he has hypnotized the gullible Alberta into forgetting that she gave it to him. Nothing in the story has prepared us for this ending, which borders on the supernatural. Also, Sweet Prophet's reaction when Alberta tells about her dream seems to indicate that her numbers payoff is a complete surprise to him. Combined with Sugar's belief in Prophet's ignorance this creates a double red herring.

Sweet Prophet has been presented to us as a member in good standing of Himes' corps of charismatic and unscrupulous street charlatans. He is much more flamboyant than any of the others, but he is also more buffoonish. With his grotesquely curling nails, purple mink-trimmed cape, buck teeth, and long, grizzly white hair, Sweet Prophet is positively clownish. He lacks the sinister madness of Reverend Short *(The Crazy Kill)* or the slick majesty of Deke O'Malley *(Cotton Comes to Harlem)*. Only the white hair provides a clue to the evil that lurks within his supposedly holy exterior.

Most of his appearances suggest only that he is a crooked showman. The sudden knowledge that he is also a hypnotist is as unsatisfying as his having the final words of the story. Himes leaves the reader with the distinct impression that Sweet Prophet is somehow going to get away with his duplicity. This is underscored by the fact that Coffin Ed and Grave Digger have very little part in the story and are not the ones to bring Sweet Prophet to book for his crimes.

More suspension of disbelief must be called up concerning the character of Sugar Stonewall. He is presented to us early in the story as a lazy, good-for-nothing Black boy who is getting along thanks to the intelligence and character of Alberta, with whom he lives. Sugar believes in his own stupidity and helplessness to a large degree. Early in Chapter 9, after Alberta has been taken to jail, and Sugar is locked out of their apartment, he dispassionately analyzes his situation:

He didn't have anything valuable enough to sell. He didn't have the talent to pick pockets, if there had been anybody's pocket to pick. He didn't have the nerve to rob anybody. He wasn't strong enough to mug. He hadn't made any connections with other women since he had had Alberta; he had been too lazy. He was a naturally lazy man.

Sugar has no thought of solving his problem by himself. He quickly comes to the conclusion that:

The main thing now was to get his woman back. Let her do the worrying. She'd find them some place to stay and something to eat. She might even find her money back. She was a strong, resourceful woman. He could depend on her.

After having made it abundantly clear that his male protagonist in this story is not only lazy but hopelessly inept, Himes confuses his audience by having Sugar make some astoundingly accurate deductions about what is going on. This first occurs in Chapter 12 after he has met Dummy and the young whore. Sugar immediately realizes that a lot of people know about the money Alberta won and that probably several of them are actively engaged in trying to find it. He also realizes that the deaths of Rufus and the Jew are connected to the theft of the money.

Later, in Chapter 21, he explains to Coffin Ed and Grave Digger how he realized that Alberta came to have such a large sum of money. Sugar believed that the only reason he was thrown out was because Alberta had come into money and didn't want him to find it. He claims that when he saw her praying beside her bed later, he knew she had money because he "...figgered right away that she had hit the numbers for a big stake...she hadn't had nothing before worth praying about."

The next day, when Alberta told her dream at the baptism, Sugar intuitively knew that the three exploding pies represented her having hit the money row at all three numbers houses. The avaricious look on Sweet Prophet's face suggested to the young man that the all-knowing street preacher had not gotten his hands on the whole sum. This kind of reasoning on the part of an avowed loafer, philanderer, coward, and self-confessed dope, is nothing short of miraculous. It is doubtful that Sherlock Holmes could have broken down the primary aspects of the case on the basis of so little information.

Sugar shows intellectual mettle on other occasions, as well. He rather quickly cooks up the scheme for posing as an African witch doctor in order to get into Rufus Wright's apartment and carries it off with a certain aplomb. During the course of this episode, he manages to outwit Mammy Stormy (herself an accomplished member of the Harlem underworld), the building janitor, and the janitor's nubile young wife.

Sugar is something of an anomaly in the Harlem canon, because he is a man fulfilling a female role. Most of the eight Harlem novels feature a male protagonist who is the archetypal square: dark-skinned, not particularly bright, but hard-working and honest. This male figure is typically played off against a light-skinned hustler who is brazenly unfaithful, duplicitous, and avaricious. For the first time and only time, Himes reverses the roles. In *The Big Gold Dream*, it is Alberta Wright who is dark-skinned, hard-working and dim-witted. Although she is referred to as the dependable and strong-willed member of the couple, she is also gullible and easily manipulated by the criminals in the story.

Sugar takes the role previously fulfilled by Imabelle and Dulcy Perry. He is apparently good-looking, but he is completely undependable. He admits that he has been "shacking up" with Alberta for eight months, and during that time he has done nothing but be her bedmate in return for her financial support. When Coffin Ed takes him to task for sleeping all day while Alberta goes out to work he explains, "You see boss, I been sick."

His other activities seem to include little except gambling and hanging out in bars. While he is too lazy to actively go out looking for other women during his abundance of spare time, he suffers no qualms about having sex with the janitor's wife at Rufus Wright's apartment building.

The *Big Gold Dream* is ostensibly about the role of organized gambling in the life of Harlem, and Himes goes to some lengths to show how it has become interwoven into the fabric of the city. Gambling, like prostitution, is so much an accepted part of life in the ghetto that there is room for healthy competition. There are no less than three active numbers houses constantly at work and constantly on the move to escape detection by the police or enemies.

Himes also shows an impressive knowledge of the numbers game in Chapter 18 when he has Dummy visit the Hotel Woodbine in his search for Slick Jenkins. Himes uses most of a full page to explain all the mechanics of the common man's game of chance. Having lived in the underworld as a gambler's apprentice, Himes fully understands the importance of this simple game in the day-to-day life of the urban poor.

Playing the numbers and similar games like punchboards have long been a part of lower class life, particularly during the Great Depression when these cheap and simple forms of gambling provided the urban poor with something to invest a few hopes in. "Hitting the number" has been, for many years, a symbol of changing luck and economic salvation for those living on the lower rungs of the economic ladder.

It is probably no accident that Himes played this symbol of economic salvation off against the more conventional salvation of organized religion. In Harlem, and indeed, every place that poor people pray to God for hope and peace, salvation is usually equated with money.

Much comment has been made in the recent past about television evangelists like Jim Bakker who actively draw parallels between God's love and the accumulation of wealth by the common man. In point of fact, the parallels that evangelists draw between God's love for mankind and man's material gain are probably a gauche interpretation of the Protestant Work Ethic. Since the time of the Puritans, Americans have been led to believe that hard work and trust in God will eventually lead to economic salvation. The tendency to pray in conjunction with playing the numbers is just a natural extension of that concept.

Himes realistically depicts this in Alberta's actions. Her dream about the three pies exploding is, to her, a sign from God that she should play the money row at all three of Harlem's numbers houses. Her gratitude is such that she not only decides to be baptized but also to give the winnings to Sweet Prophet, whom she sees as the Lord's representative on earth.

Alberta's feelings are underscored by Sugar Stonewall who tells Digger and Ed that she must have hit the big money because "she hadn't had nothing before worth praying about." Although Sugar, like all of Himes' gold-diggers, is too pragmatic to have any religion himself, he recognizes the connection between a big gambling win and the Lord's blessing among his fellow Harlemites.

Himes could not have been a religious man himself, because his view of organized religion as a corrupt and self-serving business enterprise occurs over and over in the Harlem series. This view reaches its maximum potential in this particular novel. As if to presage this viewpoint, the story begins with Sweet Prophet exhorting his flock to believe that "faith is a rock! It's like a solid gold dream!" Prophet follows up this exhortation with the more telling comment that "on this dream every church in all the world is built." In this way, Himes is suggesting that all churches are no more than elaborate money gathering machines that make promises of salvation to the poor in exchange for their hard-earned money.

Black religion has always tended to be an emotional experience, and Himes creates a colorful picture of a street full of disenfranchised lower-class Blacks standing on the hot pavement waiting for the Lord's blessing. As Alberta tells how her faith was rewarded, the other people in the street take up the cry of "Money! Money! Money!" because they are so excited that one of their own number has been touched by God.

Himes also depicts the marked sensuality of this kind of religious display. It is something that he has already shown in Reverend Short's church when the congregation goes into a fit of rolling ecstasy. At Sweet Prophet's revival, Himes draws attention to the fact that "the converts, most of whom were women, were seized by uncontrollable ecstasy. They danced and screamed and shouted and moaned, carried away with emotion, caught up in a mass delirium."

As they pray and tear off their clothes, Himes seems to be saying that the religious frenzy of these women is, in part, a sheer lust for money or material wealth. Alberta seems to substantiate this when she drinks the "blessed water" and begins to shout "I got Him inside of me! I got God inside of me. I can feel Him inside of my stomach!" Her lust for money has been so well rewarded by God's blessing that the ecstasy is almost sexual to her.

Himes does not feel contempt for Alberta and those like her; rather he seems to pity them. He reserves his contempt for Sweet Prophet and his followers and takes a number of opportunities to underscore this contempt. His first opportunity comes when Sergeant Ratigan of Homicide visits the Temple to question Sweet Prophet about Alberta's "death." Sweet Prophet denies that anyone would have deliberately killed "a great cook and a steady wage earner" like Alberta. Only God could have called her to Heaven "—as useful as she was to everybody." The duplicitous parson comes very close here to admitting how useful Alberta has been to him.

Another opportunity comes in Chapter 19 when the pious Black woman emerges from Sweet Prophet's Temple. Himes notes that "she looked like a sister who would say 'Amen' at the drop of a hat. The pious expression on her face fought a losing battle with a flaunting pride; her soul was saved and she knew it."

Although this is a minor character, she represents for Himes a microcosm of the world of self-satisfied religious people. These differ from the Albertas of the world because they have achieved some measure of financial security, and it has made them self-satisfied, arrogant, and extremely avaricious. He points up these aspects of her character when she finds the envelope Slick dropped outside the door to the Temple:

...suddenly her whole demeanor underwent a complete change. Greed replaced the pious expression on her face. Her dignity gave way to stealth.

Her cupidity replaces all manner of common sense, making it child's play for the well-named Slick to trick her out of Sweet Prophet's weekend "take." Her desolation when she discovers how she was tricked seems well-deserved, because both she and the reader realize that Sweet Prophet will understand that, in the course of being cheated, she was herself attempting to cheat him.

Himes ends this story with probably his slyest dig at religion. Alberta, who has already died and been resurrected earlier in the story, parodies God's seven day creation. After being wounded by Slick and Susie, she is hospitalized and rests for six days. On the seventh day, she gets up, arms herself with a kitchen knife, and visits the Anti-Christ in the form of Sweet Prophet. Her mind cleared of the trance that made her forget Prophet's theft, she symbolically stabs him in the side which hurts but does not kill him. Perhaps Himes is trying to tell us that nothing, not even holy intervention, can rid us of the Sweet Prophets of the world.

Digger and Ed seem to have very little to do with this story and, as in *The Crazy Kill*, the case could have been solved without them. Himes does not even bother to develop their characters or personalities here. They have a smaller part in this story than any other one in the canon, including *Imabelle*. They have nothing to do with the opening action and have no decisive part in the solution of the crime. Two of the most significant interrogations are conducted by white police sergeants.

They are twice robbed of the glory of physical confrontation with the criminals. When they visit Alberta's apartment to rescue her from Slick, "Grave Digger (leads) with Coffin Ed at his heels. Their pistols swung in gleaming arcs like the swords of warriors of old," but they arrive only to find the wounded Alberta in an empty room.

When they finally track Slick and the murderous Susie to their lair, for once the two detectives fire their guns in vain. Slick shoots his own confederate in the back when the detectives barge in. Himes suggests the impotent frustration the two have felt because they cannot arrest Sweet Prophet when he has them brutally beat Slick half to death.

The Big Gold Dream was probably Himes' most ambitious story to date. By concentrating on the manners and mores of the ghetto community and relegating Ed and Digger to a very minor role, he already seemed to be trying to move away from the detective story format. The story has little to do with the rousing, shoot-em-up kind of crime portrayed in previous books and, indeed, there is far less violence here than in any of the others.

His juxtaposition of religion and organized gambling shows a predisposition to use symbolic elements in the story to illustrate the complex issues in ghetto life. The rather flamboyant and ridiculous character of Sweet Prophet Brown seems to presage the symbolic characters that Himes would introduce later in *Cotton Comes To Harlem* and *Blind Man With A Pistol*.

Because of his marked use of symbolism and humor, *The Big Gold Dream* is the most amusing book in the Harlem series. However, it suffers from many weaknesses, not least of which is inconsistency in the makeup of some major characters and a conclusion that is weak and lacking in credibility. We know from his autobiography that at this early stage in the series, Himes was writing as quickly as he could in order to cash in on his newly-found popularity among his European audience. Undoubtedly the unevenness in this book results in part from his desire to quickly make money after so many years of financial distress.

His pace did not slacken, but his next effort would show a great deal more consistency in plot and in character. His attempts at experimentation would cease for a time, and he would return to a more traditional crime format with his detectives back in the forefront of the story.

Chapter IX
Digger's Temptation

"If you want to dance, go to the Theresa ballroom," she said in a cool contralto voice. "There's a matinee this afternoon."

"She was rather short and busty, with a pear-shaped bottom and slender legs. She had short, wavy hair, a heart-shaped face, and long-lashed, expressive brown eyes; and her mouth was like a red carnation...She wore gold lame slacks which fitted so tight that every quiver of a muscle showed...Her breasts stuck out from a turtleneck blue jersey-silk pullover as though taking dead aim at any man in front of her. "I was just relaxing a bit," Grave Digger lisped. "We've had a hard night."

She glanced at his swollen lips and broke out a slow, insinuating smile. "You shouldn't love so strenuously," she murmured.

Grave Digger felt the heat spread over his face.

Himes' original title for *All Shot Up* was the somewhat unevocative *Don't Play With Death*. Perhaps the break-neck pace, the violence, and the convoluted plot made more of an impression on the editors at Gallimard, because when it was issued in 1960, the title had been changed to *Imbroglio Negro*.

Of all the Harlem stories that Himes had written up to this time, this one has the most confusing plot. It was typical of Himes to jump backward and forward in time in all of these stories, but he seems to make greater use of this device here. The story is certainly the fastest-moving of the eight novels, and the increased number of time jumps contributes greatly to the story's overall pace.

Unlike any other Harlem novel, the story opens near midnight on a cold, snow-covered winter night. A man engaged in stealing a tire near Convent Avenue is surprised by the passage of a gold Cadillac. The occupants include an effeminate, well-dressed Black man named Baron, a merchant seaman named Roman Hill, and the tire thief's erstwhile girlfriend, Sassafras.

Before he can react, an old woman emerges into the street and is knocked down by the Cadillac, which immediately accelerates and drives away. The old woman has just managed to stagger up to a bent-over position in the street when a large black sedan roars up, hits her squarely in the backside and sends her sailing off into the darkness.

When the thief notices that the occupants of the black car are uniformed police officers, he starts running away, rolling his stolen tire in front of him like a hoop.

124

The occupants of the Cadillac are forced to the side of the road by the black sedan. Three uniformed cops, two of whom are Black, jump out with drawn guns and arrest the trio for hit and run. Baron offers the cops money and Sassafras' sexual favors to let them go.

The cops feign interest in the bribe and place Roman and the girl in their car. Before Baron realizes their intent, they knock him unconscious and take his money. The trio then jumps into the Cadillac and drives away with it. Outraged, Roman gives chase in the police car. The tire thief comes up on a motorcycle at this point and, seeing this reversed chase in progress, he bursts into laughter.

At the Harlem police precinct station, Lieutenant Anderson receives reports of multiple disturbances, but only one of them commands his instant attention. A double murder has occurred at the Paris Bar on 125th Street. One of the victims is reported to be Casper Holmes, an important Black politician. Anderson puts out a call for Digger and Ed and heads for the crime scene.

The two Black detectives meet Anderson at the scene where they discover two men shot and Casper Holmes unconscious. Ed recognizes one of the dead men as a notorious homosexual.

Inside the bar, which happens to be a homosexual hangout, a man explains to Ed that he saw two Black men and a white man dressed as policemen. The homosexual claims the trio pulled off a heist before escaping in a black sedan.

Shortly thereafter, a bartender comes forth with a further explanation. He tells them that it all started when a male erotic dancer called Snake-Hips began dancing outside the bar in order to taunt his cast-off lover. It seems that the dancer had recently taken on a new lover called Black Beauty and wanted to rub it in. The bartender identifies Black Beauty as the constant companion of a Broadway dandy named Mr. Baron.

The bartender also supplies the surprising news that Casper Holmes was a semi-regular customer of the bar. It seems that Holmes had gone out past the dancing Snake-Hips carrying a pigskin briefcase. He was just past the doorway when the dark sedan pulled up and two cops jumped out to grab him. As Holmes protested, one cop sapped him while another stole the briefcase.

At this point, another man appeared on the street and began shooting at the cops. When it was over, Snake Hips and the intruding gunman were both dead in the snow. The bartender noticed only that the dark sedan's license plate was a Yonkers issue and that the white cop had the bullying manner of a southern white. The bartender also finally admits that he was Snake Hips' cast-off lover and bursts into tears over his loss.

Digger and Ed decide to take the bartender downtown for more questioning. Outside, they find out from Anderson that the intruding gunman was actually a Pinkerton detective. Before they can head downtown, a radio call comes in about the hit and run on Convent Street.

At Convent Street they find the body of the old Black woman imbedded in the convent wall. In quick succession, they make several discoveries. First, upon removing the body from the wall they discover that the old woman is actually a young person dressed up in old woman's clothes. Shortly thereafter the coroner arrives and during his examination reveals that the corpse is male. Later they will discover from the homosexual bartender that the corpse is Black Beauty.

While all this is going on, Ed notices a car jacked up nearby and surmises that a local tire thief probably witnessed the kill. He observes that anyone stealing tires in that weather must have a "hot skirt" to support.

When they return to the precinct, Anderson explains that the secretary of the national committee of Casper Holmes' political party had left $50,000.00 in organizational expense money at Holmes' office at about ten-twenty P.M. the previous evening. Holmes had hinted that he might take the money home with him rather than leave it in his office safe over the weekend. The concerned secretary took the liberty of asking Pinkerton to detail a man to unobtrusively cover Holmes for the night.

The detectives reason that the heist was too professionally handled to have been organized in just a few hours time. Far too much preparation had been involved.

Digger is convinced that the hit and run is somehow connected with the heist. In both instances, homosexuals were viciously killed. The viciousness combined with the homosexuality angle is too much coincidence. They also have an idea that the tire thief could help them if he could be identified.

Himes jumps his story back in time here to the point where Roman and Sassafras take up the chase for the gold Cadillac. Shortly after they lose their quarry, Baron comes to consciousness in the back of the car and demands to call the police. After some argument, Roman drives Baron to a bar where he manages to elude them.

After some fruitless searching, Sassafras suggests going to see Lady Gypsy, the transvestite fortune teller. Lady Gypsy, who is also a stool pigeon, calls Digger and Ed to tell them that the drivers of the black sedan with Yonkers plates are at his shop.

When the detectives arrive, they find Gypsy unconscious. After they bring him to, he relates to the detectives the whole story of the hit and run, the fracas with the phoney cops, and the rest. He explains that Roman Hill had been driving the Cadillac, which he had purchased from Baron. Gypsy identifies Roman's female companion as Sassafras Jenkins.

Roman, it seems, had met Baron on the Brooklyn docks. Two months back, Baron had given Roman a lift in his own Cadillac and Roman mentioned a desire to own a car like it. When Baron heard that Roman had saved $6,500.00, Baron promised to get a Cadillac for him for that exact amount.

Lady Gypsy tells the detectives that he doesn't know Baron, but knew his friend Black Beauty as a working pimp. Sassafras, on the other hand, is just a working girl who always has a racket going on the side. He tells Digger and Ed where she can be found.

The scene jumps back yet again to just after the time Roman and Sassafras have slugged Lady Gypsy. Telling him that she knows a man who knows more about double-dealing than anyone in Harlem, Sassafras offers to take Roman to him. The man is, of course, the tire thief who witnessed the hit and run.

Roman is somewhat suspicious of the fact that his erstwhile girlfriend has a key to a strange man's place, but her artful lying and her seductive powers quickly take his mind off of his questions. Soon they are locked in a sexual embrace.

On the way to Sassafras' crib, Digger and Ed spot a man in a motorcycle and sidecar combination. In the sidecar are two auto tires. The late hour, the bitter cold, and the tires make the detectives suspicious and they begin to follow the cyclist. Spotting the tail, the motorcyclist is soon careering down the icy streets with the detectives racing after him.

At a fateful moment, the cyclist tries to maneuver between two trucks, hoping that he can elude them. Ed fires his revolver at the fleeing man but hits, instead, the tire of one of the trucks. The truck driver, hearing his tire go, hits his brakes. This action serves to throw off the motorcyclist's timing. As he veers to miss the truck, he hits three sheets of stainless steel that are projecting from the truck and is decapitated.

By this time, Sassafras and Roman have spent their passion, eaten, gotten drunk, and had sex again, after which they fall into a deep sleep. Digger and Ed discover the lovers in this post-coital slumber. Upon awakening Roman they find themselves with a tiger by the tail. As tough as the detectives are, the giant seaman gives them a terrific battle before they subdue him. In the confusion, Sassafras escapes.

Later that same Sunday morning, the detectives visit Casper Holmes in his hospital room, in spite of his efforts to keep them out. They explain to the politician all that has transpired, including the connection among Roman, Sassafras, the mysterious Baron, and the phoney cops. They explain further that a white man named Bernard Kaufman who acted as a notary in the sale of the Cadillac is also involved.

When they tell Holmes about the deliberate killing of an old woman who turned out to be Black Beauty, Holmes reacts visibly. Sensing an advantage, Ed bores in with the news that Black Beauty has been identified as one Junior Ball and that Holmes' wife made the identification and funeral arrangements.

Holmes, regaining his composure, gets tough and pretends indifference to the news, explaining that Junior Ball was his wife's cousin. However, Holmes gets inexplicably angry when Ed wonders why a trio of bandits who just robbed Holmes of fifty grand would deliberately run down and kill his wife's cousin.

Holmes insists that the robbers must be outsiders. Also, since nobody except Holmes and the party secretary knew about the money, the leak had to come from outside the city. All Holmes wants now is revenge for the insult on his own turf. He wants the case solved with as little publicity as possible.

Later that same day, Digger and Ed visit Casper Holmes' apartment where they meet his wife Leila. A striking, sensual beauty, she tantalizes both men, especially the usually sensible and forthright Digger. Mrs. Holmes denies any knowledge of Baron or her cousin's shady private life. The attraction between Leila and Digger is so strong, however, that she becomes flustered and sends them to one Zog Ziegler in order to get them out of the apartment. Ziegler, it seems, was Black Beauty's associate in a dress designing business.

By the late afternoon, the police top brass have just finished interviewing Casper Holmes. Alone finally, he receives a call from the Pinkerton Detective Agency. The agency man informs Holmes that the national party secretary, has arranged for Pinkerton to pick Casper up when he leaves the hospital.

Hanging up from that call, Holmes quickly calls Joe Green, the biggest numbers banker in Harlem. He informs Green that he is sneaking out of the hospital at seven-thirty that evening in H. Exodus Clay's hearse and asks Green to detail two strong-arm men to cover him. After Green agrees, Holmes calls Clay and arranges for Jackson to drive him to his office.

Following these calls, Holmes contacts Leila and tells her he will be home around eight P.M. He orders her to hang around until nine P.M. After that she can go where she wants. She is to tell anyone who calls in the meantime that he is still in the hospital in a coma.

After receiving a call from the party secretary, Holmes makes one more call to someone named Johnny. He tells Johnny to meet him at his home around ten P.M. and instructs the man to use his own key to get in.

At almost that same moment, Leila Holmes receives a second phone call. Expecting Casper, she is surprised to find a redneck southern voice at the other end. The voice frightens her with its undercurrent of sadism. The caller tells Leila that if Casper wants to get his fifty grand back that he will have to talk to the caller and his gang. When Leila tries to stall, the line goes dead.

At six-twenty P.M. the same cracker voice calls Clay's funeral home. The voice identifies himself as a Pinkerton detective. The cracker instructs Clay that he is sending three men to the funeral parlor to guard the ambulance that is going to pick up Casper Holmes. What Clay doesn't realize is that the voice has called sixteen other ambulance services before getting the desired response. Clay, not knowing any better, informs the voice that the job doesn't require any gun-toting detectives, inadvertently betraying Holmes to his enemies.

Meanwhile, Digger and Ed have become very suspicious of Holmes. They decide to remove Roman Hill from jail and take him around to help them find and identify Baron. They travel across the Brooklyn Bridge to where Leila has told them they will find Zog Zeigler. Once there, the detectives send Roman inside with instructions to pretend to be a friend of Black Beauty's and to ask for him by the name of Junior Ball. They tell Roman that once he is inside, he is to ask when Mr. Baron will be in.

Back at Clay's funeral parlor, tragedy is about to strike. Joe Green's strong-arm men are waiting in their car for the hearse to get underway when out of nowhere a drunk appears and begins to urinate on their car. An altercation ensues, causing the two leg-breakers to lower their guard just long enough for them to be attacked and killed by the cracker and his two pals. The three killers commandeer Green's Cadillac and follow the hearse down the street.

Using a ruse to escape the reporters clustered at the hospital, Holmes has himself loaded into the waiting hearse and orders Jackson to take him to his office. Believing that the following Cadillac contains Joe Green's boys, Holmes has Jackson signal to them before he alights from the hearse and disappears into his office. Once Jackson has gone, the three thugs enter the building behind him.

By this time, Roman has emerged from Zog Zeigler's building somewhat dazed from the experience of being heavily courted by high-class homosexuals. Apparently, no one there knew Baron, and when he did not appear, Roman left. Ed and Digger know that something is about to break. Calls to the hospital and to Leila avail them nothing. The hospital has been instructed to give out no information about Holmes, and Leila deliberately lies to them.

Ed notes that if he were Casper, he would get out of the hospital as soon as he could. Roman mentions at this point that Holmes has already left the hospital. He had heard the homosexuals at Zeigler's house talking about Casper's call to Johnny which let them know he would be home by eight P.M. It is thirteen minutes before eight at that very moment.

Thinking feverishly, the two detectives realize that Casper would probably use a private ambulance to leave the hospital, or perhaps a hearse. Thinking instantly of H. Exodus Clay, they race to the nearest phone to call him. Clay informs them about the plans and about the call from the man he thought was a Pinkerton detective. Another quick call to Pinkerton's confirms their worst fears.

Ed and Digger quickly come up with a plan that will require the help of Roman and Sassafras. With a little persuasion, they get Roman to tell them where to find the girl.

Shortly thereafter, the detectives call Casper Holmes' apartment and one of them imitates the voice of Bernard Kaufman, the phoney notary public who helped Baron to swindle Roman. Leila feigns ignorance about their questions and quickly hangs up. The detectives expect this and station themselves and their two prisoners across from the apartment.

Soon Leila Holmes comes out and hurries toward the corner of Fifth Avenue. When she comes under a street light, Sassafras instantly recognizes her as Baron. After a short struggle, the detectives subdue Leila and tell her that Casper is in danger.

Chagrined at her unmasking, Leila asks how they figured her out. Ed explains that Baron had to be a woman or he'd have been known to the homosexual clique. Roman's visit proved that no one in the clique knew her.

Digger and Ed explain to Leila that Casper's life will depend on how quickly she tells them what they need to know. Leila explains that she recognized the phoney white cop after the hijack of the gold Cadillac. She had seen him talking to Casper the previous Friday morning. She then remembered Casper putting in a long-distance call to Indianapolis the night before, right after he'd gotten word of the money from the party secretary.

Leila figured out that Casper had hired the criminals to stage the robbery on his behalf. She believes that the cracker and his friends have kidnapped Casper because he must have tried to double-cross them.

A few minutes later, Leila enters Casper's office and is grabbed by one of the two Black men in the gang. She quickly tries to take control of the situation by rubbing her body against that of the gunman. Between the smell of her perfume and the rubbing, the gunman is soon afire with lust.

The office has been torn apart in the search for the money, and Casper is spread-eagle on the carpet with his arms and legs tied to the furniture. He has been stripped and beaten.

The white man has cut Casper's eyelids off and is threatening to cut off his testicles as Leila arrives. When she identifies herself, the cracker immediately decides to kill her. Rubbing up against her black captor, Leila pleads for her life.

The Black gangster swears he will not allow Leila to be killed, and an argument ensues between him and the cracker. Leila works to keep up the tension, and the situation becomes even more confused when the second Black man tries to act as peacemaker.

In desperation, Leila lunges for the window and pulls up the shade. The cracker stabs her before Ed and Digger shoot all three men. Only the cracker survives the battle.

The detectives untie Casper who gets to his hands and knees. When his gaze locks onto that of the cracker, he grabs a gun from the floor and kills the white man. Ed, crazed with anger, almost clubs out Casper's brains until Digger intervenes.

Leila lies on the floor clutching the knife in her abdomen as Digger comforts her and strokes her hair. His tender feelings for her are obvious but, in his businesslike way, he tells her "it's all over but the lying."

Soon Casper is back in the hospital bandaged from head to his toe. He calls in his attorney and instructs him to get any charges against Roman dropped. Hill is to be reimbursed for the $6,500.00 he lost and placed on the first ship out. Casper also instructs the attorney to file a claim in Roman's name for the $6,500.00 found on the cracker's body and to have H. Exodus Clay keep all of the effects on the killers' bodies for Casper's personal inspection.

By noon that same day two detectives from the Automobile Squad strike a Cadillac showroom where they have located the gold-colored Cadillac, but no one knows how it got there. One of the company's oldest salesmen, Herman Rose, closely resembles the description of Bernard Kaufman, but without Roman's identification the police have to leave him alone.

Other police have turned Casper's building upside down, but there is no sign of the money. Digger and Ed are forced to admit that they can't prove a thing against the wily Black politician.

Later that evening, they explain what they know to Lieutenant Anderson. It seems that there was no relation between Casper's swindle or the caper Leila was pulling in her Baron persona. Leila had met Rose when Casper bought his own Cadillac. When she met Roman and found out about his money plus his desire for a Cadillac, she got Rose and Black Beauty together to help her separate the big seaman from his savings.

Rose's part was finished after the transfer of the car. Leila was supposed to take Roman down the deserted street where Black Beauty was waiting to fake the hit and run. Afterwards, they would return the car to the showroom and keep Roman's money.

The three hoodlums, fresh from their fake robbery of Casper, rounded the corner in time to see the fake hit and run. On the spur of the moment, they decided to grab a car that couldn't be reported as stolen. They deliberately killed Black Beauty so nobody could go to the police about the hijack. The killers eventually took the car back to the showroom themselves for convenience sake.

Ed and Digger believe that Leila is innocent of any involvement in Casper's caper. In fact, they believe that Leila actually hates him because he is a homosexual. The implication is that Casper has used Leila as a front all these years in order to protect his secret life. Paradoxically, Leila admired Casper for his achievements and did not want him hurt.

The only question left unanswered is the whereabouts of the money. Suddenly, the detectives get an idea and take off for Clay's mortuary. Once there, they ask Clay for the effects belonging to one Lucius Lambert. Clay is reluctant to help, but eventually shows them the effects.

They discover nothing of any value except a box of stockings. Removing the lid, they discover fifty thousand dollars inside. Lucius Lambert, it seems, was the homosexual known as Snake Hips, killed outside the bar where Casper was robbed. He was also the only one to whom Casper could have passed the money before being sapped.

Ed observes that, "This boy would never have been dancing on the street half dressed on a night as cold as Saturday just to bitch off that square bartender."

They also note that Casper probably counted on their not finding out Snake Hips' real name. In order to pay Casper back for his duplicity, Digger and Ed take the money and donate it anonymously to the *New York Herald*

Tribune Fresh Air Fund, which sends young ghetto boys to the country on vacations. To Casper they send a telegram which reads "crime doesn't pay."

With this book, Himes relied much more on fast pacing than thoughtful plotting. The story has none of the symbolic elements Himes experimented with in *The Big Gold Dream,* and it displays all of the violence and sexual titillation that made the series so popular. Although Himes presented strong, colorful characters, the story still lacks consistency, and a number of important questions are left unanswered at the conclusion.

If the story is outstanding for any reason, it must be for the violence. Before the story has progressed much beyond the first few chapters, three people are dead, and another two have been knocked unconscious. The violent scenes in this story all share a strong element of macabre absurdity.

The sense of absurdity is best exemplified in the death of Black Beauty. The manner of his death is absolutely comical. Later, when the body is discovered embedded in the wall the comedy is continued when the medical examiner changes his identification of the victim over and over again. The victim is transformed from old woman to young woman and finally young man before it is finally determined that it is actually a notorious homosexual and female impersonator.

Digger and Ed's chase of Sassafras' boyfriend through the snowy streets of Harlem is a classic of example of Himes' use of black humor:

He wheeled sharply to the left, but not quickly enough. The three thin sheets of stainless steel...formed a blade less than a quarter of an inch thick. This blade caught the rider above his woolen-lined jacket, on the exposed part of his neck, which was stretched and taut from his physical exertion, as the motorcycle went underneath...the blade severed his head from his body as though he had been guillotined.

His head rolled halfway up the sheets of metal while his body kept astride the seat and his hands gripped the handlebars. A stream of blood spurted from his severed jugular, but his body completed the maneuver which his head had ordered and went past the truck as planned.

Not satisfied with this, Himes goes on to tell how the truck continues down the street and climbs the steps of a "big fashionable Negro church" which has out front the announcement "Beware! Death is closer than you think!"

Himes seems to be on something of a roll throughout this whole scene. Digger and Ed wreck their car and are superficially hurt, prompting Digger to comment, "I'd have been better off with the Asiatic flu." The headless body, now on its second page of text, finally gives out of blood and crashes the motorcycle into a credit jewelry store with a sign that reads, "We Will Give Credit to the Dead." This kind of giddiness is unusual, because although we are used to excessive violence in this series, it is out of the ordinary for Himes to make such a running joke out of it.

This tendency to make violence and gore funny is an interesting aspect of Himes' personality and is something he shares with very few other writers. Possibly this trait developed during his days on the street and in prison. We know now that people who are faced with death and bloodshed, such as police officers and emergency room personnel, also tend to make jokes about such things. Modern thought explains this kind of behavior as a way to relieve stress. Himes used so much of his writing as a way of working out his personal feelings that perhaps his comical depictions of mayhem were his way of mitigating the violence he carried inside himself.

Himes lets us even further into the lives of his detectives in this novel, providing us with insights not previously seen. A particularly interesting scene takes place early in the story when the two detectives are enjoying a hot meal in Mammy Louise's pork store. For the first time in the series, someone intimate with the Black detectives takes them to task for their violent ways:

"You p'licemens," she said scornfully. "Gamblin' an' carryin' on and' whippin' innocent folkses' heads with your big pistols."
"Not if they're innocent," Grave Digger contradicted.
"Don't tell me," she said argumentatively. "I has seen you." She curled her thick sensuous lips.
"Whippin' grown men about as if they was children."

Later, Mammy moans:

"Trouble, always trouble in dis wicked city. Whar ah comes from—"
"There ain't no law," Coffin Ed cut her off as he put on his jacket. "Folks cut one another's throats and go on about their business."
"It's better than gettin' kilt by the law," she argued. "You can't pay for one death by another one. Salvation ain't the swapping market."
"Tell it to the voters, Mammy," (Ed) said absently..."I didn't make these laws."

As the two detectives begin to rush from the room to answer a radio call, something happens that serves as testimony to Mammy's conviction that Digger and Ed are out of control. A bulldog that she keeps gets frightened by their sudden movement and jumps at them. Without any thought on his part "Grave Digger's long, gleaming, nickel-plated revolver came out in his hand like a feat of legerdemain..." but Mammy drags her foolish pooch out of the way before any damage is done.

This is almost a throw-away scene. By this point in the series, we have grown to know Ed and Digger and even feel some affection for them. Each has shown flashes of humanity and even regret over the ills of the city. This knowledge of their intrinsic decency, combined with the reader's acceptance of violence as their method of purging Harlem has anesthetized us (and them) to their ritual bloodletting. The fact that a dog could come so close to death just for standing in their paths underscores vividly the fact that these two men have totally lost their perspective. They are no longer simply the agents of the law; they have become a law unto themselves. Anyone in their way can be judged and executed simply for being in the wrong place at the wrong time.

Perhaps more interesting than this realization is Himes' depiction of Digger's unbridled passion for Leila Holmes. When Leila enters the room, she begins flaunting her considerable sexuality in order to place the detectives at an uncomfortable disadvantage. Her animal magnetism, combined with her haughtiness, only tends to heat Digger's blood. He angers her with his close questioning, but her temper only causes him to bore in harder. The antagonism between them is a flimsy mask for the building sexual tension:

She kept staring into Grave Digger's hot, rapacious gaze until her body seemed to melt; and she sat down again as though from lack of strength.

By the time that the interview is over, the tension between them is so thick that Leila is near tears.

Later, after Leila is wounded in the fight with the three gangsters, Digger's lust for her turns to tenderness as he comforts her. The story ends with Leila still in the hospital fighting for her life, and we never find out whether or not Digger and Leila rekindle their desire for each other.

Digger surprises us again in the story when he and Ed stop at a lagoon in Central Park where boys and girls are skating on the ice. Digger remarks to his partner that it "reminds me of Gorki."

"The writer or the pawnbroker?" Coffin Ed asked.
"The writer, Maxim. In his book called *The Bystander*. A boy breaks through the ice and disappears. Folks rush to save him but can't find him—can't find a trace of him. He's disappeared beneath the ice. So some joker asks, 'Was there really a boy?' "

Coffin Ed looked solemn. "So he thought the hole in the ice was an act of God?"
"Must have."
"Like our friend Baron, eh?"

In many ways, this conversation is the most startling element of the story. The tradition of the hard-boiled dick requires that he sometimes display some trace of intellectuality, but it is a particular surprise coming from Digger. Although he is the more thoughtful of the two detectives, the crudity of his speech and his poverty-stricken background seem to leave little room for this sudden knowledge of a writer as esoteric as Gorki.

It is also interesting that Himes would give his detective the opportunity to express this parallel that exists between the murder case and the Russian novel. Besides highlighting this hitherto unrevealed subtlety in Digger's character, Himes takes this opportunity to give the reader a hint that the mysterious Baron does not exist at all. Digger apparently has some notion at this particular point in the story, but Leila's unmasking is a surprise to everyone else.

In addition to this literary awareness, we discover in this story that the heroes share both a sense of honor and a sly sense of humor with some of their literary forebears. When they discover the whereabouts of the money Casper has stolen, they resist the urge to keep it, even though it would make them both rich by Harlem standards. Instead, they give it to charity and send a mocking note to their powerful antagonist.

Casper's political power is absolute. With a few phone calls, he is able to remove potential witnesses against Leila and himself. By so doing, he so hopelessly muddles the case that all the detectives in New York cannot clear it up. Digger and Ed know that they are too weak to pull Casper down, but, in the tradition of such puckish heroes as Til Eulenspeigel, they tweak his nose to show him they have not been fooled.

For the first time, we get some understanding of how Digger and Ed got onto the police force. During their initial interview with Holmes we find that he apparently had something to do with their getting on the force. Digger and Ed, quick to exert their independence from anyone, point out their distinguished army records and high civil service exam scores had as much to do with it as Casper did.

Himes created some of his most compelling characters for this story, none of them more so than Casper Holmes. Holmes is depicted as the most powerful political figure in Harlem, a man who has come up from the bottom and now has it all. He owns an entire floor of an exclusive apartment building and is married to a beautiful show-girl. He has been so successful in getting the vote out in Harlem that he is courted by white politicians and is on a first-name basis with the national party secretary.

But Casper is not what he seems. In spite of his greatness and the significance of his accomplishments, Holmes is one of Himes' worst characters. Although he has black skin, he is one of several ambiguous actors in the series. Along with whiteness, homosexuality was another Himesian signal for an evil or unscrupulous nature. Even though Casper is a powerful Black politician who has done much for Harlem, at bottom he is an egotistical and self-serving scoundrel whose main concern is his own enrichment. Once we realize that he is a closet homosexual, we are tipped off to the fact that he is not what he seems in other realms of behavior as well.

During the course of this story, Holmes racks up an impressive list of crimes. He steals $50,000.00 from the party and consorts with thieves and killers. In addition, he is indirectly involved in the deaths of seven people, the attempted murder of two more, and is the actual murderer of yet another.

On top of all this is the taint of his homosexuality. Although Himes never says anything openly against homosexuality, he indirectly condemns it by the kinds of homosexual characters he creates. All are prostitutes, killers, or at best moral weaklings. In spite of the fact that Holmes radiates masculinity and power, he is soiled because he shares a secret with a group of people whom Himes considers unsavory.

One question that is left unanswered about Casper Holmes is why he steals the money in the first place. It is never explained why he concocts this elaborate plot, participates in all of these crimes, and risks his own death. Holmes seemingly holds all of Harlem in the palm of his hand. When Digger and Ed approach the door to his apartment and read the brass panel with Holmes' name, Digger comments that it "might just as well say Jesus Christ." To such a man, $50,000.00 must be a trifling sum.

It is interesting to note that *All Shot Up* is the only one of the eight Harlem stories to take place in the dead of winter. In every other story the action takes place in the summer, and the sizzling heat seems to underscore the passion of the characters as they grasp for and lust after missing treasure. Here the frigidity of the weather was Himes' way of providing a backdrop that would hint at the essentially cold-blooded nature of Casper Holmes, his secret sexuality, and his crimes.

Leila Holmes shares with Casper a compelling personality, unexplained questions, and sexual ambiguity. With her "pear-shaped bottom," breasts that stick out from her pullover "as though taking dead aim at any man in front of her," and a "mouth like a red carnation," she is Himes' sexiest woman to date. The fact that Digger falls under her power proves that she is unusual.

This hypersexuality is underscored by a wide leather belt with gilded designs about her waist. The designs "depicted a series of Pans with nude males and females caught in grotesque postures on their horns." And yet, almost from the beginning, there is a subtle suggestion that all is not right with her.

A careful reader will remember that an early description of Baron includes short, wavy hair just like Leila's and "eyes that were unusually expressive for a man" but which fitted well in his heart-shaped face.

The question that looms largest about Leila is why she is masquerading as a man and engaging in a con game? As the wife of the most powerful politician in Harlem, money could not be the answer, yet Casper, himself, is engaged in a similar but larger game. Himes never satisfies our curiosity about either of them.

Leila's true sexuality is never explained, either. Although she and Digger light fires in each other, Leila has apparently been cross dressing for more than a year, and, in addition, there have been mysterious dealings with her cousin, Black Beauty, and his homosexual partner, Zog Zeigler. Himes leaves the story with Leila in the hospital, her recovery as much in doubt as the reasons for her inexplicable behavior.

Roman Hill is another archetypal square. He is as masculine as Johnny Perry but as stupid as Jackson. Like Johnny, he attempts to solve the mystery on his own, but he lacks the sophistication to figure out all of the political and sexual trickery that is going on behind the scenes.

Sassafras Jenkins is also an Himesian archetype, but she seems more like a Harlem version of a wood nymph than a typical gold digger. As a schemer she lacks the cunning present in Imabelle and the viciousness that later surfaces in Ginny (*Heat's On*) and Iris O'Malley (*Cotton*). Although she is known to the police as a prostitute, she seems to be simply a fun-loving girl who lives with one man after another as her means of support. She is possibly the most harmless and likeable character of her type in the series.

Himes had a penchant for depraved, knife-wielding killers, but the "cracker" is the first such character to appear with white skin. Other vicious crackers would appear in *Cotton*, but they would lack the depravity and mongrel appearance of this one. It is appropriate that, in this story of sexual ambiguity, this character is virtually the only one who is immune to Leila's charms.

Just prior to the climactic gunfight in Casper's office, the Negro gunman is willing to jeopardize the entire caper because of his attraction to Leila. The cracker is totally indifferent and wants to kill her from the outset. This lack of interest in her charms, coupled with his business deal with Casper, provides a strong suggestion that this vicious character may be a homosexual himself. His symbolic rape of Leila with a switchblade knife tends to add weight to this notion.

This novel tells us more about the detectives, and we see genuine growth in their personalities. At the same time, they are faced with a well-defined crime that must be solved, and the pace of the story is quickened by their efforts to track down witnesses and also unmask the imposters.

With all of its strengths, the story is plagued with weaknesses. The motivations of two of the most important characters are never clear, and the story ends with no real explanation of why the crimes were committed in the first place. Himes' failure to explain major plot elements in some of these early stories has to be linked to the haste in which they were written.

The weaknesses in this particular story may have been a signal that although Himes was happy for the celebrity and money the series was bringing him, he was nevertheless tired of writing formula fiction. He was over halfway through the series and was nearing a critical juncture in his relationship with it. In the story that would follow *All Shot Up*, Himes would return to his original themes and produce his most coherent story thus far.

Chapter X
Brothers In Arms

The youth skidded forward on his hands and elbows, scraping off the skin, and Coffin Ed closed in.

Now the two jokers decided to take the youth's part. They turned toward Coffin Ed grinning confidently and one said in a jocular voice, "What's the trouble, daddy-o?"

Their eyes popped simultaneously. One saw the nickel-plated revolver and the other saw Coffin Ed's face.

"Great Godalmightly, it's Coffin Ed!" the first one whispered.

Nineteen sixty-one marked the end of the first flush of feverish activity that had produced the Harlem Domestic series and made Himes a financially successful writer. His sixth entry in the series was originally entitled *Be Calm* and Gallimard issued it that way, calling it *Ne nous énervons pas.*

While all of the previous five stories share some characteristics with each other, the book that would be published in America as *The Heat's On* has some marked similarities with *For Love of Imabelle.* Most of the characters in *Heat* are bizarre, narcotics-using lowlife. A two-timing high-yellow woman precipitates much of the action, and most of all, the detectives are separated through misadventure for much of the story. Once again, bad judgment causes one to be seriously wounded, and a routine police case turns into a quest for personal revenge by the other.

As the story opens, Pinky, a giant-sized, milk-white albino Negro, and Jake, a hunch-backed dwarf, are standing outside Riverside Episcopal Church on Riverside Drive.

For some reason, Pinky is pressing Jake for assurances of friendship. While Jake puzzles over this, it becomes clear that Pinky has turned in a fire alarm because several fire engines are converging on the spot. Jake begins stuffing heroin packets into his mouth to prevent the police from finding them on him.

When the cops and firemen arrive, the sexton of the church rushes out to tell them that Pinky is the one who has turned in the false alarm. Jake finally breaks free and begins to run away, only to be caught in mid-stride by the arrival of Coffin Ed and Grave Digger. They see that he has been swallowing heroin and hit him in the stomach hard enough to make him vomit it up. They spread out a handkerchief to catch the vomit and heroin packets, and the dwarf passes out on the grass.

The two detectives notice the altercation and go over to investigate. Although the Negro boy's feeble-minded attempts to explain himself are making the fire captain angrier and angrier, the two detectives eventually are able to make sense of his story. He believes that his stepmother and her African lover are in the process of murdering his father. He claims that he pulled the fire alarm simply to call attention to the crime.

This admission creates a brawl, and most of the firemen attack the huge albino with axe handles. It is all that Ed and Digger can do to prevent his murder, and in the confusion he escapes. Unnoticed by virtually everyone is the unconscious body of Jake Kubansky the pusher, who is trampled in the melee. Frustrated and angered by the stupidity of the firemen, the two detectives go to investigate Pinky's claims.

About a block down, they enter the basement of a white apartment building in order to find Pinky's father Gus, who is janitor of the building. At Gus's apartment they find a young African watching with relish as a sexy, cat-eyed high-yellow woman does a suggestive dance.

Although the woman treats Digger and Ed with complete contempt, they discover that she and Gus are going to Ghana. She shows them luggage tagged for the Queen Mary.

They also discover a huge, ferocious dog that Ginny, the woman, says belongs to Pinky. When Digger presses her about Pinky's relationship to her, she explains that Pinky is not Gus's son, only someone for whom he felt pity and kept around. More questioning reveals that Pinky is a heroin addict (something they had already guessed) and that the young African sold Gus a plantation in Ghana. The money from this purchase is supposed to have come from the sale of a farm left to Gus by his first wife.

Ginny takes note of all the sirens outside and asks about the cause of the excitement. When Digger explains Pinky's accusations, Ginny erupts with fury, claiming that Pinky is jealous of Africans because he isn't black. The detectives have heard sillier things in Harlem, and they depart.

Back at the station house, they discover from Lieutenant Anderson that Pinky is still on the loose. He also astounds them with the news that Jake is in the hospital.

After dinner, the two detectives return to Gus's house on a hunch. There, they see the African walking Pinky's gigantic dog into the park and return shortly thereafter without it. They experience a rare moment of indecision over this puzzling event and indulge in an even rarer quarrel before going home.

The scene shifts backward in time to an hour after the melee at Riverside Church and follows Pinky to an old house at the end of an unfinished street in the Bronx. The frantic sounds of a piano pounding out a boogie beat emanate from the gabled attic.

His knock is answered by an old man named Uncle Saint. When Pinky requests an audience with Sister Heavenly, the gruff old man sends him upstairs. Pinky finds her in the attic treating a sick old man with cocaine while she oversees others being treated for impotence.

Finally Heavenly's work is at an end for the evening, and she listens as Pinky tells her the story about Ginny and the African's plan to kill Gus and steal his farm in Ghana. She is skeptical about his story, but she can see that he believes it implicitly.

Pinky further explains that there is a map to a buried treasure in Ghana that is hidden in Gus's trunk and that the trunk is to be sent to the wharf that very morning. The African and Ginny plan to kill him before the expressmen come for the trunk.

Moving with great speed, the old woman gets dressed. She gives Pinky a knockout drop, and as he lapses into unconscious, Uncle Saint takes Heavenly away in an old limousine.

When they arrive at Gus's apartment, Heavenly goes inside to look for him. She figures that if the old man has anything of value, he will likely have it on him. Saint privately disagrees with her. He believes that Gus is a go-between for smugglers and, for some reason, is more likely to have gold or diamonds hidden in the trunk. Saint reasons that such a square trick would be likely to fool even experienced Federal agents.

As he waits, an express truck pulls up and two men enter the building. Inside, Sister Heavenly has covered Ginny and the African with her revolver, and she makes them admit the expressmen when they buzz for entry. Unfortunately, the expressmen pick up the trunk and depart without seeing or speaking to anyone.

Without waiting for Heavenly, Saint follows the truck to the wharf. Because he followed too closely, he is forced to stop in front of a black Buick sedan parked near the French Line dock. As he watches in the rear view mirror, a big man gets out of the Buick, approaches Saint, and tries to shoot him with a silenced derringer. Saint, using a ventriloquist's trick, startles the man into letting down his guard and kills him with a shotgun he carries. As another man begins shooting at him, Saint drives away in a panic. After several close calls with the police, he gets safely back to Sister Heavenly's house in the Bronx.

That same morning, Digger and Ed are called down to the police commissioner's office where they find that they are accused of the death of Jake, the dope-pusher. In spite of all the remarks they make in their own defense, they are suspended from active duty pending an investigation.

Back in the Bronx, Uncle Saint discovers that Sister Heavenly has somehow beaten him back home. Heavenly confronts Saint and Pinky with the surmise that they have been on a wild-goose chase. Pinky reacts angrily to this and accuses them of trying to steal the map and kill Gus themselves. Heavenly responds that she saw Gus talking to the expressmen and watched him give them the map to mail. Pinky is astounded into silence by this news.

Before the discussion can progress further, they are interrupted by Angelo, a detective from the local precinct who tells her about Saint's exploits and the shotgun killing on the docks. He extorts money from her to cover it up before leaving.

Returning to the house, Heavenly announces her intention of going to the docks to see Gus and Ginny off. As soon as she leaves, Saint disguises Pinky with a dye job that turns his skin purple and a ridiculous ensemble of clothing. Heavenly, who has watched this from a neighboring home, follows Pinky to Gus's apartment. She stations herself on a convenient park bench and waits where she can see the entrance.

In the meantime, Digger and Ed have decided that they must take action to clear themselves and have also returned to Gus's apartment. There they discover Pinky's dog lying near the iron gate to the front entrance. When they note that the dog has a bad head wound, they realize that the African must have taken the dog to the park on the previous night to kill it.

Entering the apartment, they find the African's body on the floor and the apartment systematically ransacked. They realize that the killers could still be in the apartment. Digger wants to get out and call the homicide squad, but Ed insists on finding some weapons and continuing the investigation. Before they can make much headway, Ed is sapped from behind, and Digger is shot twice. A Black maid enters the basement at a crucial moment and saves their lives with her screams.

Down at the wharf, the Queen Mary is about to sail, and Pinky is searching for Gus' trunk. In spite of his outlandish appearance, Pinky decides to wait for the African to arrive and follow him to the trunk's location. When the African fails to show up, Pinky decides to go to his apartment. When he arrives there, however, he is warned by an old Black woman that two white police detectives are in the building. Pinky quickly retires down the street to a tobacco shop and numbers drop run by Daddy Haddy. Pinky convinces Daddy to send his boy, Wop, down to the building to wait for and warn the African about the cops. This accomplished, Pinky leaves in the opposite direction.

Back at Heavenly's house, Uncle Saint has decided to avenge himself on Heavenly for all of the years of mistreatment he has suffered by breaking into her safe and escaping from New York. He digs up a bottle of nitroglycerine that he has saved for years and prepares a charge to blow the safe open. At a crucial moment, he gets tangled up with a pet goat and blows up not only the safe, but the entire house and everything in it.

Sister Heavenly is standing outside as two white men emerge from Gus' building. When she sees Grave Digger brought out on a stretcher and hears that the African has been murdered as well, she leaves quickly, finally realizing what is going on and determined to profit from it.

When she discovers that the explosion has wiped her out and left her without resources, she is forced to seek shelter and make other plans. As she taxis down Riverside Drive however, she notices an S.P.C.A. truck taking away Pinky's giant dog, Sheba. Without wasting another moment, she calls the S.P.C.A. and makes a request for the dog. They promise her the dog, but when she calls back thirty minutes later, Heavenly discovers to her chagrin that a detective has taken Sheba away.

The story drops back in time to earlier that same afternoon. Against instructions, Ed escapes from the hospital and returns to his home in Astoria. Before he leaves the house, he makes a call to Lieutenant Walsh at homicide. Ed explains that the gunmen are after a shipment of heroin that Gus, Ginny, and the African may have stolen. Walsh is skeptical because enough heroin to cause multiple murders would have been noticed by now. He warns Ed to stay off the case.

Ed, however, has no intention of staying out of it now. Before leaving his neighborhood, he breaks into Digger's house and takes his revolver. He then embarks on a series of inexplicable errands. At a local pharmacy he buys a large package of milk sugar. From there he goes to a sporting goods store in Brooklyn where he buys a square yard of rubberized silk, which he uses to wrap the package of milk sugar, and a small canvas bag to carry it in. From there he goes to the S.P.C.A. to retrieve Pinky's dog.

He then embarks on an odyssey to find Pinky. After visiting and beating a pimp half to death, he visits Kid Blackie's gymnasium. At the gym, Blackie tells Ed that he hasn't seen Pinky but that Ginny was there earlier with two white gangsters in a gray Buick. They were also looking for Pinky. Blackie does not know where Pinky might be, but he fills Ed in about his aunt, Sister Heavenly, whom he identifies as a faith healer and heroin pusher. He informs Ed that Daddy Haddy can tell him how to find Sister Heavenly. Unknown to Ed, Sister Heavenly has been following him in a taxi.

At 6:07 P.M., Ed pulls up at Daddy Haddy's and, finding it locked, breaks in. He is not surprised to find Daddy murdered and the store ransacked. As he leaves, he finds a little girl trying to entice the dog out of his car. Ed vaguely realizes that it is strange that the girl is calling the dog by name, but the concussion he got earlier prevents him from thinking clearly. Before he can focus his thoughts, he also notices Wop standing at the corner looking at the sky. Suspicious of such behavior, Ed begins to follow, then chase the kid.

Thanks to the interference of a street idler, Ed is able to collar the boy, and he drags him back to the car. Finding the dog gone, Ed threatens the boy with dire punishment unless he tells where the dog has gone. Terrified, Wop confesses that Sister Heavenly is behind it all.

The scene switches back to Sister Heavenly, who now has Sheba in the taxi with her. After purchasing chloroform and some surgical equipment, she has herself driven to a fleabag hotel where she rents a room and takes the dog upstairs. She then chloroforms the dog and dissects it on the floor of her room. After inspecting every inch of the dogs entrails, she leaves the hotel.

By this time, Coffin Ed has driven Wop out to Sister Heavenly's house where they find nothing but a police barricade and rubble. Realizing that he will find no clues here, he takes the boy on a "junkie's tour of Harlem." Because Wop is well-known as Daddy Haddy's courier, Ed uses him to gain entrance to cribs and dope dens all over town. Once inside, he uses terror tactics to make the inhabitants talk. By eleven P.M., however, he still has nothing to go on.

He has only one place left to go—the whore house run by Madam Cushy. Having heard on the radio that Grave Digger has died of his wounds, Ed is in wretched shape emotionally and physically. He is bent on vengeance and is in no mood to brook further insolence from anyone. When Madam Cushy refuses to help him, he takes her at knife-point and risks a gun battle with her bodyguards to make her talk. He discovers that Ginny is hiding out there and forces Cushy to give her up.

Ed quickly overpowers Ginny and brutally strips and tortures her until she agrees to talk. Twenty-three minutes later, Ed has the full story. Soon they are back at the apartment building on Riverside Drive where the case began.

He painstakingly sets a trap, utilizing the bag of milk sugar that, unknown to anyone else, he had brought earlier in the day and left on top of the elevator cab. At a signal from Ginny, Ed is attacked by the two killers who shot Digger. He kills both before a third gunman shoots him from behind. Before Ed can retaliate, the hall is filled with detectives who dispatch the third gunman.

The detectives, who turn out to be U.S. Treasury agents, decide that Ed's trap might work twice. Informing Ed that narcotics czar Benny Mason is waiting outside with his chauffeur, they decide to send Ginny out to him with Ed's bag. This time, the bag will contain real heroin that they have brought along with them. Realizing that the Feds plan to frame her for the murder of the African if she refuses to help, Ginny reluctantly agrees to go along with the sting.

As she approaches the gangsters' car outside, however, Sister Heavenly attacks and stabs her to death. Benny Mason and his chauffeur see this and shoot Heavenly. Mason is quickly taken into custody by Treasury agents.

While all this is happening, the homicide detective working with the T-men explains that they have been following Ed all day because they realized, as Ed did, that he and the gangsters were going to eventually meet up with each other. He also explains that Grave Digger is still alive, the shock of which sends Ed into a dead faint.

Later, Ed explains all that he learned that helped him to crack the case. First of all, the African was simply an innocent bystander—he had no real place in the case at all.

After the trunk disappeared from the apartment, Ginny never was able to find out what had happened to it. When Gus failed to return, Ginny began to worry. Following Sister Heavenly's visit to her apartment, Ginny sent the African out to look for Gus and to take him to the dock. Subsequently he was murdered.

Sometime later, the two white gangsters showed up claiming to be police detectives. Once she was in their power she was taken to an apartment in the Village where she was searched and questioned about the whereabouts of the heroin. In order to escape their torture, she made up a wild story about Gus having taken the heroin to Chicago. After she told them this story, the gangsters called Benny Mason who came right up to the apartment. They bound and gagged her and left her in the Village, while they returned to her flat to search for the heroin. It was during this search that the African was murdered. Digger and Ed also surprised them during this search and were nearly killed themselves.

Ed also explains that although the Feds had been covering the docks, they didn't cover it well enough. He relates how when the hoods returned to the flat in the Village with Benny Mason, Benny promised Ginny protection if she cooperated. Mason, it seems, was the boss of the narcotics racket, and he had been using Gus to pick up smuggled narcotics when they arrived in port. Ginny did not know this—she had genuinely believed the story about Gus inheriting a tobacco farm in North Carolina.

The narcotics had been dropped overboard to Gus in a small motorboat at eleven P.M. two nights before the action began. Gus was supposed to pass the million-dollar package on to Mason in the trunk that was eventually picked up by the expressmen. Gus knew where to go for the drop thanks to a map sent by Benny Mason shortly before the drop. Coincidentally, the drop was made by Jake Kubansky who was killed at the beginning of the story.

Benny Mason confessed to the Treasury men that the trunk had been empty when his men got it off the express truck. Ginny had believed that Gus had run off with the heroin, but Mason did not. Gus had no friends who would take a chance on hiding him from Mason. Having watched the apartment continuously, Mason was certain that the drugs were still in the apartment building.

The detectives have trouble believing this. They have taken everything in the building apart and found nothing. They are forced to face the fact that Mason, however, believed that the heroin was still there.

Just as the detectives are about to break up, a uniformed cop comes in to announce that a Railway Express truck has arrived with a delivery. On Ed's advice, all of the detectives hide themselves. At once, they jump out to discover Pinky, dressed in an ill-fitting uniform. He is carrying a large green trunk that has not previously been seen by anyone. When the detectives break the trunk open, they find the long-missing Gus inside, his neck broken.

Pinky tearfully explains that when he discovered that Gus was going to Africa without him Pinky killed him in a rage. Pinky also confesses that the murder occurred at eleven-thirty on the night of the narcotics drop. Gus had with him five big black eels, which the detectives realize were the containers of the smuggled heroin.

Pinky rationalized pinning the murder on Ginny and the African because he knew they were cheating on Gus. They realize from his ramblings that the treasure map he had talked about earlier was in reality the map that Benny Mason had given Gus to find the narcotics drop. They also discover that Pinky had thrown the heroin-packed eels into an incinerator and burned them up without ever realizing their contents.

Out of curiosity, Ed asks Pinky why Gus wouldn't take him to Africa. Pinky claims that Gus had said Black Africans wouldn't like a white colored person and would probably try to kill him.

Thus are all the loose ends finally tied into a neat bundle. Contrary to earlier news, Digger is recovering from his bullet wounds in the hospital. Ed and Grave Digger are cleared of any wrong-doing in the death of Jake Kubansky and are reinstated onto the force. Ed, however, is left to ponder a society that forces policemen to use brutal methods to curb crime then castigates them for it.

The Heat's On is ostensibly about narcotics trafficking in New York City, but on another level, it has more to do with race and skin color. There is an early indication of how much confusion skin color can cause when we first see Pinky confronted by white firemen. His negroid features combined with his milk white skin and cream colored hair present such a bizarre picture that the white men can't figure out what he is. When they realize that he is actually Black, they become abusive and attempt to hurt him.

Not much later, when Digger and Ed meet Ginny, Gus's high-yellow sexpot wife, her contemptuous remarks to them are all racial. First she commands, "You niggers better get away from that window or I'll call the police." When she realizes that they are the police, she heaps on them the greatest contempt she can muster by sneeringly referring to them as "nigger cops."

Her comments become even more abusive when Digger tells her that Pinky has accused her of trying to murder Gus. She explodes with "The dirty mother-raping white nigger!" She complains that he is falsely accusing them because "He don't like Africans is all. He's just envious 'cause he ain't got no color in his own fishbelly skin."

Digger and Ed shake their heads at this logic, complaining:

"Now I've heard everything," Grave Digger said. "Here's a white colored man who puts in a false alarm that Riverside Church is on fire, getting half the fire equipment in New York City on the roll and all the police in the neighborhood up here—and why? I ask you why?"

"Because he don't like black colored people," Coffin Ed said.

"You can't blame that on the heat," Grave Digger said.

What is interesting about this interchange is that Ginny is rationalizing away her own bigotry by trying to pass it off on Pinky. As a light-skinned Black with regular features, Ginny continually expresses hatred and contempt for others of her race. Even though Pinky has pure white skin, his features mark him as a "nigger." This attitude is prevalent in all of the light-skinned Negroes in Himes' Harlem, from Imabelle through Iris O'Malley. They hold themselves apart from darker Blacks and express outright hatred for them.

Knowing this, there is some irony in Gus's death. His is the most mysterious murder and the only one not directly connected with narcotics trafficking. He refuses to take Pinky with him to Africa with him because "He said all them black Africans wouldn't like colored people white as I is, and they'd kill me." In a rage that is half sorrow, Pinky murders the only father he has ever had.

In this story, Africa is looked upon as a place to which American Blacks can escape. This is a theme that Himes will enlarge upon in *Cotton Comes to Harlem*. In order to escape to the fatherland, Gus places himself in jeopardy by committing perhaps the only real crime of his life by helping Benny Mason recover narcotics. Pinky sees Africa as an escape, too, and in his rage and disappointment at being left behind, he is driven to commit murder and to attempt to place the blame on others.

In many ways, *The Heat's On* is a reprise of the major themes found in *For Love of Imabelle*. Each story features an amoral light-skinned Black woman. Each story also features a completely bizarre character who is addicted to cocaine and heroin "speedballs." *Heat*, in fact, has two such characters in Pinky and Uncle Saint. Both novels include among their casts cold-blooded murderers who are drug addicts. In both novels virtually everyone but the detectives is dead when the story comes to a conclusion.

Also noteworthy is the fact that virtually all of the major and minor characters have been launched on a passionate, headlong search for a valuable treasure. Pinky claims, at one point, that there is a map to a buried treasure. Even though his perspective is twisted, there is, in point of fact, a map that leads Gus to the drop point for the heroin "treasure." Himes uses the map as a red herring to further confuse the case.

As was the case in *Imabelle*, when all of the bodies have been taken to the morgue, the detectives discover that the treasure that had cost so much to so many no longer exists. It had been destroyed before the action in the story took place. Pinky, in the best traditions of the Himesian sucker, never realized that he held a million dollars in his hands before he burned it up in the incinerator.

Possibly the largest point of comparison between the two novels lies in the fact that one of the detectives is taken out of action during the story, leaving the other one to pick up his fallen brother's weapon and set out on a ride for vengeance. In each case, the fallen partner's near demise is the result of poor judgment. In *Imabelle*, the pair attempt to arrest an entire gang by themselves. In consequence, Coffin Ed is badly wounded. In *Heat,* the pair enter a danger zone where a crime is actually in commission. Having been suspended from the force, they are unarmed and unprepared for the prospect of meeting dangerous killers. Coffin Ed's insistence on going into the basement results in Grave Digger's serious injury.

In both novels, the detective who is left to carry the standard follows the case in his own inimitable manner. Grave Digger is certainly the brains of the team, and in *Imabelle* (and again in *Real Cool Killers)* he uses his deductive abilities to follow up leads. Only rarely does he rely on the submerged brutality in his personality to force information or cooperation out of a suspect.

It is obvious that Ed cannot crack a case with his brains as Digger does. From the moment he leaves the hospital, it is clear that if he can solve the case, he will do so through brute force. Himes prepares us for this as he describes Ed's ritual preparation for his crusade:

His shoulder holster hung from a hook inside the door of his clothes closet. The special-made long-barreled, nickel-plated .38 caliber revolver, that had shot its way to fame in Harlem, was in the holster. He took it out, spun the chamber, rapidly ejecting the five brass-jacketed cartridges, and quickly cleaned and oiled it. Then he reloaded it, putting a U.S. Army tracer bullet into the last loaded chamber...From the shelf in the closet he took a can of seal fat and smeared a thick coating on the inside of the holster. He wiped the excess off with a clean handkerchief...He chose a knockout sap from the collection in his dresser drawer...He slipped a Boy Scout knife into his left pants pocket. As an afterthought he stuck a thin flat hunting knife with a grooved hard-rubber handle, sheathed in soft pigskin, inside the back of his pants...and snapped the sheath to his belt.

Before long, he has visited Red Marie and Red Johnny (the redness symbolizing that prostitution is their stock in trade) and pistol-whips Johnny to a bloody pulp. Himes describes in sickening detail how Ed has to use a spoon to dig the broken teeth and bloody tongue out of Johnny's throat in order to keep him from strangling to death. Soon after that, he spends several hours travelling through Harlem beating and threatening others.

By the time Ed finds Ginny, he is nearly wild with grief and self-hatred for his part in Digger's imagined death. This guilt pushes him so far over the edge that he commits hideous torture. Later, after he has shot two men to death, Ed delivers a strange plaint to his wife and Lieutenant Anderson. Along with the near-shooting of the dog in *All Shot Up,* Ed's speech in *Heat* stands as one of Himes' little monuments to how badly his heroes have been brutalized by their environment and how little they understand how much their work has changed them:

Coffin Ed said, "What hurts me most about this business is the attitude of the public toward cops like me and Digger. Folks just don't want to believe that what we're trying to do is make a decent peaceful place for people to live in, and we're going about it the best way we know how. People think we enjoy being tough, shooting people and knocking them in the head."

Recognizing the futility of trying to explain to Ed just where he and Digger have gone wrong, Lieutenant Anderson simply changes the subject.

In comparing this story to others in the series, it is worth noting that young love does not provide any sign of regeneration or a reaffirmation of life and hope. This was something, in fact, that Himes would not include in any of his later stories. Perhaps he felt that such redemption was no longer possible in his fictional world or in the increasingly turbulent real world, either.

The evil of narcotics pervades every corner of this novel, providing some indication of how widespread the problem was in the early 1960s. We also begin to understand the deep disgust that Himes himself must have felt about it. With but a few exceptions, all the characters in *The Heat's On* are addicts, and most of the remaining few have been somehow tainted by their association with the others. While the whiteness of Pinky's skin is an early indication of the symbolic evil that he represents, it is clear from the early pages of the story that he is not the typical sucker who simply acts as the catalyst for the story. We see him associating with a thoroughly depraved pusher in the opening page, and, not much later, he is injecting "c & m speedballs" into his own veins. Any innocence of which we may have suspected him is wiped out by these revelations.

The fact that, unlike any of the other stories, *Heat* takes us out of Harlem and into greater New York, suggests the far-reaching power of the evil that narcotics represents to Himes. The character of Benny Mason, the white drug czar, hangs over the story like a menacing presence as well. It is clear that, since Mason and his hired killers are all white men, Himes sees narcotics as a disease which the white world has used to infect, weaken, and further subjugate the Black community.

Himes uses Digger to make an effective comment on this when the assistant district attorney points out to him that he and Ed are accused of killing a man suspected of the "minor crime" of dope dealing. Perhaps the fact that a member of the white establishment says this is what provokes Digger to such outrage:

"You call dope peddling a minor crime?...All the fucked-up lives...All the nice kids sent down the drain on a habit...Twenty-one days on heroin and you're hooked for life...Jesus Christ, Mister, that one lousy drug has murdered more people than Hilter. And you call it *minor!*...And who gets into the victim's blood? The peddler! He sells the dirty crap. He makes the personal contact. He puts them on the habit. He's the mother-raper who gets them hooked. He looks into their faces and puts the poison in their hands. He watches them go down from sugar to shit, sees them waste away. He puts them out to stealing, killing, starts young girls to hustling—to get the money to buy the kicks. I'll take a simple violent murderer any day."

The district attorney's man heaps more irony on the situation when he demands Digger and Ed's indictment for brutality on the grounds that "the public is indignant." Only the intervention of the cynically amused police commissioner saves Digger and Ed from injustice. Later, when they complain to their white boss, Anderson thoughtlessly throws more coals on Digger's blazing rage by insisting that it will all blow over because "it's just the newspaper pressure. We're suffering from the customary summer slack in news...The papers are on one of their periodic humanitarian kicks."

Digger reacts to this with a bitter, telling blow when he comments, "Yeah, humanitarian. It's all right to kill a few colored people for trying to get their children an education, but don't hurt a mother-raping white punk for selling dope."

In every novel in the Harlem Domestic series, Himes introduces one character that dominates the story and is truly unforgettable. In *Heat* it is Sister Heavenly. In spite of her old, wizened appearance, Heavenly projects a considerable force that steals every scene she enters. Heavenly is undoubtedly the most interesting of all Himes' villains because she is completely self-made.

Most of the other villains Himes created are rather two-dimensional, and, for that reason, their backgrounds were of little interest. Others, like Ulysses Galen, are killed early in the story and we only get to know them through the words of others. Himes gives us a chance to look in on Sister Heavenly's thoughts and reminiscences and through them see her origins.

Heavenly, whose name is undoubtedly an indication of her effect on her clients and former lovers, explains that she grew up on a cotton farm in the south. With a candor that is reminiscent of Himes' own, she relates that she was "too cute and too lazy to hoe the corn and chop the cotton" and so took off with a pimp to become a whore at fifteen. After she became a whore, she used skin lightening creams on a regular basis until she had virtually turned herself white.

As she became lighter in color, her means of supporting herself became more pernicious. By the time we meet her, she is ostensibly running a faith-healing pitch, but this is really a cover for pushing narcotics. She pays protection money to corrupt policemen and is able to support herself handsomely.

As corrupt as she is, Sister Heavenly has a great deal more style than many of Himes' other bad women. She is in total command of her environment and of the men who come into her life. Since she became a successful faith healer, she has kicked men out when they no longer pleased her. As tough as she is though, she is as mild-mannered as a preacher's wife. Her strongest oath when vexed is "Now, ain't that just lovely!" With her beaded handbag, locket watch, and parasol, she is easily able to move in and out of polite society, fooling police officers as she goes.

When Uncle Saint blows up her house and all of her wealth, she is more disgusted by this blow than shaken by it. As Himes points out: "Sister Heavenly was a fatalist. If she had ever read *The Rubaiyat of Omar Khayyam*, she might have been thinking of the lines:

> The moving finger writes,
> and having writ moves on;
> Nor all your piety nor wit
> Nor all your tears
> Shall cancel half a line of it..."

Once, in a moment of sarcasm, she describes herself as "one of the devil's mistresses," and her later behavior makes the description apt. Before she is through, she will have disemboweled a dog and searched its entrails for heroin, stabbed another character in the heart, and engaged in a running gun battle with a pair of white gangsters. Through it all, she maintains her calm, fatalistic demeanor, even as she lies dying with a bullet in her spine.

Himes provides us with some of his darkest humor in this story, as most of it has to do with violent death. Much of this comes through Uncle Saint, Sister Heavenly's cast-off lover and part-time chauffeur. Saint, as depraved a character as can be found in the series, is a drug addict who possesses strength and weakness in equal quantities. He hates Heavenly with a deep passion, but lacks the resolve to leave her. His desire to outwit her and, perhaps to hurt her pride as much as she has hurt his, provokes him to take long chances.

Saint is typical of many of the old timers that populate Harlem in that he understands the uses of the white man's contempt. When he attempts to get through the toll gate with his bullet-riddled car, he puts on a convincing act as a crazy old darky to get him past suspicious and skeptical police officers. This ploy is one that Himes uses several times in the series, most notably in *Imabelle* and *Cotton*. Earlier in the story, Saint gets the better of a white gunman by falling back on a ventriloquist's trick (certainly a unique ploy in the history of crime fiction).

Himes provides his most hilarious surprise when Uncle Saint tangles with a stubborn goat while attempting to blow up Sister Heavenly's safe with nitroglycerine. His hatred for the goat is so much greater than his common sense that he literally destroys himself in an attempt to blow up his four-legged tormenter. With a justice that is truly poetic, Himes wipes the old outlaw from the scene and sends him to the land of the saints.

The Heat's On is certainly one of the more entertaining of the Harlem canon and includes one of the more engrossing mysteries in the series. It is a much more coherent story than many of the others because the motivations of the characters are so clearly laid forth. The story is also strengthened by the fact that although there are no real clues to the solution of the mystery, there are no deliberate attempts to confuse the reader either.

The story is also of interest because once again Himes provides us with a finer focus on his two detectives. Digger and Ed show indecision a few times during the story, and at least once Digger displays an unaccustomed irritation with his partner, Ed exhibits a broad range of emotion, including shame, regret, and guilt over his part in Digger's injury. More important, for the only time in the series Ed gets to carry the ball alone as he hunts for the killers.

On the minus side, *Heat* is a very derivative story, containing many elements, situations, and characters that hark back to Himes' first book in the series. It is a much darker story than *Imabelle*, however, with no redeeming conclusion and no characters left to live happily ever after. A realistic writer like Himes, who seldom ended his protest novels on a hopeful note, may have felt that this was an unnecessary element in the story. What is more likely is that the ending to this story reflected a deepening pessimism that becomes even more evident in his later work.

This story is important also because it marks a division in the series. We noted earlier that this story included many of the themes that one tends to associate with Himes. At the same time, he managed for the first time to avoid many of the weaknesses that are apparent in earlier stories. An objective appraiser would have to say that Himes had gone as far as he could go with the kind of novel that he had been writing.

Perhaps Himes realized this himself, because he did not write another Harlem novel for several years. One could say that Himes may simply have tired of writing formula fiction, and the money that he was then making should have made it unnecessary for him to continue. Himes had been writing for thirty years by this point. It had been the only thing to sustain him through all of his trials and tribulations. It is impossible to believe that he was no longer interested in writing when he had finally achieved the success he had sought for so long.

Himes had already shown a predisposition to experiment at earlier points in this series. His cessation at this point in the series suggests that he was ready to do something much more original and needed the time to do it well. Consequently, when the next Harlem story appeared several years later, it was evident that Himes would no longer be writing pure crime drama laced with protest elements. His work would begin to reflect a deepening re-interest in writing socio-political fiction. This resurgence of interest would cause him to edge the crime elements from the center stage and replace them with something much more compelling.

Chapter XI
Return To Africa

The voice from the sound truck said:

"Each family, no matter how big it is will be asked to put up one thousand dollars. You will get your transportation free, five acres of fertile land in Africa, a mule and a plow and all the seed you need, free. Cows, pigs and chickens cost extra, but at the minimum. No profit on this deal."

A sea of dark faces wavered before the speaker's long table, rapturous and intent.

"Ain't it wonderful, honey?" said a big black woman with eyes like stars. "We're going back to Africa."

After 1961, Himes' literary reputation had improved to the point that he found he could take a break from writing. Like many other writers, before and since, he discovered that he was now selling so well that he was even able to place manuscripts that had been unsaleable earlier. In 1962, for example, he was able to publish his sex farce, *Mamie Mason*, through Plon. A year later he published what is virtually his last piece of "serious" protest fiction, *Une affaire de viol* through Les Yeux Ouverts.

The financial freedom he had gained through the first six entries in the Harlem Domestic series probably allowed him the leisure to put more thought into his writing than had been possible earlier. It also gave him the ability to choose his publishers, rather than simply taking what was offered him.

In 1964, Himes produced what is for many the quintessential title in the Harlem series. Although it was not the first of the series to appear in this country in hard cover (*The Heat's On* had that honor), it was the first to gain any widespread critical attention and was later turned into a successful motion picture. It was issued by Plon as *Retour en Afrique* and a year later by G.P. Putnam under its more famous title, *Cotton Comes to Harlem*.

This book achieved for Himes some of the most positive critical recognition that he had ever received. Nat Hentoff noted in *Book Week* that *"Cotton Comes to Harlem* is paced like a hard-edged, up tempo Charlie Parker blues...Himes is skilled at quick-action prose that skims but seldom stumbles."[1] M.K. Grant was even more effusive when she wrote in *Library Journal* that "the book to watch this month is Chester Himes's *Cotton Comes to Harlem*...The humor is rough, the escapes hairbreadth, the sex rampant and the dialogue authentic."[2] Even the dean of crime fiction critics, Anthony Boucher, conceded that although he had reservations about "this carnival of gallows humor," he still found that the plot had "many splendidly strange notions."[3]

Himes was at his peak in this story, and it shows. For the first time, he was able to fuse together the drama of the protest novel with the dash and excitement of his own self-developed crime format. To complete the mix he added in touches of humor and satire that made this a totally unique story.

The novel begins with a large group of Negroes standing in the middle of an empty lot listening to a voice amplified through a sound truck. Reverend Deke O'Malley is offering the group a chance, at $1,000.00 a family, to return to Africa and resume an idyllic agricultural life that is free of the injustice and hypocrisy of white America.

Posters of the ship that will take the faithful to Africa and an armored car to guard the donations dominate the area. Pretty young women operate tables to sign people up for the trip, and a cook is off to one side preparing barbecued ribs. Soon O'Malley's people have collected $87,000.00.

Several things occur in rapid succession. First two big Black men who identify themselves as detectives with the district attorney's office show up with instructions to take O'Malley in for questioning. At approximately the same time, a meat truck arrives, ostensibly to resupply the cook with more ribs. When the truck doors open however, it is full of masked men with southern accents and submachine guns. One of O'Malley's men is killed before the gunmen scoop up the collected trip moneys and take off in their truck.

O'Malley, the detectives, and the armored car guards give chase in the armored car, but the lighter meat delivery truck quickly gets out of sight. As it turns left at 137th Street, the back doors of the meat truck burst open and a bale of white cotton slides out into the street. Before the gunmen can stop to retrieve it the armored car comes into view and they are forced to flee. Later, the cotton is found by an old Negro rag picker named Uncle Bud who, with the help of an obliging white policeman, loads the cotton into his cart. He takes it to Goodman's junk yard and trades it for $25.00.

A short distance away, a pair of con men are engaged in a con called the *holy dream*. One man has engaged a prissy, fat, church-going sister in a quasi-religious discussion. While he has the woman enthralled, his partner is behind her with a razor blade, cutting away her dress to expose the purse hidden between her legs.

As the partner reaches for the exposed purse, she realizes what is going on and strikes him. As he instinctively runs into the street he is run over by the fleeing meat truck. Now out of control, the truck crashes into a telephone pole.

At almost that same moment, Grave Digger and Coffin Ed are in Lieutenant Anderson's office getting an assignment. That assignment is to cover Deke O'Hara, a.k.a. Reverend Deke O'Malley. We discover that O'Hara/O'Malley is actually an ex-convict who had informed on a syndicate operation in order to get a shorter sentence. There is reason to believe that the syndicate has a contract out on O'Malley.

Because O'Malley has managed to gain the confidence of the solid citizens, he has gotten approval for police protection from his enemies. This is to be Digger and Ed's assignment. Just as their conference with Anderson is drawing to a close, they receive word of the robbery at O'Malley's rally.

At the crime scene, Digger and Ed discover very little that will help them. They have a strong suspicion that the two Negro detectives were imposters, and they feel sure that the heist was not orchestrated by the Syndicate. They decide that the only thing to do is to find Deke.

Himes takes us into Deke's own mind at this point. He explains how Deke had originally decided to impersonate a preacher in order to hide out from the Syndicate. He soon discovered that the Syndicate had no real interest in him. His chance reading of a biography of Marcus Garvey and the original Back-to-Africa movement gave him the idea for a con game.

His plan had been to use the two phoney detectives to impound the money so that he could keep it out of the bank and in his own hands. Deke in fact knew nothing about the white hijackers at all.

After he and his men split up Deke returns to his own apartment building, but some sixth sense warns him away. His senses prove correct when he telephones from a block away, and his wife, Iris, warns him that Digger and Ed are there waiting for him.

Before they can have the call traced, Lieutenant Anderson contacts them and sends them over to where both the meat truck and the armored car have been discovered smashed and empty. They take a few moments to try to reason with Iris in order to enlist her aid, but she contemptuously rejects their pleas and makes it clear that she has no interest in the problems of poor Black people. When a white detective arrives from the precinct to guard Iris, Digger and Ed depart for the crash scene.

At the scene of the wrecks, Digger and Ed find the area sealed off by homicide detectives. As they examine the trucks they discover strands of unprocessed white cotton caught on a loose screw. The bodies of two men are nearby; one of them is a member of the bogus pair of detectives who came to take Deke away from the rally. The other is the sneak thief named Early Riser. Because Early worked with a partner named Loboy, the homicide men believe that he may be able to tell them something.

Himes switches the scene back to Deke O'Malley just after he has been warned by Iris. Like the cops, he has no idea what is going on or why. He supposes that the Syndicate could have done it just to frame him and ruin him financially.

He calls the wife of John Hill, a young recruiting agent killed during the robbery, and enlists her aid. He arranges to stay with her in order to avoid the police and ostensibly to clear himself. Lonely and eager to help, she agrees.

Mable Hill is young, beautiful, and "square." Already distraught over the death of her young husband, she is quickly overcome by O'Malley's looks and charisma, and soon they are in bed together.

Digger and Ed follow Loboy's trail into Spanish Harlem to a whorehouse. They take him back to the crash site where he identifies the driver of the meat truck as a big white man but can tell them no more.

The next morning, a startling sight awaits the residents and familiars of Seventh Avenue. Signs proclaim a newly-remodeled storefront as the headquarters of the "Back-to-the-Southland-Movement." Other signs and posters proclaim the good life to be had by Negroes in the south, as contrasted to the starving millions in Africa. The posters offer free fare back to the south, high wages, and a $1,000.00 bonus for each family of five able-bodied persons. A smaller sign, posted in the lower corner of one window, reads "Wanted, a bale of cotton."

Presiding over this operation is Colonel Robert L. Calhoun, a white-haired and goateed gentleman outlandishly dressed in the costume of a southern planter.

Barry Waterfield, the remaining member of Deke O'Malley's bogus detective team, enters the office on Deke's orders and tells the colonel about Deke's Back-to-Africa movement. Barry obliquely suggests that he wants to double-cross O'Malley in order to receive a payoff from Calhoun. They strike a deal to meet underneath the subway extension to the Polo Grounds near the Harlem River at midnight that night where Calhoun will trade money for the Back-to-Africa subscription list.

Following Waterfield's departure, Calhoun is visited by Bill Davis, an honest recruiting agent for the Back-to-Africa campaign. He orders Calhoun to get out of town immediately. Calhoun takes the threat calmly, and Davis leaves. A half-hour later, hostile pickets begin marching in front of Calhoun's office, and a race riot begins to brew. Before it can get completely out of hand the police arrive and break it up.

Afterwards an ingenuous-looking young Negro named Josh gains audience with Calhoun. Josh explains to the colonel how Uncle Bud brought the cotton to Goodman on the previous night and arranges to let Calhoun into the junk yard at ten P.M. that night.

Back at Iris O'Malley's apartment a white detective is guarding against her escape. Using her considerable sexual allure, Iris seduces him and escapes wearing only a raincoat.

She makes her way to Barry Waterfield's apartment where she discovers that Deke has moved into Mable Hill's apartment. Her face contorted with rage, she goes directly to Mable's. Once there she bursts in and violently upbraids Deke for cheating on her. Mable, who has nearly loved Deke to death by this time, is feeling deeply possessive of the erstwhile preacher and is prepared to fight for him.

A cat-fight erupts between the two women, and before Deke can intervene Iris snatches a revolver from his hand and kills Mable. Wild with rage and panic, Deke beats Iris unconscious and flees the apartment.

Soon the police have Iris in jail for Mable's murder. Digger and Ed have her brought to the interrogation room. Iris is angry at Deke and is ready to do anything to get even with him. She tells the detectives all about Deke's scheme, tells them where to find the other members of his gang, and agrees to help them put Deke in prison.

Meanwhile Barry Waterfield has arranged to close the deal he had made earlier with Calhoun. As he leaves his building, he is followed by detectives who have been assigned to follow him. Digger and Ed join the chase, but due to a variety of circumstances they lose him.

They realize that because Deke's gang doesn't have the money yet, they can't be staging a getaway. Therefore they must be going to wherever the money is. Digger realizes that if they are going to a rendezvous and are not worried about being seen, they must be meeting underneath the bridge at the Polo Grounds.

The scene shifts to the Polo Grounds where Deke and his gang are already under the bridge. Deke spots his gunmen around before giving Barry a phoney list of subscribers. With this, he hopes to find out what Calhoun knows about the missing money.,

When the meet takes place, Calhoun's three men take Barry to Calhoun. The Colonel asks Barry without preamble where the cotton is. Barry remembers in a flash the sign in the window of the Back-to-the-Southland office and, in an effort to save his life, blurts out that Deke has it.

At a gesture from the Colonel, his men make a move to kill Barry with a knife. As Barry struggles, Deke's men start shooting, and in the process Barry and several of Calhoun's men are killed. Everyone bolts from the scene, but through a piece of luck Digger and Ed manage to capture Deke.

Back at the precinct station, the two detectives bring Iris in to confront Deke. Iris lies outrageously, even going so far as to accuse him of Mable Hill's murder. She concludes by providing the detectives with forged documents that will prove that the Back-to-Africa campaign was a swindle. By the time Iris leaves the room, Deke is a beaten man.

As the detectives confer in Anderson's office they begin to realize that none of the major players in the case has the money. Their frantic search for it is the reason for all of the recent excitement.

Later they get a call to investigate a dead man in a junk yard. When they arrive they discover a corpse named Josh Peavine. When Goodman the junk yard owner arrives, they discover that the only thing missing is the bale of cotton he bought from Uncle Bud. At the mention of cotton, the detectives recognize a vital clue.

Digger is awakened on Monday morning by the news that Deke O'Malley's two gunmen have broken him out of jail and killed two police officers. When he and Ed arrive at the station, their old enemy the police commissioner tells them that he is giving them a free hand to go out and bring O'Malley in.

In a private conference with Precinct Captain Brice, Digger suggests that they take Iris O'Malley out of jail to help them find Deke. The captain refuses to take the responsibility. He will only allow them to do it at their own risk. Angered by his cowardice, they decide to do it anyway.

They provide Iris with clothing and some skin dye that will turn her light skin dark and take her out past the jailer. They take her down the street in the car and let her out on the corner with only one instruction: when she contacts Deke she is to tell him that she knows where the bale of cotton is. She is puzzled by this instruction, but she agrees. Digger and Ed disguise themselves and go into hiding.

Iris in the meantime, has gone to the apartment of Billie Belle, a beautiful professional dancer who is Iris' lesbian lover. Billie helps her redisguise herself before she goes back out to find Deke.

Digger and Ed are still in hiding. They see an advertisement in the *Harlem Sentinel* for a bale of cotton, but when they call the number, it is Colonel Calhoun's voice that answers. Somewhat later they talk to a stool pigeon who takes photographs while pretending to be a blind man. He shows them a photo he took recently that shows Colonel Calhoun and his men being met on the street by the murdered Josh Peavine. They realize that they now have Calhoun cold on a murder charge, but they are still unsure of why he is involved in the hijacking.

Having followed Iris to Billie's, they stake themselves out in order to pick Iris up when she leaves. At nightfall, the disguised Iris leaves the apartment and walks down the street to O'Malley's Star of Ham Church with the two detectives behind her. She enters the church and goes to an apartment in the building.

Hidden inside the church, O'Malley and his two gunmen hear Iris enter. O'Malley is tied to a chair, and the two gunmen are threatening him. They think that Deke is double-crossing them, and they are holding him prisoner until they get the money.

After a brief wait, Digger and Ed sneak into the church on sock feet. They hide between the pews and wait for Iris to come back down. Iris finally appears and uses a signal which opens the hidden door to the hideout where O'Malley's gang is waiting. In the conversation that follows, it is clear that everyone now knows that the missing money is in the bale of cotton. What they don't know is where the cotton has gone. They tie Iris up with the intention of torturing the information out of her.

Before they can begin however, they hear Coffin Ed and Digger above thanks to a special sound system that picks up noises in the church. The two killers go up into the church where gunfire erupts. Both gunmen are hit and die horribly from the burning phosphorus in Digger and Ed's tracer bullets. In the process the church catches on fire. Down below the hate between Iris and Deke has also burst forth, and they have thrown their chair-bound bodies at each other in a grim effort to kill one another.

The fire brings more police and firemen, and eventually order is restored. Iris finally tells the detectives that the bale of cotton can be found at the Cotton Club. When the detectives arrive at the club, they find Billie doing a seductive, nude dance with the cotton bale. After her performance, she offers to sell the bale of cotton to anyone in the audience for $1,000.00. Colonel Calhoun emerges from the audiences to pay Billie for the cotton and has it wheeled outside.

Digger and Ed follow Calhoun to the Back-to-the-Southland movement office. After Calhoun leaves the office in his limousine, Digger and Ed break in and wait for him to return. However, when Calhoun and his nephew return and begin to search the bale, they are enraged to discover that it is empty. This proves to be enough for Digger and Ed and they step out to arrest the pair for the murder of Josh Peavine. They answer Calhoun's denial with the news that the cotton fibers will prove it for them.

Calhoun plays into their hands by trying to bribe them. They offer him twenty-four hours to get out of town in exchange for $87,000.00. Calhoun agrees to give them the money, but he is amazed that they will waste it on a bunch of mere Negroes.

Two days later, the two weary detectives return to the station with the money and make their report. They withhold enough truth to make it look as if Calhoun outsmarted them while they waited for him at his office. The commissioner and Captain Brice are both angry enough to have them drawn and quartered, but they are faced with the fact that the pair have completely cleared up the case, brought in virtually all of the criminals, and recovered the money.

The only unanswered question is how Billie got the bale of cotton. She is brought in and explains that she found Uncle Bud sleeping in his cart one day, and the sight of his white, nappy old head reminded her that she needed a bale of cotton for her exotic dance. He offered to get her one for $50.00. She had given him the money, and he had delivered the cotton to the club that same night. She had not seen Uncle Bud again since that time. Later she saw the advertisement in the *Harlem Sentinel* about a bale of cotton and had called the number. She had spoken to Calhoun and had agreed to sell it to him for $1,000.00.

The detectives receive citations for bravery in the case, and a barbecue is held in their honor by the Back-to-Africa group. They figure out that Uncle Bud found the money inside the bale of cotton before he took it to Billie. Later they discover that he took the money to Dakar where he has purchased some land, cattle, and a large number of wives. One happy man has returned to Africa.

Himes achieved in this story his most coherent plot and his most consistently humorous story. Although there are several murders, there is much less reliance on graphic violence and more on character interaction and satire to carry the story along.

A major focus of this story is Black heritage and the Negro's longing to return to a time when he wasn't an outsider. The dream of a return to Africa is an important part of the heritage of the American Black. The African country of Liberia, created by former slaves in the early 19th century, is a reflection of that long-time dream.

Deke O'Malley's Back-to-Africa campaign is so named in order that he can use the luster of the most famous of all Black nationalist movements, that begun by Marcus Garvey in the early 1900s. Garvey was a Jamaican Black who lived in London prior to World War I. During that period, his contacts with Africans stimulated his interest in the idea of an African homeland. After returning to Jamaica, he established what he called a Universal Negro Improvement Association and eventually moved the headquarters to New York City.

In Harlem he founded the Black Star Steamship Line with the purpose of creating stronger bonds between American and Caribbean Negro communities. Later he published a militant weekly newspaper in which he expressed his ideas of Negro separatism. By the 1920s, Garvey was elected leader of what he called the African Republic, a government-in-exile. As he reached his peak of power, however, he was brought down by financial problems and was eventually sent to Atlanta Federal Prison for mail fraud.

Garvey's sentence was commuted in 1927 by President Calvin Coolidge, and he was deported to Jamaica. He spent the rest of his life trying to keep his movement alive. During the 1960s when the term "AfroAmerican" was in vogue, Garvey was certainly a symbol to the militant young Blacks who craved "Black Power."

Himes makes it clear that, with all this historical and emotional baggage attached to it, a movement espousing a "Back-to-Africa" movement would be sure to attract sentimental and gullible squares. It is worthy of note that the re-creation of this piece of Black heritage, combined with O'Malley's looks and charisma, create such emotional force that his followers ignore the fact that O'Malley has been denounced by the remaining members of the original Garveyite movement.

As he has before, Himes has also made religion a focus of this story. He has taken his typically jaundiced view of it, depicting the purveyors of religion as charlatans and thieves and the worshipers as upstanding but naive fools. This is especially evident in *Cotton* because unlike Reverend Short and Sweet Prophet Brown, Deke O'Malley is an ex-convict and a former member of the Syndicate. A consummate con man, O'Malley comes to Harlem fresh from serving time (as did Garvey himself) in the Atlanta Federal Penitentiary and in no time at all, sets himself up as the minister of the mythical Star of Ham church.[4]

When O'Malley is taken into police custody on perfectly legitimate charges, the natural mistrust of white authorities by poor urban Blacks makes it a foregone conclusion that they will believe O'Malley is being railroaded. They come very close to fomenting a riot in order to secure his release. This gullibility on the part of the Black citizenry reflects a deeper pessimism in Himes and suggests the hopelessness he felt for his race. In this story the urban poor have been abused and subjugated for so long that they automatically believe in anything that a Black spiritual and political leader will say, even when it is obvious that it is not a good thing.

Himes makes other more subtle jabs at religion, the foremost of which is the bond between sexuality and Negro religion. Early in the story when Early Riser and Loboy are working their scam on the fat church sister, Loboy is talking in a charming and seductive manner about adultery. The more that Loboy talks about the sinfulness of adultery, the more sexually excited the Black sister becomes:

John (Loboy) leaned forward and touched her on the shoulder like a spontaneous caress. His voice thickened with suggestion. "But Jesus say, 'Commit all the 'dultry you want to, John. Just be prepared to roast in hell for it.' "
"He-he-he," laughed the church sister and slapped him again on the shoulder. "He was just kidding you. He'd forgive us for just one time," and she suddenly switched her trembling buttocks, no doubt to demonstrate Jesus's mercy.

At the same time, Himes takes the opportunity to remind us of the connection between sexuality and money. The sister carries her money in a purse that rides near her sex organs:

The black thighs bulged in all directions so that just below the crotch, where the torso began, there was a sort of pocket in which one could visualize the buttocks of some man gripped as in a vice. But now, in that pocket, hung a waterproof purse suspended from elastic bands passing up through the pants and encircling the waist.

Himes has made this connection before. In *The Crazy Kill*, Chink Charlie roots in the money on Dulcy's bed, almost as a foreplay to the sex he expects to have with her. In *The Big Gold Dream*, the women at Sweet Prophet's street baptism are overcome with sexual ecstasy at the prospect of becoming materially wealthy as a result of "having God inside" them.

Deke O'Malley later uses this religio-sexual connection in his seduction of Mable Hill. It is obvious from the time that she comes on stage that O'Malley's spiritual seduction of Mable probably predates the death of her husband, John.

Mable and John are archetypal squares in that they have risen above their poverty to a kind of middle-class status. Believing in the Protestant Work Ethic, they are great believers in God and the bounty that He has in store for them as a result of their work on His behalf. Following John's death, which results while he is working for God, Mable is suffused with the interrelationship between hard work, material gain, religious devotion, and sex.

Mable clearly sees O'Malley as God's servant. Her sexual submission to him is part of God's master plan to set things right for the people of Harlem. Thus when O'Malley penetrates her, she has no trouble believing that she is taking part in a kind of holy esctasy. A naive young woman, her continual confusion of sex with a holy ritual proves to be her tragic flaw and ultimately results in her death.

Himes always makes a point of mocking race hatred among Blacks. As in every Harlem novel, the light-skinned characters who strive for material gain and social prestige are all morally bankrupt. Iris O'Malley is certainly the most outwardly bigoted of such characters and represents for Himes those Blacks who have turned their backs on their darker and less fortunate brothers.

Himes delights in displaying the selfishness he believes is inherent in this group when Grave Digger tries to explain to Iris that their main mission is to effect the return of the money to the Harlem poor. He tries unsuccessfully to appeal to her by suggesting a sense of community:

> Eighty-seven colored families—like you and me—
> "Not like me! [exclaims Iris],

thereby asserting her apartness from other Negroes with great force. Grave Digger later characterizes Iris as one of "these half-white bitches" who for the detectives (and for Himes), represent both selfishness and cultural rejection. Himes symbolically exacts revenge when Digger and Ed rub black dye all over her skin before helping her to escape from jail. She is then so black that her lesbian lover, Billie, calls her a "Topsy." Later, Coffin Ed opines that "by this time that yellow gal has damn sure got that dye off, much as she hates being black."

Race hatred by whites is very much a part of this story as well. Himes satirizes white southern supremacists in this story with the character of Colonel Robert L. Calhoun. This character, who dresses in the anachronistic costume of a white suit, white planter's hat, and "CSA" signet ring, pretends to love Blacks while openly calling them "boy" and "nigger." His Back-to-the-Southland agency projects a dream world of prosperous lives for those Negroes who return to the south to pick cotton.

Himes makes little of the fact that Calhoun's advertising posters display Black prosperity that is equal to although completely separate from that of whites. The reader already recognizes the absurdity of such a promise. At the same time Himes makes a subtle comparison between the false promises of the white supremacist and those of the crooked Black minister. O'Malley has also promised a prosperous life for Negroes who separate themselves from whites by returning to Africa. Each scheme finds Harlemites eager to participate but unable to recognize the impossibility of any life that is equal while physically separate from the rest of the world.

Possibly the greatest irony in this story is Himes' use of a bale of cotton as the repository of a missing treasure when it is so symbolic of the historic enslavement of Blacks by southern aristocrats. It is certainly no coincidence that cotton is white, Himes' representative color for evil.

The fact that Harlem Blacks would remember the south with nostalgia and consider returning to another kind of enslavement there suggests that many Blacks may have forgotten their own history. In their haste to escape the lives of desperation that they have found in northern slums, they would willingly sell themselves back into servitude. Only Coffin Ed and Grave Digger seem to recognize this as they remark that the same cotton that was responsible for Black enslavement in the south is now killing them in the north.

In spite of the fact that Colonel Calhoun is both a bad man and symbolic of an historic evil, Himes uses him to maintain that the evil is more an inability by whites to recognize Blacks as fellow human beings with needs, desires, and motivations similar to their own. When Grave Digger forces Calhoun to trade $87,000.00 for his freedom, the Colonel expresses surprise:

> "Incredible! You're going to give them back their money?"
> "That's right, the families." [said Grave Digger]
> "Incredible! Is it because they are nigras and you're nigras too?"
> "That's right." [Grave Digger]
> "Incredible!" The Colonel looked as though he had got the shock of his life.

Through this interchange Himes makes it clear that Calhoun, a symbol of repression, doesn't realize that Black people would play by the same rules of human decency as white men. The fact that a "nigra" could possess enough personal honor to want to alleviate the suffering of others of his race is "incredible" to Calhoun. Without this understanding, Himes seems to say, true equality between the races, to say nothing of peaceful co-existence, is impossible.

Himes later makes the observation through his heroes that the belief that Blacks can return to Africa is an anachronistic one. At the end of the book, the citizens who have recovered their money throw a big barbeque in honor of Ed and Digger. During the celebration:

> ...the detectives were presented with souvenir maps of Africa. Grave Digger was called upon to speak. He stood up and looked at his map and said, "Brothers, this map is older than me. If you go back to this Africa you got to go by way of the grave."

The crowd fails to understands Digger, but his meaning is that the Africa that American Negroes came from no longer exists. It is part of their heritage, but they cannot go back to it. As poorly as they have been treated in America, Negroes are now Americans with a unique viewpoint—that of a Black people living in a white society. As appealing as a return to Africa would be, American Blacks could not live there now as anything but strangers.

Digger and Ed are more in the forefront of *Cotton Comes to Harlem* than in any previous story. Their role has been significantly expanded to allow them to act not only as righters of wrongs, but also as social critics. When they visit the scene of the wrecked trucks for example, they ask a homicide detective if there are any witnesses to the wreck. The white detective answers, "Hell, you know all these people, Jones. All stone blind." In a clever take-off on Ralph Ellison's famous novel, Coffin Ed answers roughly, "What do you expect from people who are invisible themselves?"

Himes' style of protest throughout this series has been to graphically describe scenes and streets in Harlem that show the degradation and hopelessness of the inhabitants. He rarely comments on what he describes, letting the descriptions speak for themselves. In this book, however, Ed and Digger comment, often forcefully, on the squalor that they see around them. For example, Grave Digger displays great frustration as he and Ed view a miserable neighborhood:

"All I wish is that I was God for just one mother-raping second," Grave Digger said, his voice cotton-dry with rage.
"I know," Coffin Ed said. "You'd concrete the face of the earth and turn white folks into hogs."
"But I ain't God," Grave Digger said, pushing into the bar.

Later, as they walk through a squalid tenement seeking information, they are hit by the smell of urine in the hallway. Coffin Ed notes that "what American slums need is toilets." As he is assailed by other odors that include "cooking, loving, hair frying, dogs farting, cats pissing, boys masturbating and the stale fumes of wine and black tobacco," Grave Digger insists that "that wouldn't help much."

The two detectives also get an unusual opportunity to philosophize when they visit Big Wilt's Small Paradise Inn. As they take the opportunity to relax over a few drinks, they watch an unusual scene in Harlem, a group of Blacks and whites dancing together. As they listen to the jazz, the two men seem to be hearing something more than the music. Jazz is a music invented by Negroes but loved by the world. In this one place, racial differences seem to be forgotten as the universal language of music goes on:

"Somewhere in that jungle is the solution to the world," Coffin Ed said. "If we could only find it."
"Yeah, it's like the sidewalks trying to speak in a language never heard. But they can't spell it either."
"Naw," Coffin Ed said. "Unless there's an alphabet for emotion."
"The emotion that comes out of experience. If we could read that language, man, we could solve all the crimes in the world."
"Let's split," Coffin Ed said. "Jazz talks too much to me."
"It ain't so much what it says," Grave Digger agreed. "It's what you can't do about it."

Although each detective has displayed sensitivity to and expressed pain at the terrible conditions under which their people must live, neither has ever spoken so eloquently on the subject of racial harmony or noted so forlornly how distant that goal seems. It is their most poignant commentary in the series and, considering all of the bitterness that is expressed in this particular book, it casts the detectives and Himes, himself, in a momentary light of nobility.

In spite of their expanded role as commentators on and philosophers of the Black condition, Himes still emphasizes his detectives' link with the six-gun heroes of the past. When Back to Africa adherents, Back-to-the-Southland marchers, and a gang of hoodlums threaten a riot in front of the jail, Ed and Digger are called in to quell the disturbance, alone. In a scene that is reminiscent of a hundred western movies, Digger recognizes Colonel Calhoun as the driving force behind the impending trouble and sends his white hat skittering down the street with a string of well-placed pistol shots. It is a scene of comic reversals, since the man in the white hat is the villain while the black hatted, Black man is the hero.

Himes uses his most common plot device, the missing treasure, in this novel, but he infused it with new life by adding some clever twists. For once, the missing treasure is not a myth created in the mind of a feverish junky or avaricious female.

It is only after Digger and Ed have vanquished the villains and for a change sent most of them to jail or into exile, that they realize that the $87,000.00 has been recovered by the comical Uncle Bud. There is an hilarious justice in the rag picker's discovery of the money and his subsequent use of it to go to Africa and set himself up as a latter-day King Solomon, complete with one hundred wives.

Himes was near the end of his active writing career with this story, yet *Cotton Comes to Harlem* shows his imagination and wit at a peak. His style had matured to the point that he could write a coherent story that avoided overabundant violence and could rely more on careful pacing and character interaction.

Moreover, he created some of his most memorable characters in this novel and displayed a fine sense of satire. Always quick to exploit the humor in a character or a situation, Himes developed a story that is a perfect blend of humor, suspense, and social protest.

Chapter XII
A Different World

Like wildfire the rumor spread.
"DEAD MAN! DEAD MAN!..."
"WHITEY HAS MURDERED A SOUL BROTHER."
"THE MOTHER-RAPING WHITE COPS, THAT'S WHO!"
"GET THEM MOTHER-RAPERS, MAN!"
"JUST LEAVE ME GET MY MOTHER-RAPING GUN!"
An hour later, Lieutenant Anderson had Grave Digger on the radio-phone. "Can't you stop that riot?" he demanded.
"It's out of hand, boss," Grave Digger said.
"All right, I'll call for reinforcements. What started it?"
"A blind man with a pistol."
"What's that?"
"You heard me boss."
"That don't make any sense."
"Sure don't."

Nineteen sixty-nine marked the end of Chester Himes' career as a novelist, but at the same time it also marked his greatest critical success. According to Michel Fabre, Himes had been working for some time on a novel which would show Harlem in the midst of a kind of racial cataclysm.[1] He produced a story entitled "Tang" (in the collection entitled *Black on Black)* in which the use of artillery in a downtown area to kill a single Black sniper precipitated an end to white societal domination. This story led to the production of a book length work entitled *Plan B* which, to date, has never been published in English.

It is not clear why, but Himes did not attempt to publish these projects. Instead he borrowed elements from both works and came up with the novel which he published as *Blind Man With A Pistol. Blind Man* is in many ways a confusing work because it rejects much of what we have come to expect from traditional crime stories and even what we have come to expect from Himes himself. The reasons for the murders that occur are obscure, and because the detectives fail to identify the murderers, much less bring them to justice, the reader is likely to view the book as unsatisfying at best and at worst as incomprehensible.

As was historically the case with Himes' work, the book attracted its share of unkind comment, most notably from Richard Rhodes in the *New York Times Book Review*. Rhodes noted that reading it was "like reading Ralph Ellison's *Invisible Man* without the spiritual progress that alleviates the horrors of that novel. [Himes'] Harlem blacks look and sound like...idiots and psychopaths and punks...Such blindness to alternatives produces a story that demonstrates but does not qualify."[2] Rhodes concluded from his reading of the book that Himes was prejudiced.

Other critics saw in Himes' work the things he had doubtless wanted them to see from the beginning of his career. D.F. Lawler noted enthusiastically that "the people, the sounds, the problems, the vulgar vicious language of the Harlem Ghetto are strikingly and realistically presented...But above all, the very atmosphere of Harlem is conveyed. In this the author is supreme...The language itself is frequently violent and sometimes repellant; but the injustices and the crimes stand out with such stark reality that it should be read by any who think or plan to work in 'the Inner City.' "[3]

Shane Stephens gave Himes his greatest praise when he wrote in *Washington Post Book World* that "Of all the black American writers now working in the vein of imagination, Chester Himes alone seems to have carved out for himself an area of confrontation that is applicable—and meaningful—effective social protest and effective art."[4]

The book opens on a dilapidated three-story brick house that has been condemned and is unsafe for human habitation. On the front of the building however is a sign that proclaims FUNERALS I ERFORMED. Passing police and local residents have both ignored the building, while noticing the regular comings and goings of women dressed in solid black nun's vestments.

A new sign appears without warning one day, bearing the message FERTILE WOMENS, LOVIN GOD, INQUIRE WITHIN. Two white patrol officers who notice the sign investigate and discover inside a fat, half-naked cretin with a hare lip stirring a foul-smelling stew over an open fire. When they attempt to question him, he attacks the officers, and they club him to the ground. As he falls, a horde of Black nuns and naked Black children emerge to investigate the commotion.

The stunned policemen radio headquarters for help, and as they wait for reinforcements, they are visited by a very old man dressed in a spotted long-sleeved white gown. He identifies himself as Reverend Sam, a Mormon. He explains that the nuns are all his wives and the children, including the cretin, are all his.

A squad of detectives arrives, and they eventually discover fifty children. Sam admits to having eleven wives, a twelfth having died recently. His new advertisement stems from his belief that he needs an even dozen wives in order to keep things going. Sam and his large family are supported by the daily efforts of the wives who go out to beg.

The detective sergeant in charge sends Sam to jail. Shortly thereafter he discovers three graves in the cellar, each containing a partially decomposed female body.

After this somewhat inexplicable series of events, Himes begins a series of complicated scene changes, none of which is even remotely close to the others chronologically. The scene shifts first to the corner of 125th and Seventh. A square white man is standing on the corner intently watching a crowd of flashy, homosexual "sissies." Their wantonly explicit behavior has so aroused the white man that he can hardly bear it. He enters a nearby lunch counter patronized by the sissies and, after some words with the counterman, he goes off with a homosexual wearing a red fez.

Some time later, Coffin Ed and Grave Digger round a corner and spy a Black man in a red fez running down the street with a pair of pants over one arm. The two detectives are making jokes about what such a sight can mean when they see the white man stagger out of an alley without his pants. The detectives discover that he is dying from a slashed throat. His only word in response to their request for information is simply "Jesus."

After more detectives arrive, Digger and Ed follow a trail of blood stains to an apartment building. Eventually they find an ornately furnished apartment with an obscene mural and copious amounts of blood on the floor and walls.

Digger, Ed, and a white detective sergeant named Ryan interrogate several Black families living in the building. About all that they discover is the name and address of the building superintendent, one Lucas Covey.

They quickly find Covey, an arrogant and effeminate West Indian. He claims to have been at the Apollo Theatre and Frank's Restaurant earlier but has no alibi. He admits knowing about the basement room where the murder took place but insists it was occupied only in the winter by the man who fired the boilers. Covey seems surprised to hear about the murder.

When they return to the murder scene Covey insists that, with all the blood in the room, the other tenants must have heard the fight taking place. Digger and Ed return Covey back to his apartment and leave him. On a pretense, however, Coffin Ed goes back to the apartment. After about a minute and a half, Digger follows Ed and discovers him beating the truth out of Covey. The badly beaten man admits that he rented the apartment to a respectable Negro businessman named John Babson. Babson is a secret homosexual who goes by the name "Jesus Baby" when he is on the prowl. Digger and Ed turn Covey over to Sergeant Ryan and have him held on suspicion.

Other things are afoot in Harlem besides murder however. One of these events is about to be set in motion by a young Black man named Marcus Mackenzie. In a scene that takes place after the murder, he has assembled a large group of young whites and Blacks. Making use of his military training, he has organized them into a phalanx which will march through the streets of Harlem with a message of brotherhood.

Marcus is very sincere and very stupid. He has spent a great deal of his life studying the Bible and has come to the conclusion that Christian love is the answer to the race problem. With the help of Birgit, an oversexed middle-aged Swedish woman with whom he is in love, he has organized an event which he believes will bring the races together.

In another part of town, Doctor Mubuta, an African charlatan, is delivering a lecture to a room full of people. While the noises of a riot seep in from outside, Mubuta exclaims that the only solution to the Negro problem is for the Black race to outlive the white. He predicts that one day the white race will be enslaved to the numerically superior Black race.

Mubuta's audience is an eclectic one, consisting of men and women of both races. Mister Sam, a successful ninety-year-old pimp, is there because he is impotent and wants Mubuta to cure him with a ghastly home-brewed rejuvenation potion. Sam's lust for a teenaged white cracker girl has induced him to bring most of his life savings in a gladstone bag in order to pay for this elixir.

His friend and chauffeur, Johnson X, is scornful and tries to talk his friend out of making such an absurd purchase. When Sam announces that he plans to marry the cracker girl, his present wife, Viola, is so enraged by the news that she tries to kill the girl. A melee erupts, and nearly everyone in the room is killed. Doctor Mubuta grabs the money and attempts to flee through the door, but he is cut off by a Black man in a fez who kills him and takes the money.

Somewhat later, Digger and Ed visit the scene of this crime and interview Anny, a white woman who was in the room during the cutting spree. She explains that she is married to Mister Sam's son. She and her husband realized that the rejuvenation scheme was a trick Sam was playing on his wife to pay her back for having an affair with his attorney, Van Raff. During the fight, Anny and her husband escaped upstairs to their apartment where they waited until it was over.

Anny provides them with another piece of news that they find especially disturbing. A young Black girl named Sugartit was also present. She is the girlfriend of the Syndicate's district boss. Digger and Ed know that something is wrong. The Syndicate could not be involved in such a bizarre and useless drama.

Dick, Mister Sam's son, explains that the Syndicate has always been behind his father's activities. Sam acted as both figurehead and fall guy in case anything went wrong. Dick admits that he was well acquainted with his father's crooked business activities and also with the con game he was running with Mubuta to fool Viola and Van Raff.

On another street corner a fat Black man is delivering an impassioned and incoherent speech about Black Power to a large crowd. When he appeals to the crowd for money to help in the fight, many give him all that they have.

While all this is going on, a black Cadillac limousine pulls up to the curb. Inside are two dangerous-looking bodyguards, two Black men dressed as clerics, and Doctor Moore, a handsome, gray-haired Black man dressed in expensive clothing. His men take the money that has been collected and load it into the Cadillac.

From there Moore and his men drive to an apartment building in a good neighborhood. Once inside, the young clerics don kitchen garb and begin to prepare a meal for Moore. Deeper in the apartment, Moore talks to several beautiful women who are prostitutes in his employ. Moore complains to them that they are not bringing in enough money from their activities. He also complains that his Black Power pitch isn't doing too well, either. He expresses the idea that, in order to make the pitch more productive, he needs a dead man to make the common Blacks in the streets angry enough to revolt.

In yet another part of town, a short, fat black man with a hare lip known as the Prophet Ham enters the Temple of Black Jesus. Inside the chapel, Ham finds a group of ministers whom he castigates for wasting their time praying and waiting for a white Messiah. Ham wants them to fight. Ham quickly organizes the group and places a young preacher named Duke in charge. He orders Duke to organize a march with banners that read "Jesus Baby" and to get girls involved in order to attract more male followers.

We find Digger and Ed in Lieutenant Anderson's office with Anderson and Captain Brice, their crooked precinct commander. Brice takes both detectives off the Mister Sam murder case. He makes it clear that he doesn't want them working a case that involves the Syndicate. Instead, he orders them to investigate a number of brushfire riots that have been cropping up all over town. Strangely enough, Lieutenant Anderson backs Brice up. The two detectives are infuriated because they realize that they are deliberately being prevented from investigating the murder.

The pair leave the station, and we pick them up further out in Harlem. They are watching from the sidelines as the Black Jesus group, Marcus Mackenzie's marchers, and the Black Power people are about to converge. Digger and Ed have not taken much of this too seriously until the fighting starts. Without warning a riot breaks out, and in an attempt to stop it, Digger and Ed are both badly beaten up.

Himes jumps back in time and picks the detectives up in Lieutenant Anderson's office the morning after the murder of the white homosexual. Anderson informs them that the murdered man was a producer of off-Broadway plays named Richard Henderson. He was married and shared an apartment with his wife off Times Square.

The two detectives are frustrated when Anderson urges them to go easy on the investigation and not stir up any trouble. The pair hotly accuse Anderson of asking them to drag their feet and not find anything out. Anderson, of course, denies this.

They decide to look for the man in the red fez whom they saw leave the murder scene. They enter the lunch counter where the white man was last seen alive and interrogate the homosexual counterman. Eventually they decide that he is John Babson, alias Jesus Baby, and take him into custody.

The scene changes to the front of the Amsterdam Apartments. A panel truck bearing the name of a television sales outlet pulls up, and the two delivery men alight with a crate containing a television set for Barbara Tyne in Apartment 406.

Two loiterers offer to help the delivery men carry the set up to the fourth floor. Their knock is answered by Miss Tyne, a beautiful Black woman dressed only in a robe. Her surprise over the set is so great that she pitches forward in a dead faint, exposing her pubic area in the fall. The four men exclaim with excitement, bringing up nearly everyone from the street.

In the excitement of gazing at Miss Tyne's crotch and bringing her back to consciousness with liberal doses of whiskey, nobody in the crowd notices a man's straw hat on the sofa. The owner is nowhere in sight. Miss Tyne comes to finally and manages to get everyone out of the apartment, with the exception of the two delivery men. A half hour later the pair are seen carrying the television crate back down the stairs. For some reason it is still heavy.

Himes shifts the action back to the point where the detectives have taken John Babson into custody. Babson is cooperative with them because he is sexually attracted to Digger and Ed and believes the attraction to be mutual. By alternately playing tough and seductive with Babson, the detectives keep him badly off balance. Finally they spring Richard Henderson's name on him and threaten to beat him. After a stunned silence, he confesses to knowing Henderson as a producer and offers to take them on a tour of the places where Henderson hung out looking for other homosexuals.

He escorts them to the Five Spot Nightclub on St. Marks Place where they are seated in a conspicuous place by the bouncer. Seated nearby are two beautiful lesbians whom they have seen earlier in the day. Without any warning, one of the lesbians jumps up on a table and begins to do a wild belly dance in time to the hot jazz coming from the bandstand. As she begins to strip off her scanty outfit, Babson gets uncomfortable and leaves the table for the bathroom.

The club goes wild as the bouncer ineffectually attempts to get the stripper to put on her clothes. The shouting and laughing are suddenly interrupted by cries from the street. When Digger and Ed get to the sidewalk, they discover that the stripping lesbian's companion has cut Babson's throat. She refuses to explain why she killed Babson.

Witnesses supply the information that she was accusing Babson of being a police spy and a stool pigeon while she was cutting him. The stripping lesbian, when questioned, identifies herself as an ostensibly respectable woman, married for nine years to a meat-packing executive. Before they can book her as a material witness, an old man, identified as her husband, appears and bails her out. The husband of the stripping lesbian turns out to be Jonas "Fats" Little. Little is known to the detectives because, since the Depression, he has used his sausage business as a front for numbers running and a Syndicate heroin operation.

Another confusing scene shift takes place in the middle of the foregoing action, returning us to where Digger and Ed were attempting to quell the riot. They are watching helplessly when they are confronted by four Black youths. A Black man wearing the red fez of the Black Muslims hangs slightly behind them.

Somehow they get the kids to back off, but someone else bombs their car with a Molotov Cocktail. Their clothes catch on fire, and soon they are left alone in the street with no car and few clothes left intact.

The battered detectives go to the apartment of Barbara Tyne, who Ed claims is his wife's cousin. When Digger sees Barbara, however, he realizes that she is not only a professional hooker, but also Ed's sometime girlfriend. He is miffed that his partner never confided in him.

Barbara lends them two sets of rather flashy looking clothing which she claims belong to her former "husband." Before they leave the apartment, the two detectives watch a television news broadcast in which Black and white leaders urge all rioters to go home. Ed and Digger recognize the Prophet Ham, Doctor Moore, and Marcus Mackenzie on the platform.

Returning to the station house, the pair go into conference with Anderson. Anderson still wants them to find the person responsible for instigating the riots. The two detectives, already angered and disgusted by what they see as a deliberate stall, blast Anderson. They insist that, since the real cause of the riot is bigotry and hatred, there is no single person for them to arrest.

Anderson accuses the two of dragging their feet on the Henderson murder case. They refuse to take the blame, however, and confront Anderson with the theory that nobody really wants Richard Henderson's murder solved. Digger insists that it will uncover an interracial homosexual scandal. Anderson's obvious embarrassment tells them that they have solved one mystery, at least. They leave the station and go home.

The next morning, Anderson greets them with the news that Covey has come in and identified Babson's body as that of the mysterious Jesus Baby. Covey also claims that he is the man who rented the murder apartment from him. As far as the authorities are concerned, the Henderson murder case is closed.

Unfortunately, a man named Dennis Holman steps forward and identifies himself as Babson's landlord. He asserts that Babson is innocent because they were in bed together at the time Henderson was being killed.

Digger and Ed decide to take Holman over to Covey and confront him with the new evidence. When they reach Covey's apartment, however, they discover that he has been shot dead at close range. The circumstances indicate he was killed by someone he knew and trusted.

Digger and Ed decide to visit the Black Art Bookstore on Seventh Avenue. With the help of the owner they make contact with Michael X, the minister of the Harlem Mosque. Michael X tells them that the man behind the riots is a big-time gangster known as Mr. Big, a man whom he refuses to identify further. He insists that if they want to know more about Mr. Big, they should ask their bosses. Digger warns him that such talk could get him killed, and the interview ends.

The next scene takes place in Fo-Fo's "Sporting Gentleman's Club" where a dice game is going on. A blind man who wants to hide his affliction is shooting the dice. Since he cannot see, he is quickly cleaned out. He leaves the game and walks blindly into the street. His inability to see causes havoc everywhere he goes. Eventually he manages to get onto a subway coach.

On the coach, he hears another Negro, Fat Sam, having a bitter dialogue with himself. Sam is pouring out his frustration and rage against the white race. Sam sees the blind man facing in his direction and imagines that the man is staring at him. He hurls abuse at the blind man and, of course, the blind man has no idea that he is being addressed. Eventually, a senseless argument erupts and is further complicated by the needless involvement of a large white man.

Sam and the white man get into a scuffle, during which the white man inadvertently slaps and knocks down the blind man. The blind man pulls out a huge revolver and begins shooting into the coach, accidentally killing a Negro preacher. More shots are fired, and a panic ensues as people trample each other in their haste to escape the car.

Out on the street a demolition crew is destroying a number of tenements in order to reuse the land for commercial property. The watching Harlemites are bitter because the evictees have no where else to live. Digger and Ed are stationed across the street from the building, shooting the rats that run out of the condemned buildings.

Some white cops, standing at one end of the street are watching the detectives at work and are arguing about racial issues when they see Fat Sam run up from the subway leaking blood from several wounds. They come very close to shooting Fat Sam before their attention is directed to the blind man. Hearing this the blind man fires and kills a policeman, provoking the police to kill him. A riot erupts, and soon everything is completely out of control.

An hour later, as Grave Digger is reporting in to request help from Anderson, he explains to his commander how it all began with a blind man shooting a pistol. Anderson as usual is mystified, but for a change, so is Digger.

The thing that is the most readily apparent about *Blind Man With A Pistol* is that Himes has completely slipped the bonds of the traditional detective story. Here the formerly indomitable Digger and Ed are deliberately prevented from even coming close to solving the case. The all-pervasive corruption that seems to meet the detectives at every point in their lives makes the book more reminiscent of movies such as *Chinatown, Serpico,* and *Prince of the City* than the works of Chandler or Hammett. In this more pessimistic (and perhaps realistic) world, no matter how honest, brave, or persevering the detective is, he is no match for the weight of the evil that bears down on him. His mere survival is considered a victory.

Himes has retained only one element of his usual style in this story, and that is the constant shifting back and forth in time between events. Here, the detectives are concerned with the murder of the homosexual, Richard Henderson, the multiple killing at Dr. Mubuta's con game, and the riots. All are taking place at different times, and nowhere does Himes provide the reader with any realization of how the different investigations relate to each other chronologically. The shifts happen so often and so suddenly that Himes manages to intensify the nightmarish qualities of the novel.

The pervasive corruption is represented in microcosm by the appearances of Barbara Tyne. When we first meet her, she is a prostitute working in the employ of the sinister Doctor Moore. The amorality of her character is apparent in the way in which she parades naked in front of Moore. Without a doubt she is or has been Moore's mistress as well as his employee. Her job is not simply to make money as a call girl. She also frequents high-class parties where she works to meet and seduce wealthy men. Her motive in doing so is to bring them under Doctor Moore' sway.

The next time we meet Barbara she is receiving the delivery of a box containing a television set. Her nude fainting spell is undoubtedly a ruse to conceal the fact that she is hiding someone in her apartment. Although we never discover who has been hiding there and is subsequently smuggled out by the television delivery men, her connections suggest only one possibility. She is in the employ of a gangster who is using the Black Power movement for his own ends. Men wearing the Black Power fez have been involved in all of the major crimes under investigation. Because a thread of homosexuality seems to run through everything going on, it is clear that Barbara Tyne has been hiding the mysterious Jesus Baby from the police.

Knowing all of this, it comes as something of a shock to discover that she is also Coffin Ed's good-time girlfriend. The fact that Coffin Ed has hidden this secret love of his from his brother-in-arms and chief confidante suggests a number of things to us. First, his engaging in a sexual liaison with a woman of obviously low morals signals a significant breach in the hard-boiled detective's code of ethics. It is a breach that Ed is clearly ashamed of, since he hides it from Digger. Even worse, Ed has probably unknowingly (but possibly knowingly) allowed information about his investigations to get into the hands of Doctor Moore and through him to the unidentified Mr. Big.

It is obvious from the beginning of this story that Himes felt a deep pessimism at this point of his life. While his bitterness toward whites remained unabated, his feelings have taken on a particular edge in this story. He seems to be indicating that Blacks, perhaps because they have been degraded and

subjugated for so long, have become their own worst enemies. In his preface
he explains this feeling:

A friend of mine, Phil Lomax, told me this story about a blind man with a pistol
shooting at a man who had slapped him on a subway train and killing an innocent
bystander peacefully reading his newspaper across the aisle and I thought, damn right,
sounds just like today's news, riots in the ghettos, war in Vietnam, masochistic doings
in the Middle East. And then I thought of some of our loudmouthed leaders urging
our vulnerable soul brothers on to getting themselves killed, and thought further that
all unorganized violence is like a blind man with a pistol.

Bearing this in mind, the beginning of the novel is particularly telling.
The dilapidated house is symbolic of the ruined world that Blacks have been
allotted by the whites. Himes indulges in a bit of irony when he gives us
one cop's impressions of the disgusting hovel:

As they picked their way around the house through knee-high weeds dense with
booby traps of unseen bottles, tin cans, rusted bed springs, broken emery stones, rotting
harness, dead cats, dog offal, puddles of stinking garbage, and swarms of bottle flies,
house flies, gnats, mosquitoes, the first cop said in extreme disgust, "I don't see how
people can live in such filth."

Of course, this description is nothing new to the reader. Himes has inured
us through seven other Harlem novels to the fact that the urban Black often
has no real life choices. If he lives in filthy, dilapidated surroundings, this
isn't what he has picked for himself; it is what was left for him.

The mass of naked, half-savage children that the policemen find feeding
at a trough like animals not only reminds us of the animal state in which
Blacks were forced to live during the days of slavery, but is also symbolic of
the emotional and philosophical slavery in which they still live.

Many of the children suffer from ringworm, a parasitic disease that attests
to their poverty. Himes also tells us that most of the boys had "elongated
penises for children so young," which seems to bear witness to the early age
at which poor Blacks begin to engage in sexual activity. For the urban poor,
the mass of illegitimate children spawned by youthful, unmarried fornication
represents one more ill that keeps the Negro enslaved and poor.

The eleven Black nuns who have borne all of these naked children seem
to suggest the matriarchal society that the Black world has become. Women
without husbands whose days are filled with the necessity of feeding their
children, these women represent the millions of welfare mothers that populate
the ghetto, doing whatever is necessary to support their young.

Reverend Sam's policy of simply advertising for another wife when one
dies suggests an interchangeability about them and bears witness to their relative
facelessness within their own society. It is, after all, not a Black woman's face
or personality that has ever mattered in the world. It is only her ability to
bear more children into one kind of slavery or another.

The enigmatic Reverend Sam seems to represent a number of things. Himes has never shown a high regard for Black religion in his work. He presents Reverend Sam to us as one more religious charlatan who justifies his life of ease and sexual indulgence with religious double-talk. When the police first begin to question him, one of their first questions concerns the name of the church that ordained him. His only reply is: "What difference did that make?" In the tradition of Himes' other charlatans, he has created his own church and made himself pastor. Sam's nuns beg and hustle on the street because that is how they support his "church" and themselves. For Sam, it is no different philosophically from the methods that the white church uses to support white nuns.

It is worth noting that Sam wears a spotted white robe. Since we know that white is Himes' symbolic color for evil, it is clear indication that Sam is not a good character. The spots on the robe are further proof that his character is tainted. The final discovery of the three graves in the basement of the tenement leaves us with no doubt that he is a classic Himesian exploiter who has preyed on his own people in order to create a life of ease for himself.

This opening chapter seems to have nothing to do with the rest of the story. In fact, Himes is using it as an allegory to suggest why Harlem is on the verge of an explosion. The domination of the Black race by the whites has created an intolerable situation of slums, degraded women, illegitimate children, and hopeless conditions. Making matters worse are the small group of Black hustlers who, finding no way out of the ghetto for themselves, remain behind to exploit, manipulate, and cheat the helpless thousands who are trapped with them. In this roundabout way, Himes has set the stage for his final Harlem story.

Early in this book Himes provides us with what he calls an "interlude" that helps to further set the ideological stage for this book. In it he tells us:

Where 125th Street crosses Seventh Avenue is the Mecca of Harlem. To get established there, an ordinary Harlem citizen has reached the promised land, if it merely means standing on the sidewalk.

But Harlem doesn't belong just to Black people. Himes says:

...most of the commercial enterprises—stores, bars, restaurants, theaters, etc.—and real estate are owned by white people.

But it is the Mecca of the black people just the same. The air and the heat and voices and the laughter, the atmosphere and the drama and the melodrama are theirs. Theirs are the hopes, the schemes, the prayers and the protest. They are the managers, the clerks, the cleaners, they drive the taxis and the buses, they are the clients and the customers, the audience; they work it, but the white owns it. So it is natural that the white man is concerned with their behavior; it's his property. But it is the black people's to enjoy. The black people have the past and the present, and they hope to have the future.

The winning of that future is essentially what this story is about. Behind the story of the murders is the drama of the riots which act as a dynamic backdrop for the rest of the plot. Marcus Mackenzie, Dr. Moore, and the Prophet Ham symbolically represent Himes' view of the prevailing attitudes of American Blacks.

Mackenzie is in many ways reminiscent of the "squares" in Himes' other Harlem stories. Himes gives us a capsule history of the young man, who grew up amid the drama of the 1943 Detroit race riots. Marcus entered the army, and because he was handsome, clean-cut, and quiet, he was generally well treated. Thanks to his naivete he took this experience to mean that "plain Christian love was the solution to the Negro problem." Marcus returned to America with the idea of holding an interracial march that would show members of both races working in harmony and brotherhood.

Somewhat removed in his motives from Marcus is Doctor Moore. Moore is the head of the Black Power movement and is the force behind a number of street-corner demagogues who are exhorting Negroes to march and give money in support of Black Power. Himes depicts many willing supporters among this Negro proletariat.

But Moore takes the money collected by his shills and drives to a comfortable apartment building. We get some insight into his character when, during a discussion of the night's menu, one of Moore's subordinates informs him that there is only margarine to go with the corn bread. Moore grimaces with distaste and tells his man to take money out of the proceeds of the Black Power movement to purchase butter.

Shortly after this conversation, Moore has a discussion with Barbara Tyne, a professional prostitute in his employ. She has been spending the day frequenting high-class cocktail parties hosted and attended by wealthy Blacks and whites, probably fund-raisers for some type of racial charity. The prostitute is plying her trade in the hopes of securing the favor and financial support of wealthy white men for Moore's benefit.

Her day has not been a good one, because she has had to compete with Black bourgeois women for these men's favors. Moore shows his true colors at this point, using thinly veiled threats to get Barbara to work harder. His reasons for urging her on have nothing to do with the Black Power movement; they are much more prosaic. "The rent isn't paid and I'm behind with my Caddy."

He also makes it clear that the Black Power movement isn't bringing in the kind of money he really needs. He tells the prostitute that "these Harlem folks ain't serious. All they want to do is boogaloo." What he needs is to make them mad, and to make them mad, he says, he needs a dead man.

There is one other figure left in Himes' unholy trio, and that is the Prophet Ham, leader of the Temple of Black Jesus. Ham, a sinister fat man with a hare lip, is neither naive nor one of Himes' exploiters. Rather, he is a fanatic driven by hatred for whites. He finds plenty of supporters in Harlem because "the white Jesus hadn't done anything for them."

Ham disdains the name "prophet." According to Ham, prophets are either misfits, "squares like Moses," or race leaders. Ham considers himself a soldier. His intention is to draft Jesus to his cause. But it is a Black Jesus they will draft, and, he says, they are going to feed the white man "the flesh of the Black Jesus...until he perish of constipation if he don't choke to death first." Praying is over, he insists. It is time to fight.

Ham seems mad, yet it is clear that there is a method to his madness. When he leaves his Temple, he gets into a lavender Cadillac convertible and drives away with a fat, vulgarly sensual white woman, telling her that he has been "cooking with Jesus." Ham is in fact fomenting revolution and standing by to pick up the pieces.

Himes paints Harlem in different colors than he ever has before. It is no longer a colorful place filled with suckers and criminals. Harlem has become a kind of socio-political powder keg, waiting for a stray spark to set it off. The actions set in motion by each of these three characters will be that spark.

The nightmarish quality of the story and the sense we have that everything is going out of control is heightened by our awareness of the fact that for the first time in the series, Digger and Ed are not equal to the task. Things are happening that they are helpless to control. Even they seem to know it.

During a confrontation with some teenaged punks, we note how out of touch they seem with the events they are facing. In an effort to get the kids to go home and stay out of the riot, Coffin Ed identifies himself and Digger as police officers. Instead of reacting with either fear or bravado, the kids respond with this bald assertion:

> "Then you're on whitey's side."
> "We're on your leader's side." [Ed replies]
> "Them Doctor Toms," a youth said contemptuously. "They're all on whitey's side."
> "Go on home," Grave Digger said, pushing them away, ignoring their flashing knife blades. "Go home and grow up. You'll find out there ain't any other side."

This conservative assertion from the normally bitter and ideologically black Digger is startlingly out of place in the midst of the race hatred surrounding him.

The detectives know unequivocally that they are out of their depth in this confusing case. They remind Lieutenant Anderson that "you ought to know more than anyone else we're not subtle cops. We're tough and heavy-handed. If we find out there's some joker agitating these young people to riot,...we're gonna beat him to death." Perhaps this is why they show no surprise later on when, at the Black-Art Book Store, Michael X (who from his description is a thinly-veiled analogue of Malcolm X) tells them "you don't really count in the overall pattern."

Malcolm/Michael X, of course, counts too much. He knows the identities of the Black and white opportunists behind the riots, but he won't tell the police who they are. The rioters may be his ideological enemies, but he won't inform on them to his racial enemies, the white authorities. Unfortunately, he is too innocent to realize how vulnerable his knowledge makes him, even when Digger warns him that "people have been killed for less."

As the story comes to a close, Himes has reduced the two detectives from crime solvers and protectors of innocent Blacks to the level of mere sanitation men. The revolvers with which they have kept an uneasy peace are now being used to shoot the rats running from a demolition site.

A further irony lies in the knowledge that these buildings are the former homes of poverty-stricken Blacks. They have been evicted from these buildings by their white landlords in order that the property can be put to a more remunerative commercial use. The march of time has not only rendered the two detectives impotent to stop crime in Harlem, it has somehow worked to make them the handmaidens of the white oppressors.

This apocalyptic view of life in Harlem is made all the more sinister by two particular elements. One is the fact that to the police investigators there seems to be no connection among the murder of Richard Henderson, the multiple killings at Doctor Mubuta's gathering, and the riots. The other element is the connection that seems to exist among the unseen presence of the Syndicate, the rioting, and the homosexual scandal that bubbles beneath the surface. It is obvious that Digger and Ed do not really see the connection, and the police officials that do know are carefully keeping it secret. They deliberately misdirect the two detectives and to further confuse the issue use the trusted Lieutenant Anderson to do their dirty work.

Anderson, who has traditionally been the voice of reason in the series and who has acted as the sounding board to whom the detectives could direct their bitterness and frustration, symbolizes Himes' apparent inability to have any faith left in whites. He hints that Anderson has been promised command of the Harlem precinct and all the graft that goes with it if he will prevent Digger and Ed from learning too much. It is obvious from his embarrassment that Anderson knows the answers for which the pair are searching, but his greed has overcome his moral imperative.

Although on the surface white domination over Harlem seems to have little to do with this story, we see that the unseen "Mr. Big" is a white man whose tentacles reach into every crack and crevice of New York society. This provides Mr. Big with a sinister aura and gives the impression that, like "Big Brother," he sees everything and controls virtually everyone.

Mr. Big is undoubtedly connected with the Syndicate, which shows its head several times in the story. The first time is when we hear about Mr. Sam's life-long association with the Syndicate.

The second time we hear of the syndicate is after the police have taken the stripping lesbian into custody. Just as she is about to be booked on suspicion, she is bailed out by her husband, Jonas "Fats" Little, a notorious Syndicate associate. By a strange coincidence he is also a homosexual.

It is interesting that Himes should have postulated an association between organized crime and the homosexual subculture. These were two things for which he expressed a great deal of hatred in his writings. For him the Syndicate represented just one more way that the white world was exploiting the Black race. Prostitution, numbers running, and especially narcotics were all attached to Syndicate tentacles.

At the same time, Himes seemed to harbor a deep disgust with homosexuality, a feeling that may have its roots in his prison years. For whatever the reason, homosexuality is never depicted in a favorable light in this series. His only strong homosexual character, Casper Holmes, is a crook who uses his position to steal from his own people. All other homosexual characters in the series are of course effeminate and weak.

Himes' antipathy for homosexuals seems to have increased as he became older. When Digger and Ed take John Babson around Harlem as they search for Jesus Baby, their treatment of him is nothing short of sadistic.

It is a complicated scenario that Himes has created in this last book, and it is little wonder that his detectives cannot cope with it. It seems obvious that from a professional standpoint both of them have slowed down, too. When they allow themselves to be distracted by the stripping lesbian long enough for John Babson to be killed, we see that they are losing their touch. Later in the story they allow Anderson to prevent them from going out and beating the truth out of someone. In earlier times they would never have stood still for such an order.

At the same time we note that the magic has gone out of Digger and Ed's partnership, too. Perhaps because we know both detectives as devoted family men, the discovery of Coffin Ed's affair is an unpleasant surprise to us as well as to Digger.

Coffin Ed has never been the brainy member of the team, but when we realize that his mistress, Barbara Tyne, has probably been hiding Jesus Baby from the police, it tends to make him seem very foolish. Perhaps the killing of rats is all that the two aging detectives are good for after all.

The brief, italicized passages that Himes calls "interludes" act as bridges between some of the disjointed scenes and at times provide us with a God's eye view of things. In one of these, for example, he shows us Doctor Mubuta transacting business with a wealthy white woman. At Mubuta's direction, a cretin carries an immobile, sheet-wrapped male figure and places it in the woman's automobile. The woman's embarrassment and unease while all this is going on would seem to suggest that Mubuta has sold her a drugged or hypnotized Black man for her use in some kind of perverted pleasure.

This particular passage serves as one more reminder of how some whites continue to exploit Blacks and also reminds us that the exploitation is often carried out with the help of unscrupulous Black manipulators. When we meet Mubuta shortly thereafter speaking to Mister Sam's group, we are already prepared for the fact that he is up to no good.

Mubuta is something of an ironic character as well as a charlatan. Prior to the introduction of his rejuvenation formula, he postulates that the only way that the Negro Problem is ever going to be solved is for the Black man to outlive the white. Later, after Mubuta and the others have been killed, Mr. Sam's white daughter-in-law confesses to Grave Digger that Mubuta touched her with his solution.

Himes makes an interesting use of the name "Sam" in this story. By the time the novel has come to a close, Reverend Sam, Mr. Sam, and Fat Sam have all been on the stage once. The appearance of each character is a prelude to the death of one or more Black people. Inasmuch as "Sam" is a name that shows up in a number of his books (Fat Sam, in particular), Himes may be suggesting that he is a kind of Negro everyman. Possibly he used this device to confirm his earlier assertion that Blacks are hurting themselves as much as the white man is.

With the publication of *Blind Man With A Pistol*, Himes' career as a novelist came full circle. Ostensibly a crime story, the work is an effective protest novel which depicts in a harsh light the destructive forces that American race relations threaten to unleash in the big city.

Himes was old and in poor health by the time this book appeared, and his frustration and depression are manifest in his last novel. It is crystal clear that he held out no hope for peaceful change in America and feared the mindless violence that seemed ready to erupt, not because he feared violence *per se*, but because he knew that unorganized violence would ultimately be more destructive to the Black race than helpful.

Like all old-timers, Himes undoubtedly believed that things were worse than they had ever been and that prospects for progress were slim. In the few pieces of writing that he would produce in the fifteen years of life left to him, that bitterness and disbelief would become more pronounced.

Chapter XIII
Conclusion

Chester Himes' writing life was far from over when *Blind Man With A Pistol* was published. The 1970s would see him busy adapting *Cotton Comes to Harlem* and *The Heat's On* into successful motion pictures. In 1972 and 1976 he issued two volumes of powerful and unsparing autobiography that are both remarkable for their candor and frustrating for what they fail to reveal about his life.

Himes became something of a grand old man among younger Black writers and was known to be kind and generous in the praise, advice, and help he gave to this new crop of artists. He was particularly forthcoming to interviewers such as John A. Williams, and it is through these outspoken glimpses of Himes that we have come to better understand his background and his motivations.

As cruel as his early years had been to him, his declining years were spent in relative comfort. He remarried, and with the money he earned from his later work he built a comfortable house in Spain where he remained until his death in 1984.

His decision to write crime stories was purely an economic one, and it is possible that he held the genre in the same low opinion as many serious literary critics. He seemed to know little about the traditional hard-boiled crime story, and yet he was able to siphon off the elements that made it unique and exciting to create his own subgenre. Although other writers have attempted to write about crime in the ghetto, few have equaled Himes' originality or his ability to create a stark, compelling backdrop.

As a writer of detective stories, Himes does not get high marks when he is measured against the narrow parameters against which such fiction is usually judged. He does not dwell on deep, mysterious secrets, international conspiracies, or dilettante sleuths. In many of his stories, the mystery is rather superficial, and the detectives have very little part in the solution.

Himes's criminal Harlem should not be judged along with traditional mystery fiction. To consider him thus would be to devalue his work. Perhaps unknowingly, Himes was following in the footsteps of a select few writers who actually had some knowledge of the world that they sought to fictionalize. It comes as no surprise that the work of old timers like Hammett or Donald Goines and even newer writers like James Colbert and O'Neil De Noux is so realistic when you realize that they have experienced real life in the dangerous netherworld of urban America.

Himes' writing is particularly effective because he was able to combine realistic depictions of ghetto life and ghetto dwellers with symbolic elements that emphasize Black culture and heritage. His ability to ennoble otherwise comical characters and to create the aura of hope in an atmosphere of failure and degradation is in the highest traditions of the fiction writer's art.

At the same time, Himes created in Grave Digger and Coffin Ed two protagonists who could stand side-by-side with other romantic American heroes. It is worthy of note that the hard-boiled detective is as much a myth figure to 20th century Americans as Arthur and Roland are to Britain and France. Because America became urbanized so quickly, this mythical detective has replaced the cowboy as the definitive American hero archetype.

He is a loner with high ideals and a man who sacrifices material comfort and risks his own life and happiness to protect the innocent and the helpless. Perhaps because they are Black men upholding white laws, Digger and Ed fit this mold better than many of the white detective characters who have preceded them. Himes has told their story in a saga in which we watch them through ten years of danger. They meet death head-on more than once, inadvertently cause damage to their families because of their devotion to duty, and risk the hatred of their superiors because of their deep belief in justice. At the end of their history, we see them older, more tired, and perhaps less effective than at their beginning. In spite of that, we cannot escape the fact that they have ennobled themselves through their sacrifices.

Himes created something truly unique in this series. Unlike many practitioners who have written about the same character through twenty or thirty adventures, we never tire of Coffin Ed and Digger. Because they grow and change, Himes made them new each time we met them and charged them with a dynamism that is not evident in Travis McGee, Spenser, and other detective characters. When Digger and Ed's adventures come to a close, the reader inevitably faces it with a feeling of regret rather than one of relief.

Himes was an unusual and talented man. He was also angry and embittered, but these emotions tended to enhance his talent rather than reduce it. His entry in the field of crime writing was an auspicious one and from an historical point of view an important one. He infused a tired genre with new life and undoubtedly provided the impetus for many future writers to approach the hard-boiled story from a fresh and bold perspective.

Notes

Introduction
[1]Stephen F. Milliken. *Chester Himes: A Critical Appraisal*. Columbia: University of Missouri Press, 1976, p. iii.

[2]Marvin Lachman. "Virgil Tibbs and the American Negro in Mystery Fiction." *The Armchair Detective* 1 (April 1968), 88.

Chapter I
[1]Chester Himes. *The Quality of Hurt*. New York: Doubleday, 1972, p. 4.

[2]*Ibid.*

[3]*Ibid.*

[4]Letter, Joseph S. Himes to Robert E. Skinner, September 23, 1988.

[5]*Hurt.*, p.5.

[6]*Ibid.*, p.13.

[7]*Ibid.*, p.14.

[8]*Ibid.*, p.22.

[9]*Ibid.*, p.28.

[10]*Ibid.*, p.29.

[11]Joseph Himes letter.

[12]Owl's Head was the underworld nickname for the Iver Johnson revolver. Iver Johnson has been one of the most successful firearms manufacturers in America since before the turn of the twentieth century. Their products have always been cheap and serviceable and available in a variety of calibers. They were so called Owl's Head because the company's trademark for many years was the head of a horned owl, set in a medallion at the top of the guns' grips. They were the Saturday Night Specials of their day, something that was no reflection on their effectiveness. Robert Kennedy, for example, was killed with one in the 1960s.

[13]*Quality of Hurt*, p.39.

[14]*Ibid.*, p.59.

[15]*Ibid.*, p.65.

[16]*Ibid.*, p.62.

[17]Joseph Himes letter.

[18]*Ibid.*

[19]Chester F. (sic) Himes. "His Last Day." *Abbott's Monthly* 5 (November 1932), 33.

[20]Chester F. (sic) Himes. "Her Whole Existence: A Story of True Love." *Abbott's Monthly* 6 (July 1933), 24.

[21]*Ibid.*, p. 25.

[22]*Ibid.*, p. 56.

[23]Milliken, p. 41.

[24]Letter, Chester Himes to John A. Williams, October 31, 1962, p. 3. quoted by permission of Professor Michel Fabre.

[25]*Ibid.*, p.4.

[26]*Ibid.*, p.6.

[27]Chester Himes. "The Dilemma of the Negro Novelist in the United States." quoted in Fred Pfeil, "Policiers Noirs." IN: *The Nation* 243 (November 15, 1986), 523.

[28]*Hurt*, p. 115.

[29]*Ibid.*, p. 137.

[30]*Ibid.*

[31]Roger Callois. *Puissance du roman.* Marseille: Sagittaire, 1942, p. 76.

[32]Chester Himes. *My Life of Absurdity.* New York: Doubleday, 1976, p. 102.

[33]*Ibid.*, p.105.

[34]Pfeil, p. 523.

Chapter II

[1]William F. Nolan. *Dashiell Hammett: A Casebook.* Santa Barbara, California: McNally, 1969, p.2.

[2]Raymond Chandler. "The Simple Art of Murder." in: Raymond Chandler. *The Simple Art of Murder.* New York: Ballantine Books, p. 20.

[3]Chester Himes. "He Knew." *Abbott's Weekly and Illustrated News* 1 (December 2, 1933), 15.

[4]Edward Margolies. *Which Way Did He Go: The Private Eye in Dashiell Hammett, Raymond Chandler, Ross Macdonald, and Chester Himes.* New York: Holmes and Meier, 1982, p.60.

[5]Though Himes never specifically says so, the guns are probably a model made by Smith and Wesson from the late 1930s through the 1950s. They were made on a heavy frame to facilitate the use of specially-made high-powered ammunition and can be thought of as a forerunner of the modern .357 magnum revolver. The heavy frame and the long barrels made them ideal for head bashing, and, in consequence, they were popular with law enforcement officers.

[6]William Marling. *Raymond Chandler.* Boston: Twayne, 1986, p.96.

[7]Raymond Nelson. "Domestic Harlem: The Detective Fiction of Chester Himes." *Virginia Quarterly Review* 48 (Spring 1972), 276.

Chapter III

[1]John A. Williams. "My Man Himes: An Interview with Chester Himes." in: John A. Williams and Charles F. Harris, eds. *Amistad I.* New York, Vintage Books, 1970, p. 49.

[2]Raymond Nelson. "Domestic Harlem: The Detective Fiction of Chester Himes." *Virginia Quarterly Review* 48 (Spring 1972): 262.

[3]Jay R. Berry. "Chester Himes and the Hard-Boiled Tradition." *The Armchair Detective* 15 (Issue #1 1982): 43.

[4]James Lundquist. *Chester Himes.* New York: Frederick Ungar, 1976, p. 23.

[5]Berry, p 39.

[6]Raymond Chandler. "The Simple Art of Murder." in: Raymond Chandler, *The Simple Art of Murder.* New York: Ballantine Books, 1972, p. 20.

[7]Williams, p.49.

Chapter V

[1]Conversation with Michel Fabre, New Orleans, Louisiana, February 9, 1988.

[2]Chester Himes. *My Life of Absurdity*. New York: Doubleday, 1976, pp.120-1.

Chapter VI
[1]Chester Himes. *My Life of Absurdity*. New York: Doubleday, 1976, p.150.

Chapter VII
[1]Chester Himes. *My Life of Absurdity*. New York: Doubleday, 1976, p.120.
[2]Fred Pfeil. "Policiers Noirs." *The Nation* 243 (November 15, 1986):523.
[3]Raymond Chandler. "The Simple Art of Murder." in: *The Simple Art of Murder*. New York: Ballantine Books, 1977, p. 20.

Chapter XI
[1]Nat Hentoff. [Review of *Cotton Comes to Harlem*]. *Book Week* (March 28, 1965), 11.
[2]M.K. Grant. [Review of *Cotton Comes to Harlem*]. *Library Journal* 90 (February 1, 1965), 670.
[3]Anthony Boucher. [Review of *Cotton Comes to Harlem*]. *New York Times Book Review* (February 7, 1965), 43.
[4]Ham, of course, was the son of Noah who is traditionally believed to be the ancestor of the Ethiopians.

Chapter XII
[1]Conversation with Michel Fabre, New Orleans, Louisiana, February 9, 1988.
[2]Richard Rhodes. [Review of *Blind Man With A Pistol*]. *New York Times Book Review*. (February 23, 1969), 32.
[3]D.F. Lawler. [Review of *Blind Man With A Pistol*]. *Best Sellers* 28 (March 15, 1969), 506.
[4]Shane Stephens. [Review of *Blind Man With A Pistol*]. *Book World* (April 27, 1969), 4.

Bibliography

Most of the titles in the Harlem Domestic Series were issued in this country as paperback originals. For that reason, it was nearly impossible to find original texts from which to work. The following reprint editions were used in the course of writing this book.

A Rage in Harlem (Originally entitled *For Love of Imabelle*). London: Allison & Busby, 1985.

The Real Cool Killers. London: Allison & Busby, 1985.

The Crazy Kill. London: Allison & Busby, 1984.

The Big Gold Dream. Chatham, New Jersey: Chatham Bookseller, 1973.

All Shot Up. Chatham, New Jersey: Chatham Bookseller, 1973.

The Heat's On. London: Allison & Busby, 1986.

Cotton Comes to Harlem. London: Allison & Busby, 1984.

Blind Man With A Pistol. London: Allison & Busby, 1986.

Index